INDIANA SCIENCE FUSION

Assessment Guide

Grade 7

HOLT McDOUGAL

HOUGHTON MIFFLIN HARCOURT

ISBN 978-0-547-45168-8

2 3 4 5 6 7 8 9 10 0982 19 18 17 16 15 14 13 12 11 10
4500242668 ABCDEFG

Contents

Unit 2 Motion and Forces

Unit 3 Energy

Unit 4 Earth's Structures

Unit 5 The Changing Earth

Unit 6 The Cell

The Design Process

ISTEP+ Practice Tests

Answer Key

INTRODUCTION

Overview

ScienceFusion provides parallel instructional paths for meeting the Indiana Revised Academic Standards for Science. You may choose to use the print path, the digital path, or a combination of the two. The quizzes, tests, and other resources in this Assessment Guide may be used with either path.

The *ScienceFusion* assessment options are intended to give you maximum flexibility in assessing what your students know and what they can do. The program's formative and summative assessment categories reflect the understanding that assessment is a learning opportunity for students, and that students must periodically demonstrate mastery of the standards in cumulative tests.

All *ScienceFusion* tests are available—and editable—in ExamView and online at thinkcentral.com. You can customize a quiz or test for your classroom in many ways:

- adding or deleting items

- adjusting for cognitive complexity, Bloom's taxonomy level, or other measures of difficulty

- changing the sequence of items

- changing the item formats

- editing the question itself

All of these changes, except the last, can be made without invalidating the standard correlation of the item.

This Assessment Guide is your directory to assessment in *ScienceFusion*. In it you'll find copymasters for Lesson Quizzes, Unit Tests, ISTEP+ Review and Practice Tests, and Alternative Assessments; answers and explanations of answers; rubrics; a bubble-style answer sheet; and suggestions for assessing student progress using performance, portfolio, and other forms of integrated assessment.

You will also find additional assessment prompts and ideas throughout the program, as indicated on the chart that follows.

Assessment in *ScienceFusion* Program

	Student Editions	Teacher Edition	Assessment Guide	Digital Lessons	Online Resources at thinkcentral.com	ExamView Test Generator
Formative Assessment						
Assessing Prior Knowledge						
Engage Your Brain	X					
Unit Pretest			X		X	X
Embedded Assessment						
Active Reading Questions	X					
Interactivities	X					
Probing Questions		X				
Formative Assessment		X				
Classroom Discussions		X				
Common Misconceptions		X				
Learning Alerts		X				
Embedded Questions and Tasks				X		
Student Self-Assessments				X		
Digital Lesson Quiz				X		
When used primarily for teaching						
Lesson Review	X	X				
Lesson Quiz			X		X	X
Alternative Assessment			X		X	
Performance Assessment			X			
Portfolio Assessment			X			
Summative Assessment						
End of Lessons						
Visual Summary	X	X				
Lesson Quiz			X		X	X
Alternative Assessment		X	X		X	
Rubrics			X		X	
End of Units						
ISTEP+ Review	X		X		X	X
Answers		X	X		X	
Test Doctor Answer Explanations		X	X			X
Unit Test A (on level)			X		X	X
Unit Test B (below level)			X		X	X
End of Year						
ISTEP+ Practice			X		X	X

Formative Assessment
Assessing Prior Knowledge

Frequently in this program, you'll find suggestions for assessing what your students already know before they begin studying a new lesson. These activities help you warm up the class, focus minds, and activate students' prior knowledge.

In This Assessment Guide
Each of the units begins with a Unit Pretest consisting of multiple-choice questions that assess prior and prerequisite knowledge. Use the Pretest to get a snapshot of the class and help you organize your pre-teaching.

In the Student Edition
Engage Your Brain Simple, interactive warm-up tasks get students thinking, and remind them of what they may already know about the lesson topics.

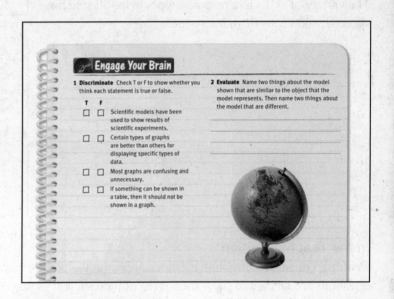

Active Reading Questions Students first see the lesson vocabulary on the opening page, where they are challenged to show what they know about the terms. Multiple exposures to the key terms throughout the lesson lead to mastery.

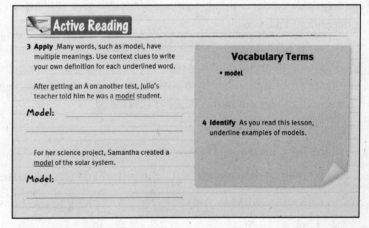

In the Teacher Edition
Opening Your Lesson At the start of each TE lesson Opening Your Lesson suggests questions and activities that help you assess prerequisite and prior knowledge.

Embedded Assessment

Once you're into the lesson, you'll continue to find suggestions, prompts, and resources for ongoing assessment.

Student Edition

Active Reading Questions and Interactivities Frequent questions and interactive prompts are embedded in the text, where they give students instant feedback on their comprehension. They ask students to respond in different ways, such as writing, drawing, and annotating the text. The variety of skills and response types helps all students succeed, and keeps them interested.

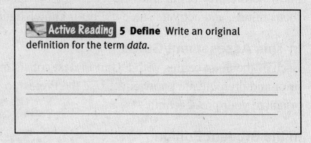

In the Teacher Edition

Probing Questions Probing questions appear in the point-of-use teaching suggestions. These questions are labeled to show the degree of independent inquiry they require. The three levels of inquiry—Directed, Guided, and Independent—give students experience that builds toward independent analysis.

Classroom Discussions Discussion is a natural opportunity to gauge how well students have absorbed the material, and to assess any misconceptions or gaps in their understanding. Students also learn from each other in this informal exchange. Classroom discussion ideas appear throughout the lesson in the Teacher Edition.

Tips for Classroom Discussions

- Allow students plenty of time to reflect and formulate their answers.

- Call upon students you sense have something to add but who haven't spoken.

- At the same time, allow reluctant students not to speak unless they choose to.

- Encourage students to respond to each other as well as to you.

Misconceptions and Learning Alerts The Teacher Background pages at the start of a unit describe common misconceptions and identify the lessons in which the misconceptions can be addressed. Strategies for addressing the misconceptions appear in the point-of-use teaching notes. Additional Learning Alerts help you introduce and assess challenging topics.

Formative Assessment A final formative assessment strategy appears on the Evaluate page at the end of each lesson, followed by reteaching ideas.

In This Assessment Guide

Several of the assessment strategies described in this book can be used either as formative or as summative instruments, depending on whether you use them primarily for teaching or primarily for evaluation. The choice is yours. Among these are the Lesson Quizzes, described here, and the Alternative Assessment, described under Summative Assessment, next. Because both of these assessments are provided for every lesson, you could use them both at different times.

Lesson Quizzes as Formative Assessment In this book, Lesson Quizzes in a unit follow the Unit Pretest. The five-item Lesson Quiz can be administered as a written test, used as an oral quiz, or given to small student groups for collaboration. In the Answer Key at the end of this book, you'll find a feature called the Test Doctor, which provides a brief explanation of what makes each correct answer correct and each incorrect answer incorrect. Use this explanatory material to begin a discussion following the quiz.

Classroom Observation

Classroom observation is one way to gather and record information that can lead to improved instruction. You'll find a Classroom Observation Checklist in Assessment Tools, following the Introduction.

Tips for Classroom Observation

- Don't try to see and record everything at once. Instead, identify specific skills you will observe in a session.

- Don't try to observe everyone at once. Focus on a few students at a time.

- Repeat observations at different times in order to identify patterns. This practice helps you validate or correct your impressions from a single time.

- Use the checklist as is or modify it to suit your students and your instruction. Fill in student names across the top and write the date next to the skills you are observing on a particular day.

- Keep the checklist, add to it, and consult it periodically for hints about strengths, weaknesses, and developments of particular students and of the class.

- Use your own system of ratings or the simple number code on the checklist. When you have not seen enough to give a rating, leave the space blank.

Summative Assessment

In the Student Edition

Visual Summary and Lesson Review

Interactive summaries help students synthesize lesson material, and the Lesson Review provides a variety of questions focusing on vocabulary, key concepts, and critical thinking.

Florida Benchmark Reviews

Each unit in the Student Edition is followed by an ISTEP+ Review test, also available in this Assessment Guide. These tests include all the items types on the statewide assessments, and the items are closely aligned to the standards. You may want to use these tests to review unit content right away or at any time later in the year to help students prepare for the statewide assessment. If you wish to give students practice in filling in a machine-scorable answer sheet, use the bubble-type answer sheet at the start of the Answer Key.

In This Assessment Guide

Alternative Assessments

Every lesson has an Alternative Assessment worksheet, which is previewed in the Teacher Edition on the Evaluate page of the lesson. The activities on these worksheets assess student comprehension of core content, while at the same time offering a variety of options for students with various abilities, learning styles, and interests. The activities require students to produce a tangible product or to give a presentation that demonstrates their understanding of skills and concepts.

Tips for Alternative Assessment

- The structure of these worksheets allows for differentiation in topic, difficulty level, and activity type/learner preferences.

- Each worksheet has a variety of items for students and teachers to choose from.

- The items may relate to the entire lesson content or to just one or two key topics. Encourage students to select items so that they will hit most key topics in a lesson.

- Share the rubrics and Presentation Guidelines with students so they understand the expectations for these assignments. You could have them fill in a rubric with their name and activity choices at the same time they choose their assignments, and then submit the rubric with their presentation or assignment.

Grading Alternative Assessments

Each type of Alternative Assessment worksheet has a rubric for easy grading.

- The rubrics focus mostly on content comprehension, but also take into account presentation.

- The Answer Key describes the expected content mastery for each Alternative Assessment.

- Separate Presentation Guidelines describe the attributes of successful written work, posters and displays, oral presentations, and multimedia presentations.

- Each rubric has space to record your reasons for deducting points, such as content errors or particular presentation flaws.

- If you wish to change the focus of an Alternative Assessment worksheet, you can adjust the point values for the rubric.

The Presentation Guidelines and the rubrics follow the Introduction. The Answer Key appears at the end of the book.

Unit Tests A and B

This Assessment Guide contains leveled tests for each unit.

- The A-level tests are for students who typically perform below grade level.

- The B-level tests are intended for students whose performance is on grade level.

Both versions of the test address the unit standards with a mixture of item types, including multiple choice, short response, and extended response. Both levels contains items of low, medium, and high cognitive complexity, though level B contains more items of higher complexity. A few items appear in both of the tests as a means of assuring parallel content coverage. If you need a higher-level test, you can easily assemble one from the lesson assessment banks in ExamView or online at thinkcentral.com. All items in the banks are tagged with five different measures of difficulty as well as standards and key terms.

Florida Benchmark Practice 1 and 2

The final tests in this Assessment Guide are year-end ISTEP+ Practice tests. They are long-form, multiple-choice tests in the style of the statewide assessments. The two parallel forms of the test make it possible for you to administer one form, reteach as needed, and administer the second form to follow up. An Answer Sheet appears with the practice tests.

Performance Assessment

Performance assessment involves a hands-on activity in which students demonstrate their skills and thought processes. A Lab and Activity Evaluation sheet appears in Assessment Tools following the Introduction. Using this rubric and the tips below, you can use many of the labs in the program as instruments for performance assessment. You may choose to make observations of performance during everyday labs and activities or to set up formal performance assessment using labs rated for independent inquiry.

Tips for Performance Assessment

- Prepare materials and stations so that all students have the same tasks. You may want to administer performance assessments to different groups over time.

- Make your expectations clear, including the measures on which students will be evaluated. You may invite them to help you formulate or modify the rubric.

- Assist students as needed, but avoid supplying answers to those who can handle the work on their own.

- Don't be hurried. Allow students enough time to do their best work.

Developing or Modifying a Rubric

Developing a rubric for a performance task involves three basic steps:

1. Identify the inquiry skills that are taught in the lesson and that students must perform to complete the task successfully and identify what understanding of content is also required.

2. Determine which skills and understandings of content are involved in which step.

3. Decide what you will look for to confirm that the student has acquired each skill and understanding you identified.

Portfolio Assessment

A portfolio is a showcase for student work, a place where many types of assignments, projects, reports and data sheets can be collected. The work samples in the collection provide snapshots of the student's efforts over time, and taken together they reveal the student's growth, attitudes, and understanding better than other types of assessment. Portfolio assessment involves meeting with each student to discuss the work and to set goals for future performance. In contrast with formal assessments, portfolio assessments have these advantages:

1. They give students a voice in the assessment process.

2. They foster reflection, self-monitoring, and self-evaluation.

3. They provide a comprehensive picture of a student's progress.

Tips for Portfolio Assessment

- Make a basic plan. Decide how many work samples will be included in the portfolios and what period of time they represent.

- Explain the portfolio and its use. Describe the portfolio an artist might put together, showing his or her best or most representative work, as part of an application for school or a job. The student's portfolio is based on this model.

- Together with your class decide on the required work samples that everyone's portfolio will contain.

- Explain that the students will choose additional samples of their work to include. Have students remember how their skills and understanding have grown over the period covered by the portfolio, and review their work with this in mind. The best pieces to choose may not be the longest or neatest.

- Give students the Portfolio Planning Worksheet found in Assessment Tools. Have students record their reasoning as they make their selections and assemble their portfolios.

- Share with students the Portfolio Evaluation Checklist, also found in Assessment Tools, and explain how you will evaluate the contents of their portfolios.

- Use the portfolios for conferences, grading, and planning. Give students the option of taking their portfolios home to share.

ASSESSMENT TOOLS
Alternative Assessment Presentation Guidelines

The following guidelines can be used as a starting point for evaluating student presentation of alternative assessments. For each category, use only the criteria that are relevant for the particular format you are evaluating; some criteria will not apply for certain formats.

Written Work
- Matches the assignment in format (essay, journal entry, newspaper report, etc.)
- Begins with a clear statement of the topic and purpose
- Provides information that is essential to the reader's understanding
- Supporting details are precise, related to the topic, and effective
- Follows a logical pattern of organization
- Uses transitions between ideas
- When appropriate, uses diagrams or other visuals
- Correct spelling, capitalization, and punctuation
- Correct grammar and usage
- Varied sentence structures
- Neat and legible

Posters and Displays
- Matches the assignment in format (brochure, poster, storyboard, etc.)
- Topic is well researched and quality information is presented
- Poster communicates an obvious, overall message
- Posters have large titles and the message, or purpose, is obvious
- Images are big, clear, and convey important information
- More important ideas and items are given more space and presented with larger images or text
- Colors are used for a purpose, such as to link words and images
- Sequence of presentation is easy to follow because of visual cues, such as arrows, letters, or numbers
- Artistic elements are appropriate and add to the overall presentation
- Text is neat
- Captions and labels have correct spelling, capitalization, and punctuation

Oral Presentations
- Matches the assignment in format (speech, news report, etc.)
- Presentation is delivered well, and enthusiasm is shown for topic
- Words are clearly pronounced and can easily be heard
- Information is presented in a logical, interesting sequence that the audience can follow
- Visual aids are relative to content, very neat, and artistic
- Often makes eye contact with audience
- Listens carefully to questions from the audience and responds accurately
- Stands straight, facing the audience
- Uses movements appropriate to the presentation; does not fidget
- Covers the topic well in the time allowed
- Gives enough information to clarify the topic, but does not include irrelevant details

Multimedia Presentations
- Topic is well researched, and essential information is presented
- The product shows evidence of an original and inventive approach
- The presentation conveys an obvious, overall message
- Contains all the required media elements, such as text, graphics, sounds, videos, and animations
- Fonts and formatting are used appropriately to emphasize words; color is used appropriately to enhance the fonts
- Sequence of presentation is logical and/or the navigation is easy and understandable
- Artistic elements are appropriate and add to the overall presentation
- The combination of multimedia elements with words and ideas produces an effective presentation
- Written elements have correct spelling, capitalization, and punctuation

Alternative Assessment Rubric – Tic-Tac-Toe

Worksheet Title: _____

Student Name: _____

Date: _____

Add the titles of each activity chosen to the chart below.

	Content *(0-3 points)*	**Presentation** *(0-2 points)*	*Points* *Sum*
Choice 1: _____			
Points			
Reason for missing points			
Choice 2: _____			
Points			
Reason for missing points			
Choice 3: _____			
Points			
Reason for missing points			
		Total Points (of 15 maximum)	

Alternative Assessment Rubric – Mix and Match

Worksheet Title: _____

Student Name: _____

Date: _____

Add the column choices to the chart below.

	Content (0-3 points)	Presentation (0-2 points)	Points Sum
Information Source from Column A: _____			
Topics Chosen for Column B: _____			
Presentation Format from Column C: _____			
Points			
Reason for missing points			
		Total Points (of 5 maximum)	

Alternative Assessment Rubric – Take Your Pick

Worksheet Title: _____

Student Name: _____

Date: _____

Add the titles of each activity chosen to the chart below.

2-point item: 5-point item 8-point item:	**Content** *(0-1.5 points)* *(0-4 points)* *(0-6 points)*	**Presentation** *(0-0.5 point)* *(0-1 point)* *(0-2 points)*	*Points Sum*
Choice 1: _____			
Points			
Reason for missing points			
Choice 2: _____			
Points			
Reason for missing points			
		Total Points (of 10 maximum)	

Alternative Assessment Rubric – Choose Your Meal

Worksheet Title: _____

Student Name: _____

Date: _____

Add the titles of each activity chosen to the chart below.

Appetizer, side dish, or dessert: Main Dish	**Content** *(0-3 points)* *(0-6 points)*	**Presentation** *(0-2) points* *(0-4 points)*	*Points Sum*
Appetizer: _____			
Points			
Reason for missing points			
Side Dish: _____			
Points			
Reason for missing points			
Main Dish: _____			
Points			
Reason for missing points			
Dessert: _____			
Points			
Reason for missing points			
		Total Points (of 25 maximum)	

Alternative Assessment Rubric – Points of View

Worksheet Title: _____

Student Name: _____

Date: _____

Add the titles of group's assignment to the chart below.

	Content *(0-4 points)*	**Presentation** *(0-1 points)*	*Points Sum*
Point of View:			
Points			
Reason for missing points			
		Total Points (of 5 maximum)	

Alternative Assessment Rubric – Climb the Pyramid

Worksheet Title: _____

Student Name: _____

Date: _____

Add the titles of each activity chosen to the chart below.

	Content *(0-3 points)*	**Presentation** *(0-2 points)*	*Points Sum*
Choice from bottom row: _____			
Points			
Reason for missing points			
Choice from middle row: _____			
Points			
Reason for missing points			
Top row: _____			
Points			
Reason for missing points			
		Total Points (of 15 maximum)	

Alternative Assessment Rubric – Climb the Ladder

Worksheet Title: _____

Student Name: _____

Date: _____

Add the titles of each activity chosen to the chart below.

	Content (0-3 points)	**Presentation** (0-2 points)	*Points Sum*
Choice 1 (top rung): _____			
Points			
Reason for missing points			
Choice 2 (middle rung): _____			
Points			
Reason for missing points			
Choice 3 (bottom rung): _____			
Points			
Reason for missing points			
		Total Points (of 15 maximum)	

Date _____

Rating Scale			
3	Outstanding	1	Needs Improvement
2	Satisfactory		Not Enough Opportunity to Observe

Names of Students

Inquiry Skills											
Observe											
Compare											
Classify/Order											
Gather, Record, Display, or Interpret Data											
Use Numbers											
Communicate											
Plan and Conduct Simple Investigations											
Measure											
Predict											
Infer											
Draw Conclusions											
Use Time/Space Relationships											
Hypothesize											
Formulate or Use Models											
Identify and Control Variables											
Experiment											

Lab and Activity Evaluation

Circle the appropriate number for each criterion. Then add up the circled numbers in each column and record the sum in the subtotals row at the bottom. Add up these subtotals to get the total score.

Graded by _____ Total _____ /100

Behavior	Completely	Mostly	Partially	Poorly
Follows lab procedures carefully and fully	10–9	8–7–6	5–4–3	2–1–0
Wears the required safety equipment and displays knowledge of safety procedures and hazards	10–9	8–7–6	5–4–3	2–1–0
Uses laboratory time productively and stays on task	10–9	8–7–6	5–4–3	2–1–0
Behavior	**Completely**	**Mostly**	**Partially**	**Poorly**
Uses tools, equipment, and materials properly	10–9	8–7–6	5–4–3	2–1–0
Makes quantitative observations carefully, with precision and accuracy	10–9	8–7–6	5–4–3	2–1–0
Uses the appropriate SI units to collect quantitative data	10–9	8–7–6	5–4–3	2–1–0
Records accurate qualitative data during the investigation	10–9	8–7–6	5–4–3	2–1–0
Records measurements and observations in clearly organized tables that have appropriate headings and units	10–9	8–7–6	5–4–3	2–1–0
Works well with partners	10–9	8–7–6	5–4–3	2–1–0
Efficiently and properly solves any minor problems that might occur with materials or procedures	10–9	8–7–6	5–4–3	2–1–0
Subtotals:				

Comments

_____

_____

_____

_____

My Science Portfolio

What Is in My Portfolio	Why I Chose It
1.	
2.	
3.	
4.	
5.	
6.	
7.	

I organized my Science Portfolio this way because _____

_____

_____

_____

_____

_____

Portfolio Evaluation Checklist

Aspects of Science Literacy	Evidence of Growth
1. **Understands science concepts** *(Animals, Plants; Earth's Land, Air, Water; Space; Weather; Matter, Motion, Energy)*	_____ _____ _____
2. **Uses inquiry skills** *(observes, compares, classifies, gathers/ interprets data, communicates, measures, experiments, infers, predicts, draws conclusions)*	_____ _____ _____
3. **Thinks critically** *(analyzes, synthesizes, evaluates, applies ideas effectively, solves problems)*	_____ _____ _____
4. **Displays traits/attitudes of a scientist** *(is curious, questioning, persistent, precise, creative, enthusiastic; uses science materials carefully; is concerned for environment)*	_____ _____ _____

Summary of Portfolio Assessment

For This Review			Since Last Review		
Excellent	Good	Fair	Improving	About the Same	Not as Good

Name _____ Date _____

Nature of Science

Choose the letter of the best answer.

1. Ricardo is preparing a science fair project about which fabrics are most absorbent. He designs a controlled experiment. What materials will he need for his experiment?

   A. microscope, a variety of liquids, stain repellant

   B. thermometer, a variety of fabrics, a heat source

   C. graduated cylinder, water, a variety of fabrics

   D. graduated cylinder, stain repellant, hand lens

2. Scientists can use many strategies during investigations, including fieldwork, surveys, models, and experiments. Which of these phrases **best** describes an experiment?

   A. mathematical analysis of data

   B. observation of animals in their natural world

   C. collection of data from an uncontrolled environment

   D. procedure with controlled conditions and variables

3. Which piece of equipment can a scientist use to measure the volume of a liquid?

   A. balance

   B. graduated cylinder

   C. ruler

   D. thermometer

4. A scientist uses a computer to make a model of DNA, the genetic material that determines inherited characteristics in living things. DNA is found inside the cells of all living things. The model looked like the figure below.

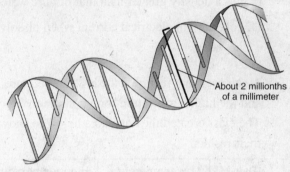
About 2 millionths of a millimeter

   Which of the following is a reason that a scientist would want to use a model to study DNA?

   A. DNA does not really exist.

   B. DNA is very large.

   C. DNA is very rare.

   D. DNA is very small.

5. Which of the following is a characteristic of both scientific laws and theories?

   A. based on scientific evidence

   B. explain natural phenomena

   C. based on opinions of scientists

   D. not subject to change

6. Which description defines a dependent variable in a scientific experiment?

   A. any factor that is controlled during an experiment

   B. factor that is measured to gather results

   C. any factor that changes during an experiment

   D. factor that is changed so that it can be tested

7. Chemists classify some substances as acids. Vinegar is an acid that is often used during cooking to flavor or to preserve foods. Which property of vinegar can you investigate through sense alone?

A. has a sour, acidic taste

B. has a pH greater than that of pure water

C. has a density greater than that of pure water

D. conducts an electrical current when dissolved in water

8. A science class recorded the low temperature and the high temperature for 5 consecutive days. The class created the data table below to show their results.

Day	Low temperature (°C)	High temperature (°C)
Monday	23	31
Tuesday	25	28
Wednesday	26	33
Thursday	24	33
Friday	26	32

What is missing from the data table?

A. labels

B. units

C. title

D. values

9. The data table below shows the number of people who lived in Greenwood in 4 consecutive years.

Population of Greenwood

Year	Number of people (thousands)
2005	208
2006	212
2007	217
2008	221

Which conclusion can be drawn from the table?

A. The population of Greenwood is increasing over time.

B. The population of Greenwood is not changing over time.

C. About four more people are living in Greenwood each year.

D. Fewer people are living in Greenwood now than in the past.

10. Marvin knows that the actual known value for the boiling point of water is 100 °C. He conducts an experiment to measure the boiling point of water in the laboratory. Which of the following results is the **most** accurate?

A. 100.4 °F

B. 102.6 °C

C. 100.4 °C

D. 102.6 °F

Name _____ Date _____

Scientific Knowledge

Key Concepts
Choose the letter of the best answer.

1. Simon is presenting a project on scientific laws and theories. Which of the following statements should he include to explain the differences between the two?

   A. Scientific theories require scientific evidence but scientific laws do not.

   B. Scientific theories are based on observations and scientific laws are based on opinions.

   C. Scientific theories explain why something happens and scientific laws describe what happens.

   D. Scientific theories are rarely changed and scientific laws are modified frequently.

2. Which of these statements best describes how scientific ideas change?

   A. New evidence leads to modification of ideas.

   B. Scientific ideas rarely change, because they are based on extensive evidence.

   C. As a scientific idea changes, it eventually becomes a scientific theory and then a law.

   D. Scientists form opinions based on evidence and decide how the idea should change.

3. A chemist wants to examine specific chemical reactions and isolate certain products using a controlled experiment. How would the chemist perform this experiment?

   A. in a laboratory

   B. out in the field

   C. by performing a survey

   D. by using scientific laws

4. The figure below shows three atomic models.

   Thomson's model, 1904   Rutherford's model, 1911   Current model

   Which of these statements about atomic models is **most likely** correct?

   A. The atomic model has not changed over time.

   B. As scientists learned more about atoms, they modified the atomic model.

   C. Scientists are still debating which of these three models is correct.

   D. Scientists think real atoms look like a combination of the three different models.

5. Which of these scientists would most likely engage in fieldwork to observe organisms?

   A. chemist

   B. biologist

   C. physicist

   D. mathematician

Scientific Investigations

Key Concepts
Choose the letter of the best answer.

1. Which piece of equipment can a paleontologist use to measure the length of a fossil?

    A. balance

    B. ruler

    C. graduated cylinder

    D. thermometer

2. During a scientific investigation, which step will a scientist likely perform first?

    A. Collect and organize data.

    B. Plan an experimental procedure.

    C. Define the problem for investigation.

    D. Defend conclusions drawn from data.

3. Malik investigates the force required to pull an object across a table. The data table below shows the data he recorded.

Mass of object (kg)	Force required (N)
1	0.20
2	0.41
4	0.80
8	?

Based on the data, what force is required to pull the 8-N object?

    A. about 0.10 N

    B. about 1.20 N

    C. about 1.60 N

    D. about 2.00 N

4. Which scientific investigation does **not** include dependent and independent variables?

    A. observing and counting bird populations

    B. studying the effect of temperature on bacterial reproduction rates

    C. investigating the effect of mass on the speed at which an object falls

    D. testing a model car's air flow resistance at different wind speeds in a wind tunnel

5. Marissa investigates how far a rubber band stretches when she suspends an increasing amount of weight from it. She collects data and analyzes it. The graph below shows her data.

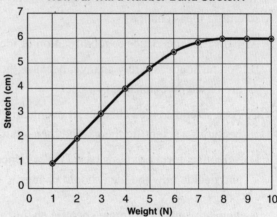

How Far Will a Rubber Band Stretch?

Based on the graph, four different lab groups come to the following conclusions. Which group's conclusion best describes the results shown on the graph?

    A. Group 1: The amount of stretch stays the same as weights are added.

    B. Group 2: The amount of stretch increases as more weights are added.

    C. Group 3: The amount of stretch is unaffected as more weights are added.

    D. Group 4: The amount of stretch gradually decreases as more weights are added.

Representing Data

Key Concepts
Choose the letter of the best answer.

1. A science class is studying seeds. They plan to measure the length, height, and mass of different types of seeds. Which of these items should the class use to record their measurements as the class takes the measurements?

   A. camera   C. graph

   B. drawing   D. data table

2. Two students measured the length of the same sample of rock, but their measurements were not the same. They want to find the cause of the difference. Which of the following possibilities should not have contributed to the difference in measurements?

   A. One student measured from left to right; the other student measured from right to left.

   B. One student used a ruler; the other student used a measuring tape.

   C. One student measured in units of cm; the other student measured in units of m.

   D. Each student used a different technique for measuring length.

3. A science class investigates how far a machine can throw a ball. The data table below shows the data they collect in four trials.

Trial	Distance traveled by ball (m)
1	10.2
2	10.3
3	10.5
4	5.0

   Based on the class's data, how can they improve the accuracy of the investigation?

   A. Erase the data for trial 4.

   B. Use a different ball.

   C. Do more trials.

   D. Change the settings on the ball-throwing machine.

4. A scientist used a model to predict the path of a hurricane. The hurricane followed a similar path but did not follow the exact path that was predicted. How does this example demonstrate a limitation of models?

   A. Models cannot be used to predict things.

   B. Models can be used to predict weather events before the event occurs.

   C. Models cannot account for how every factor may suddenly change.

   D. Models can only be used to show physical structures, not events such as hurricanes.

5. The table below lists the population of Greenwood in 4 different years.

   Population of Greenwood

Year	Number of people (thousands)
2005	208
2006	212
2007	217
2008	221

   What was the population of Greenwood in 2007?

   A. 212

   B. 217

   C. 212,000

   D. 217,000

Scientific Knowledge

Take Your Pick: *Science and Scientific Knowledge*
Complete the activities to show what you've learned about science and scientific knowledge.

1. Work on your own, with a partner, or with a small group.

2. Choose items below for a total of 10 points. Check your choices.

3. Have your teacher approve your plan.

4. Submit or present your results.

2 Points

_____ **Gathering Evidence** Suppose you are a chemist who is studying the amount of pollutants in your local river. Sketch one way you can collect empirical evidence for your work.

_____ **What Do You Think?** Using a half sheet of paper or an index card, answer these questions: *What was the most interesting fact you learned about science from this lesson? How did studying this lesson change how you thought or felt about learning science?*

5 Points

_____ **You Ask the Questions** Imagine you are tutoring sixth-graders who are studying science. Make up a practice quiz for them about scientific theory and scientific law. Your quiz should be at least five questions long. They can be short-answer, true/false, or multiple choice. Include an answer key.

_____ **A Scientific Skit** Compare a scientific theory, such as the atomic theory or the germ theory, with the use of the word *theory* in a detective or mystery story.

_____ **Defending Review** Imagine you are part of a team of scientists that has done research and published a scientific paper. One of your team members is upset because another group of scientists has criticized your findings. Present a persuasive speech explaining why the scientist should not be upset because peer review and discussion is important to establishing scientific knowledge.

8 Points

_____ **An Empirical Essay** Write a one-page essay that defines and describes empirical evidence. Make sure your essay has an introduction, a body, and a conclusion. Also include some examples of empirical evidence in your essay.

_____ **What's Your Theory?** Research a particular scientific theory. Create a commercial that promotes that theory. In your commercial, explain what a scientific theory is and how it is formed. Also include information about the theory you chose and the research that backs up that theory.

Scientific Investigations

Alternative Assessment

Points of View: *Learning Through Investigations*

Your class will work together to show what you've learned about scientific investigations from several different viewpoints.

1. Work in groups as assigned by your teacher. Each group will be assigned to one or two viewpoints.

2. Complete your assignment, and present your perspective to the class.

Scientific Investigations

 Vocabulary Look up the words *hypothesis*, *variable*, *observation*, and *data* in the glossary. Write the terms and their definitions on a sheet of paper. Add descriptions that help to explain the terms.

 Examples Using newspapers and the Internet, locate two or three articles about scientific investigations. Print or copy the articles. Then underline sections of the articles that tell about the scientific methods the scientists used.

 Analysis Look more deeply at one of the investigations in this lesson. Analyze it to try to find as many standard factors (aspects) as you can. What is the independent variable? What is one dependent variable? Could the independent variable be changed without changing the entire experiment? Could the dependent variables be changes without changing the entire experiment? What other ways could the experiment be conducted? If the investigation were changed, what might the results test?

 Observations Using the Internet or television, find a video or written description of a scientist conducting an investigation. While you watch the video, make notes about the major processes the scientist uses, and keep track of the order in which they are used. Create a poster that lists the major processes the scientist used.

 Details Write the labels *Experiments* and *Other Scientific Investigations* on a sheet of paper. Then list details about experiments and other scientific investigations. Last, use your details to sum up what you know about experiments and other scientific investigations.

Representing Data

Climb the Ladder: *Showing Your Data*

Select an idea from each rung of the ladder to show what you've learned about the different ways to represent data.

1. Work on your own, with a partner, or with a small group.

2. Choose one item from each rung of the ladder. Check your choices.

3. Have your teacher approve your plan.

4. Submit or present your results.

__ Make a Model Make a model that shows the parts of an object you would be likely to study in your science class. For example, you may decide to make a model of the parts of a cell or the structure of an atom. Your model should be as accurate and precise as possible. Present your finished model to the class in an oral presentation. Tell the model's uses and limitations.	**__ Analyze a Model** Select an existing model, such as a globe or a model in your classroom. Consider how the model is used. What are its advantages? What are its limitations? How precise and accurate is it? Show the model and share your ideas in an oral presentation to your class.
__ Develop a Line Graph Use one of the data tables from the bottom rung of the ladder to make a line graph. Make sure your graph includes all the labels, numbers, and units a line graph should have and that it accurately represents the data.	**__ Gather Data and Make a Graph** Research the average monthly temperature for the area in which you live over a one-year period. Organize the data you find in a scatter plot graph. Make sure your graph includes all the labels, numbers, and units a scatter plot should have and that it accurately represents the data.
__ Make a Data Table from a Direct Data Source Find a source of numerical data. Organize the numerical data from the source in a precise and accurate data table.	**__ Organize Data in a Table** Conduct a survey of your classmates. You might ask what flavor of ice cream they like best, what their favorite book is, or another topic of your choice. Organize the data from your survey in a correctly constructed data table. Make sure your table is accurate and precise.

Unit 1 ISTEP+ Review

Choose the letter of the best answer.

1 Scientists use computer models to study how black holes form in space. What is the MOST LIKELY reason a computer model is being used?

A. Black holes do not actually exist.

B. Black holes are too small to study.

C. Black holes are too dark to study.

D. Black holes are too far from earth.

2 Good experiments follow organized procedures. Which of these phrases describes ANOTHER CHARACTERISTIC of a good scientific experiment?

A. uncontrolled surroundings

B. results that can be replicated

C. small sample size for collecting data

D. variable procedures for obtaining data

3 A physicist at a research laboratory reports a startling new discovery. However, other scientists are unable to reproduce the results of the experiment. Which statement provides the MOST LIKELY EXPLANATION for the faulty results?

A. The results are announced to the public.

B. The conclusions are based on multiple trials.

C. The data collection was not accurate or precise.

D. Other scientists don't have as sophisticated equipment.

4 Photosynthesis is a complex series of chemical reactions that take place in a plant cell. The chemical equation below summarizes photosynthesis, which is how plants make their own food.

$$6H_2O + 6CO_2 \xrightarrow{\text{Light energy}} C_6H_{12}O_6 + 6O_2$$

Based on the above explanation, what might be a possible weakness of this model?

A. It does not show all the steps of the process.

B. It is too complicated to use for studying photosynthesis.

C. It has no value for studying photosynthesis.

D. It cannot be modified to show the more detailed process.

Go On ➡

5 Scientific investigations include many different steps. During a scientific investigation, which step occurs AFTER a scientist collects data?

A. Draw conclusions.

B. Form the hypothesis.

C. Plan the experiment.

D. Follow the procedure.

6 Indira tested whether tomato plants grew faster in part shade or full sun. The table below shows the average height of the plants in each condition after 0, 10, 20, and 30 days.

Plant Growth

Conditions	Initial height (cm)	Height after 10 days (cm)	Height after 20 days (cm)	Height after 30 days (cm)
Full sun	20	24	27	31
Part shade	20	22	23	25

What is ONE CONCLUSION Indira can draw from her data?

A. The tomato plants grew taller in full sun than they did in part shade.

B. All plants grow taller in full sun than they do in part shade.

C. Tomato plants grown in full sun will produce more tomatoes.

D. Tomato plants need to be placed in full sun in order to grow.

7 Reece completed an experiment by rolling toy cars down a ramp. Each car was a different mass. Reece recorded how long it took each car to reach the end of the ramp. He then created the table below to show his results.

How Mass Affects Speed

Car	Mass	Time
A	200	28
B	300	26
C	400	22
D	500	20

What is the MAIN PROBLEM with Reece's table?

A. The title is incorrect.

B. The units are missing.

C. The values are incorrect.

D. There are too many rows.

Go On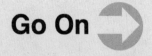

8 The kinetic theory of matter uses the motions of particles to explain why gases expand and contract at different temperatures. The figure below illustrates what happens to the same amount of gas when the temperature of the gas changes.

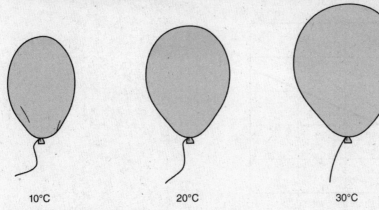

10°C   20°C   30°C

Based on the information about kinetic theory and the figure, what is the BEST PREDICTION of what will happen if the temperature rises to 40 °C?

A. If the temperature increases, then the number of gas particles will increase, causing the balloon to get bigger.

B. If the temperature increases, then the number of gas particles will decrease, causing the balloon to get smaller.

C. If the temperature increases, then the gas particles will move more slowly and get closer together, causing the balloon to get smaller.

D. If the temperature increases, then the gas particles will move faster and get farther apart, causing the balloon to get bigger.

Constructed Response

9 Jill is conducting an investigation about the television programs her classmates watch most often. She wants to know if the girls in the class watch different types of programs than the boys watch.

What data should Jill collect?

_____

_____

What is the BEST METHOD of collecting data for her investigation?

_____

_____

_____

Go On ➡

Extended Response

10 Greg grew two plants in two different soils. The graph below shows the height of the two plants over 12 weeks.

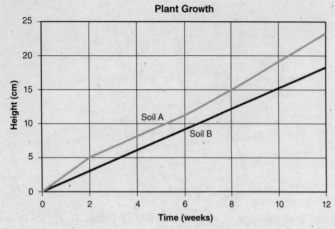

Identify the INDEPENDENT and DEPENDENT variables in Greg's experiment.

Independent variable: _____

Dependent variable: _____

Greg predicted that soil B would cause the plant to grow TALLER because it contained compost. How do the results of the experiment compare to Greg's prediction?

_____

_____

After 12 weeks, Greg noticed that the plant grown in soil B had more leaves and appeared healthier than the plant in soil A. What QUESTION can Greg ask to find out more about his observation?

_____

_____

Describe the steps you would follow to investigate Greg's new question.

_____

_____

_____

Nature of Science

Key Concepts
Choose the letter of the best answer.

1. Which statement describes how a scientist makes scientific explanations?

   A. A scientist bases scientific explanations on a large body of observations of the world.

   B. A scientist bases scientific explanations only on other scientists' opinions.

   C. A scientist bases scientific explanations on personal experience and opinions.

   D. A scientist suggests scientific explanations and makes up evidence to make them true.

2. Which description defines a dependent variable in a scientific experiment?

   A. the set of results for an experiment

   B. a factor that requires tools to measure

   C. any factor that changes during an experiment

   D. a factor that changes due to the independent variable

3. The diagram below represents a molecule of water. The circles represent atoms, and the lines represent bonds.

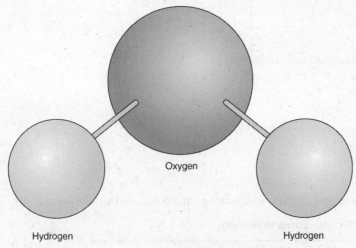

Oxygen

Hydrogen   Hydrogen

   What is the correct term for this diagram?

   A. experiment   C. visual model

   B. observation   D. mathematical model

4. A group of students measures the mass and volume of an object to calculate its density. Which procedure increases the accuracy and reliability of the group's data?

   A. repeating the experiment and analyzing all the data

   B. having group members individually calculate density

   C. changing the procedure to check whether the results are constant

   D. varying the equipment used to check whether the results are constant

5. Which of these events might lead to the modification of a scientific idea?

A. A scientist uses a computer to teach a scientific concept to students.

B. Two scientists doing the same experiment in different parts of the world under the same conditions get the same results.

C. One scientist finds evidence that she feels doesn't fit a theory. Other scientists agree that her results are valid.

D. A scientist performs an experiment and finds out that one of the chemicals used in the experiment was contaminated.

6. Jaime planted two seeds. She watered one seed with tap water. She watered the second seed with plant feed. She measured the height of the plant every two weeks. She created the graph below to show her results.

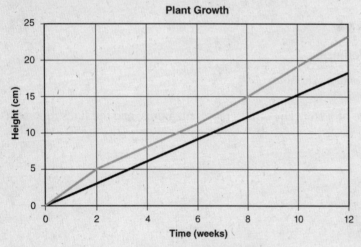

Plant Growth

Which of these items is missing from the graph?

A. key   C. title

B. x-axis   D. units

7. The table below shows the high temperature and the low temperature in a town during one week.

Daily Temperatures in Houston

Day	Low temperature (°C)	High temperature (°C)
Monday	23	31
Tuesday	25	28
Wednesday	26	33
Thursday	24	33
Friday	26	32

On which day was there the least difference between the low temperature and high temperature?

A. Monday   C. Thursday

B. Tuesday   D. Friday

8. Jim investigates how the angle of a throw affects the distance that the ball travels. The drawings below show three trials from the experiment.

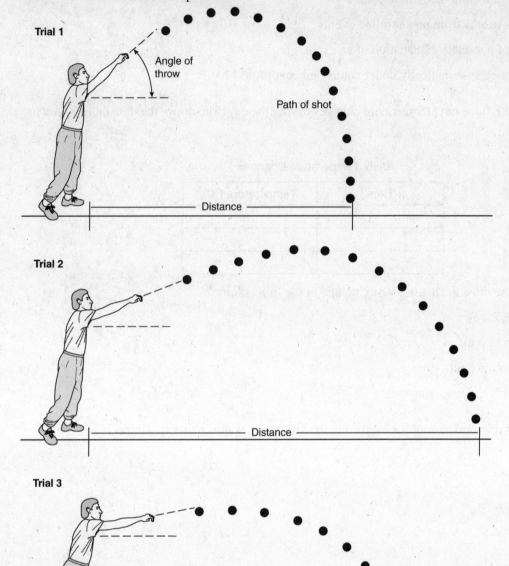

Trial 1

Angle of throw

Path of shot

Distance

Trial 2

Distance

Trial 3

Distance

Assuming Jim hurls the ball with the same force each time, what is the dependent variable in the experiment?

A. force exerted on the ball

B. distance traveled by the ball

C. angle at which the ball is thrown

D. time it takes the ball to hit the ground

9. Which description defines an experiment?

   A. prediction of something that will happen

   B. observation of results from uncontrolled events

   C. development of a testable explanation of an event

   D. procedure applied systematically under controlled conditions

10. Ming wants to determine how temperature changes during the day. She draws the data table below to record her results.

Daily Temperature Changes

Time	Temperature (°C)

   What would be the **most accurate** data to include in the first column?

   A. Early, Middle, Late

   B. 10 a.m., Noon, 2 p.m.

   C. 2 hours, 4 hours, 6 hours

   D. Morning, Midday, Afternoon

11. What is the most appropriate tool for measuring the volume of water in an experiment?

   A. milliliters

   B. beaker

   C. graduated cylinder

   D. cubic centimeters

12. A researcher finds that data from her experiment do not support her hypothesis. What should the researcher do?

A. Do more trials

B. Change the data to support the hypothesis.

C. Change the procedure to obtain the desired result.

D. Form a new hypothesis and conduct experiments to investigate it.

Constructed Response

13. List two characteristics of a reliable scientific investigation.

1) _____

2) _____

Choose one characteristic of reliable scientific investigations and explain how it can increase the accuracy or precision of the investigation.

_____

_____

_____

_____

_____

Extended Response

14. A classmate says an ice cube tray filled with hot water freezes faster than one filled with cool water when he places the trays outside on a freezing winter day. You want to plan an experiment to investigate this statement.

What is a prediction that your experiment will test?

_____

_____

Time to Make Ice Cubes

Time (min)	Temperature of hot water (°C)	Temperature of cold water (°C)
30		
45		
60		
75		

Identify the independent variable and the dependent variable in your experiment.

Independent Variable

_____

Dependent Variable

_____

Describe your experimental procedure by telling three steps you would follow.

1) _____

2) _____

3) _____

How will you know if your results support your prediction?

_____

_____

Nature of Science

Key Concepts
Choose the letter of the best answer.

1. A scientist is researching the solar system. How can the scientist best add to the empirical evidence already gathered about the solar system?

   A. The scientist can make and record observations.

   B. The scientist can debate the research with other scientists.

   C. The scientist can write an opinion column about the research.

   D. The scientist can develop a new law regarding the solar system.

2. Controlled scientific experiments include variables. One kind of variable is an independent variable and the other kind is a dependent variable. Which statement describes the difference between an independent variable and a dependent variable?

   A. The dependent variable does not change and the independent variable does change.

   B. The independent variable does not change and the dependent variable does not change.

   C. The dependent variable is the control and the independent variable is the result.

   D. The dependent variable changes based on the independent variable.

3. Why do many experiments include several trials instead of a single trial?

   A. Repetition of trials makes data easier to analyze.

   B. Repetition of trials increases the accuracy of the results.

   C. Repetition of trials increases the sample size of the experiment.

   D. Repetition of trials lets the experimenter change the experimental procedure.

4. The hinge shown below is used to model the elbow joint.

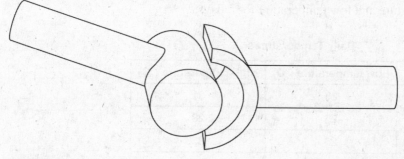

   Which feature of the model would be **most** important to understanding how the elbow joint functions?

   A. how the hinge moves

   B. how wide the hinge is

   C. what color the hinge is

   D. what the hinge is made of

5. Two scientists have different ideas about a scientific concept. What might they do to resolve their differences?

   A. Debate their ideas using evidence they have gathered through observation and research.

   B. Remain silent and hope someone will come up with confirmation for one side or another.

   C. Each will only discuss the idea with people they know will agree with it.

   D. Each will agree that the other is correct in order to remain friends.

6. Two plants were grown in two different brands of potting mix. The graph below shows the height of the two plants over 12 weeks.

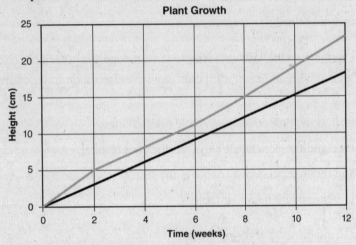

Plant Growth

Why does a key need to be added to the graph?

   A. to describe the purpose of the graph

   B. to show which plant is represented by each line

   C. to describe how often the height was measured

   D. to show which units were used to measure height

7. Trevor recorded the high temperature and low temperature for 5 days.

Daily Temperatures

Day	Low temperature (°C)	High temperature (°C)
Monday	23	31
Tuesday	25	28
Wednesday	26	33
Thursday	24	33
Friday	26	32

What was the high temperature on Thursday?

   A. 24 °F   C. 24 °C

   B. 33 °F   D. 33 °C

8. Margie conducts an experiment in which a shot-putter from the track team throws the shot several times. The drawings below show her observations of three trials from the experiment.

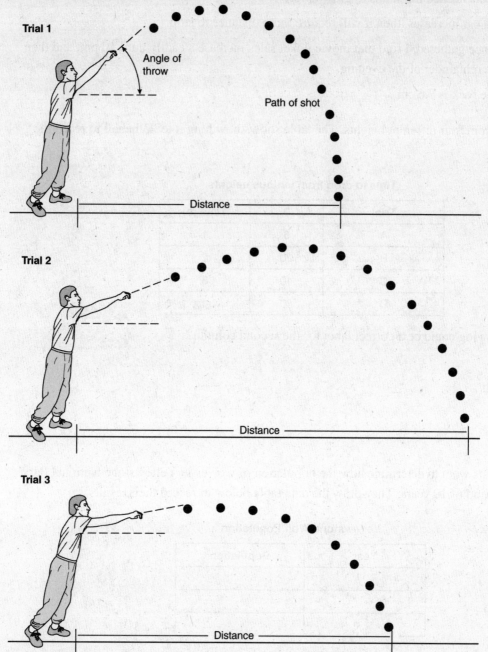

Trial 1

Angle of throw

Path of shot

Distance

Trial 2

Distance

Trial 3

Distance

Based on Margie's data, which question is she **most likely** trying to answer?

A. How much force is exerted on the shot?

B. How does the angle of the throw affect how far the shot goes?

C. How does the angle of the throw affect how long the shot is in the air?

D. How does the amount of force on the shot affect how far the shot goes?

9. Which of the following is an example of an observation?

   A. How much light is needed for plants to grow taller?

   B. If the speed of a car increases, then it will require more distance to stop.

   C. Based on evidence gathered, I find that movie ticket sales increase steadily until 10 pm, and then decrease for the remainder of the evening.

   D. The width of the rock is 7.6 cm.

10. Neil drops a ball from four different heights. The table shows how long it took the ball to reach the ground.

Time to drop from various heights

Trial	?	Time (s)
A	5	1
B	20	2
C	40	3
D	80	4

Which of the following could be a correct label for the second column?

A. Speed

B. Mass of the ball

C. Height (m)

D. Length of drop

11. A group of scientists want to determine how the population of wolves in Yellowstone National Park changes over a period of 10 years. They draw the data table below to record their results.

Yellowstone Wolf Population

Year	Population

What would be the **best** data to include in the first column?

A. Start, Middle, End

B. April, July, September

C. 2010, 2015, 2020

D. 2010, 2011, 2012

12. Ellie's class is studying tide pools and starfish. They made the following prediction:

If the water temperature in a tide pool increases, then the starfish population decreases.

Then, they recorded the following data:

Starfish Population of Tide Pools

Water Temperature (°C)	Population
10	37
12	44
16	64
20	48

Compare the results of the experiment to the class's prediction. What should they do next?

A. Change the prediction to match the results.

B. Change the data to fit the prediction.

C. Collect data at several other tide pools.

D. Change the procedure to obtain the desired result.

Constructed Response

13. A student wants to investigate to see if there is mold growing in her school. She plans to use swabs to collect samples from around the school. Then, she will attempt to grow the samples in an incubator.

What are two characteristics of reliable scientific investigations that the student should include as part of her experimental plan?

1) _____

2) _____

Choose one of the characteristics you noted above. Why should the student include this characteristic? Include an explanation of how it can increase the validity, accuracy, or precision of her results.

_____

_____

Extended Response

14. A classmate says an ice cube tray filled with hot water freezes faster than one filled with cool water when he places the trays outside on a freezing winter day.

What is a prediction you could test based on your classmate's claim?

_____

_____

Identify the independent variable and the dependent variable in your experiment.

Independent variable:

_____

Dependent variable:

_____

Name **two** other variables that you will control in the experiment.

1) _____

2) _____

Describe your experimental procedure.

_____

_____

_____

_____

How will you know if your results support your prediction?

_____

_____

Motion and Forces

Choose the letter of the best answer.

1. Which of the following describes the result of a force acting on an object?

   A. The force changes the mass of the object.

   B. The force does not cause a change in the object.

   C. The force transfers energy to or from the object.

   D. The force increases or decreases the weight of the object.

2. Imagine a weightless box floating in space. The following picture shows the forces acting on this box.

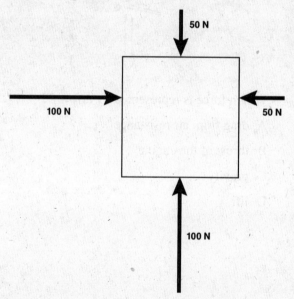

   In what direction will this box accelerate?

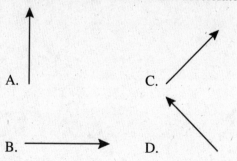

   A.

   B.

   C.

   D.

3. In a swimming race, Miho swam the first 50 m in 42 s. She swam the second 50 m in 40 s. What was Miho's average speed during the race?

   A. 0.82 m/s

   B. 1.19 m/s

   C. 1.22 m/s

   D. 1.25 m/s

4. The following picture shows forces acting on a box as it is pushed with a force of 50 N and pulled with a force of another 50 N across the floor. Sarah wants to stop the motion of the box.

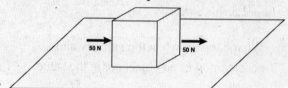

   How much force should Sarah use and in which direction should she push to stop the box from moving?

   A. 100 N down

   B. 50 N up

   C. 75 N right

   D. 100 N left

5. Imagine that a chair on the floor experiences two horizontal forces. One force measures 200 N and the other force measures –200 N. Which of the following statements describes what is happening to the chair?

   A. The chair's motion is not changing.

   B. The chair's motion is changing.

   C. The chair is not moving.

   D. The chair is moving.

6. Which two measurements are needed to determine the speed of an object?

   A. distance and time

   B. distance and direction

   C. position and time

   D. position and direction

7. What is gravity?

   A. the force that pushes all objects toward Earth

   B. the force that pulls all objects toward one another

   C. a magnetic force that is strongest at Earth's poles

   D. heat energy that comes from deep beneath Earth's surface

8. What happens when the velocity and acceleration of an object are in the same direction?

   A. The object does not move.

   B. The speed of the object increases.

   C. The speed of the object decreases.

   D. The object moves at a constant pace.

9. Jason attends a car race. In 5 s, a car reaches a speed of 100 km/h. Jason uses these data to calculate the car's acceleration. Which units will Jason use in his initial acceleration calculation?

   A. m/h

   B. km/h

   C. km/s

   D. km/h/s

10. The following diagram shows four forces acting on an airplane in flight.

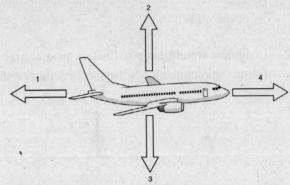

    Which force is represented by arrow 3?

    A. drag from air resistance

    B. thrust of the engine

    C. gravity

    D. lift

Motion and Speed

Key Concepts
Choose the letter of the best answer.

1. Andre boarded a train at Lincoln Station. The train left the station at 9:10 p.m. and traveled, without stopping, 6 miles to Union Station. What additional information does Andre need to find the average speed of the train from Lincoln Station to Union Station?

    A. the direction the train traveled

    B. the time the train left Union Station

    C. the initial and maximum speeds of the train

    D. the time the train arrived at Union Station

2. Which of the following is a definition of motion?

    A. a change in position over time

    B. the speed and direction of an object

    C. the length of the path between points

    D. a location compared to other locations

3. Alex is observing a car race. As a car turns a corner, it is traveling at 80 km/hr. As the car crosses the finish line, it is traveling at 140 km/hr. Which term describes these measures?

    A. speed

    B. velocity

    C. average speed

    D. average velocity

4. During a science experiment, Patti dropped a metal ball from a height of 150 m. The graph shows the distance the metal ball traveled from its initial position to where it hit the ground.

    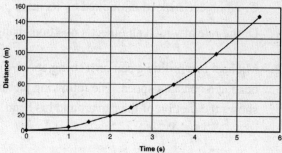

    What information does the graph give you about the speed of the metal ball over time?

    A. The ball travels at a constant speed.

    B. The speed increases as time increases.

    C. The speed decreases as time increases.

    D. The speed increases at first, and then decreases as time increases.

5. An athlete is running a 5-km race at an average speed of 8 km/h. She has to stop and tie her shoe. After tying her shoe she continues running at 8 km/h. Why would her average speed for the entire race be less than 8 km/h?

    A. The total distance she traveled increased.

    B. The total distance she traveled decreased.

    C. The total time she took to complete the race increased.

    D. The total time she took to complete the race decreased.

Name _____ Date _____

Acceleration

Key Concepts
Choose the letter of the best answer.

1. What is acceleration?

   A. the direction of motion

   B. the rate at which velocity changes

   C. an object's speed multiplied by its mass

   D. the rate at which an object's position changes

2. Michael is whirling a can on a string above his head at a constant speed. The following picture shows the motion of the can around his hand.

   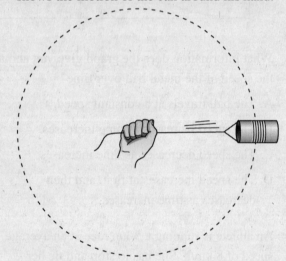

   Which statement **best** describes what happens to the can?

   A. The can is accelerating because it is changing direction.

   B. The can is accelerating because it moves faster and faster.

   C. The can accelerates because it moves slower and slower.

   D. The can does not change speeds, so there is no acceleration.

3. Measuring acceleration requires appropriate units. Scientists measure acceleration using a standardized set of units that are part of the SI system. Which are the SI units for acceleration?

   A. N   C. m/s^2

   B. m/s   D. kg·m/s

4. An ice skater moves back and forth on an ice rink. She speeds up on the straight portion of the rink. She slows down near each end of the rink and then turns around. Which statement best describes her acceleration?

   A. The skater only experiences acceleration when she is turning.

   B. The skater only experiences acceleration while skating in a straight line.

   C. The skater experiences acceleration both while skating in a straight line and while making her turn.

   D. Because the skater does not change her direction or speed, she does not experience acceleration.

5. Alex performs a lab experiment with a radio-controlled cart. He measures the speed of the cart as it accelerates along a straight track. The following table shows his data.

Time (s)	Speed (m/s)
0	0
1	1
2	1.9
3	3

   What is the average acceleration of the cart after 3 s?

   A. $2.0 \ m/s^2$ C. 1.5 m/s

   B. $1 \ m/s^2$ D. 3 m/s

Forces

Key Concepts
Choose the letter of the best answer.

1. Which of these is evidence that an unbalanced force is acting on an object?

   A. The mass of the object is changing.

   B. The object remains at rest.

   C. The motion of the object is changing.

   D. The object continues moving in a straight line at constant velocity.

2. Which property can be used to measure the inertia of a stationary object?

   A. acceleration   C. mass

   B. gravity   D. velocity

3. Luis is pushing a box of new soccer balls across the floor. In the following picture, the arrow on the box is a vector representing the force Luis exerts.

   What do the length and direction of the arrow represent?

   A. the distance and direction of the motion of the box

   B. the strength and direction of the force applied to the box

   C. the motion of the box and the direction of the force applied to it

   D. the strength and direction of the unbalanced force applied to the box

4. Which picture shows an object whose acceleration is zero?

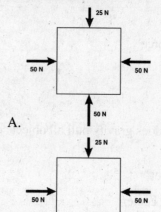

   A.

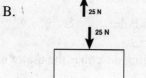

   B.

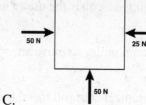

   C.

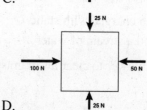

   D.

5. A rock is resting on top of a hill. The rock suddenly begins moving down the side of the hill. Why did the rock begin to move?

   A. An unbalanced force acted on the rock and caused it to move.

   B. A sudden change in gravitational force caused the rock to move.

   C. Balanced forces caused the rock to move, and then gravity kept it moving.

   D. An upward force balanced the gravitational force, so the rock began to move.

Types of Forces

Key Concepts
Choose the letter of the best answer.

1. Which of the following forces can act only when two objects are in contact with each other?

   A. electric force

   B. gravitational force

   C. magnetic force

   D. friction force

2. In what direction does gravity pull all objects on Earth?

   A. toward your feet

   B. toward Earth's center

   C. toward the North Pole

   D. toward the South Pole

3. Which of the following describes the use of an applied force?

   A. the use of a rope and pulley to move an object

   B. the use of a strong magnet to roll metal balls

   C. the use of a comb charged with static electricity to bend a stream of water

   D. the use of a leaf blower to clear away grass cuttings

4. The following table lists the weights and volumes of several items.

Object	Mass (g)	Volume (cm³)
bowling ball	3,600	5,400
golf ball	60	33
soccer ball	450	5,400
tennis ball	60	130

   Which object has the **greatest** gravitational force acting on it on Earth?

   A. bowling ball

   B. golf ball

   C. soccer ball

   D. tennis ball

5. What is the gravitational force acting on an object that has a mass of 10.0 kg?

   A. $0.2 \ kg\cdot m/s^2$

   B. $9.8 \ kg\cdot m/s^2$

   C. $10.0 \ kg\cdot m/s^2$

   D. $98.0 \ kg\cdot m/s^2$

Motion and Speed

Tic-Tac-Toe: *A Need for Speed*

1. Work on your own, with a partner, or with a small group.

2. Choose three quick activities from the game. Check the boxes you plan to complete. They must form a straight line in any direction.

3. Have your teacher approve your plan.

4. Do each activity, and turn in your results.

__ **Location**	__ **Average Speed**	__ **Velocity**
Describe your location in the classroom from the reference point of the doorway. You don't need actual measurements for this, as you can use classroom objects to describe the location. Then describe your location in the classroom from a reference point on the moon.	Calculate the average speed of a plane that travels 1,000 miles in 2.5 hours.	1. Draw a diagram that shows two objects going in the same direction but with different velocities. 2. Draw two objects traveling at the same speed but with different velocities. 3. Draw two objects with identical velocities. Describe speed and velocity in each diagram.
__ **Modeling Speed**	__ **Map It**	__ **Graph It**
Use two toy cars. Make two ramps of different lengths using classroom objects. Put one car at the top of each ramp. Release the cars together. Which car is faster? Explain why.	Draw a map of your classroom that shows the locations of the desks and other major features in the room. Describe how to get from your desk to the door and your desk to a window.	Make a graph that shows a car traveling at different rates for 10 hours. What is the average speed? What is the distance that the car traveled in 10 hours?
__ **A-Mazing**	__ **Changing Speeds**	__ **Speed But No Velocity?**
Use graph paper to draw a maze. Pick two points (the start and the finish) and find the distance between the two points if you travel though the maze. Measure the distance in a straight line (as the crow flies) from the start to the finish.	Draw a graph that shows the changing speed of a fictional runner during a 26-mile marathon. At times, the runner speeds up; at other times, he or she slows down. Occasionally the runner stops to rest or to get a drink. Show these changes on your graph.	Draw a diagram or sketch that shows an object that has traveled a certain distance at a specific speed but has zero average velocity.

Acceleration

Climb the Ladder: *Types of Acceleration*

1. Work on your own, with a partner, or with a small group.

2. Choose one item from each rung of the ladder. Check your choices.

3. Have your teacher approve your plan.

4. Submit or present your results.

__ Racing! Suppose you are a runner in a 10K race. You complete the first half of the race in 18 minutes. What is your average acceleration?	**__ More Racing!** A runner in a 5K race completes the race in 16 minutes. What is the average acceleration?
__ Speed A runner's velocity and acceleration are in the same direction. What can you say about the runner's speed? Explain in words or a diagram what happens to the runner's velocity and acceleration.	**__ Show Speed** A runner's velocity and acceleration are in opposite directions. What can you say about the runner's speed? Draw a diagram or illustration that shows the runner's velocity and acceleration.
__ Acceleration A runner changes direction. What can you say about acceleration? Explain in writing what happens to the runner's speed and direction.	**__ Centripetal Acceleration** Make a drawing that shows centripetal acceleration. Label acceleration, direction, and speed.

Forces

Mix and Match: *Forces, Motion, and Newton's Laws*
Mix and match ideas to show what you've learned about forces.

1. Work on your own, with a partner, or with a small group.

2. Choose one static situation and one involving acceleration from Column A, six topics from Column B, and one option from Column C. Check your choices.

3. Have your teacher approve your plan.

4. Submit or present your results.

A. Choose Two Situations	B. Choose Six Things to Analyze	C. Choose One Way to Communicate Analysis
___ a tire hanging on a rope	___ friction	___ demonstration
___ a bicycle leaning against a building	___ gravity	___ model
___ a car rounding a corner	___ balanced forces	___ video
___ a sailboat moving in a breeze	___ unbalanced forces	___ labeled diagrams
___ a car in a driveway	___ Newton's third law	___ skit
___ a weight lifter holding a heavy barbell overhead	___ contact force	_____
___ a person skating on ice	___ inertia	
___ a crash test dummy being restrained by a seat belt during a crash		
___ a person rowing a boat		
_____		

Types of Forces

Tic-Tac-Toe: *How Forces Work*

1. Work on your own, with a partner, or with a small group.

2. Choose three quick activities from the game. Check the boxes you plan to complete.
   They must form a straight line in any direction.

3. Have your teacher approve your plan.

4. Do each activity, and turn in your results.

__ **Poetry Slam**	__ **Celestial Objects**	__ **Charged Object Skit**
Write a poem using the word *force*. Highlight key ideas and phrases about force, including details about different types of forces and how they act on objects. If you want, present your poem as a performance.	Draw a series of diagrams showing how gravity affects the shape of objects and their movement. For example, show how the force of forward motion and gravity work together to keep an object in orbit.	Perform a skit that describes electrical and magnetic forces. Make sure you include information on how objects with like and unlike charges interact.
__ **Be the Teacher**	__ **Planetary Brochure**	__ **News Report**
Write a quiz to test how well students have learned the material in this lesson. Check that your questions cover the main ideas and that the questions are fair. Include an answer key. Give the quiz to a partner to see if it works well.	Imagine that you live on a newly discovered planet. The air is breathable, the water is drinkable, and traveling there takes a few days. However, the planet has a much lower surface gravity than Earth. Write a brochure encouraging people to visit. Describe all the benefits of living with lower surface gravity.	Write a Webcast. The topic should be related to contact force. For example, report on how friction affects sneaker performance, how air resistance influenced a baseball game's outcome, why there is a new law forbidding the use of a particular type of direct force, or how spring force is being used in a new type of toy.
__ **Comic Strip**	__ **Puzzle Time**	__ **www.force.net**
Draw a comic strip with a character who is learning about forces. Include at least three examples of everyday actions that help the character figure out how different types of forces work.	Make a crossword puzzle that uses key terms and ideas from the lesson. The puzzle should use at least ten terms including *magnetic, electrical, friction,* and *gravity*.	Design an imaginary Web page for the contact and non-contact forces. Include on your web page definitions of key terms, images, and examples.

Unit 2 ISTEP+ Review

Choose the letter of the best answer.

1 Which of the following is an example of a CONTACT FORCE?

A. electrical force

B. applied force

C. gravitational force

D. magnetic force

2 A cart is moving on a straight track. Dylan studied the effects of velocity and acceleration of this cart during four trials, shown below.

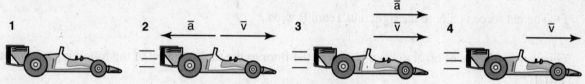

Which trial shows that the cart's acceleration DECREASED?

A. 1

B. 2

C. 3

D. 4

3 During the first two hours of a 4-hour trip, the force of the wind causes a sailboat to travel 68 km. Then the boat sails 3 km in the next hour and 25 km in the last hour. What was the boat's AVERAGE SPEED?

A. 24 km/h

B. 25 km/h

C. 32 km/h

D. 34 km/h

4 How can you find the AVERAGE ACCELERATION of an object?

A. Subtract the initial position from the final position and multiply by change in time.

B. Subtract the initial position from the final position and divide by change in time.

C. Subtract the initial velocity from the final velocity and multiply by change in time.

D. Subtract the initial velocity from the final velocity and divide by change in time.

5 During a game of tug-of-war, members of each team pull on their side of a rope. The pulling forces of each team member are shown in the tables.

Team A	Force
Member 1	70 N to the left
Member 2	70 N to the left
Member 3	90 N to the left

Team B	Force
Member 1	50 N to the right
Member 2	80 N to the right
Member 3	105 N to the right

Which statement correctly describes the NET FORCE and the WINNER of the game?

A. The net force is zero and the game is a tie.

B. The net force is 235 N to the right and Team B wins.

C. The net force is –5 N to the left and Team A wins.

D. The net force is 5 N to the right and Team B wins.

6 Gloria uses a force of 60 N to lift a box from the floor to the table. Which of the following statements is TRUE?

A. The mass of the box is less than 60 N.

B. The forces acting on the box were balanced.

C. The gravitational force on the box is less than 60 N.

D. The upward frictional force on the box is greater than 60 N.

7 Imagine a box floating in space. The following picture shows all the forces acting on this box.

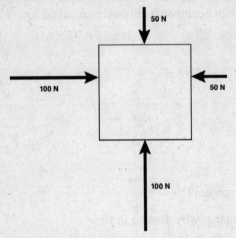

What is the net vertical force on this box?

A. 100 N upward

B. 100 N downward

C. 50 N downward

D. 50 N upward

Go On

8 Which of the following has the GREATEST effect on the gravitational force that exists between two objects?

A. mass

B. volume

C. size

D. density

9 Your weight on the moon is about one-sixth of your weight on Earth. Why do you weigh less on the moon?

A. The moon exerts a greater gravitational force because it is more dense than Earth.

B. The moon exerts a smaller gravitational force because it has less mass than Earth.

C. The moon exerts a greater gravitational force because it is closer to Earth than the sun.

D. The moon exerts a smaller gravitational force because objects are closer to its center than on Earth.

10 A metal ball sitting at rest on a table suddenly begins to roll across the table. What conclusion can you reach about the forces acting on a ball?

A. All the forces acting on the ball remain balanced.

B. There are no forces acting on the ball.

C. A balanced non-contact force acted on the ball.

D. An unbalanced non-contact force acted on the ball.

Constructed Response

11 A school bus **a)** slows down and **b)** stops for a red light. When the light turns green, the school bus **c)** pulls away in a straight line. After reaching the speed limit, the bus **d)** continues at a constant speed until reaching the next corner. The bus **e)** slows and **f)** turns the corner.

During which part of the trip did the bus experience BALANCED forces?

_____

_____

What parts of the bus trip are evidence of UNBALANCED forces?

_____

_____

Go On

Extended Response

12 A skydiver jumped from a height of 2,000 m above the ground. The graph shows the distance the skydiver traveled from her highest position during the first 5.5 seconds.

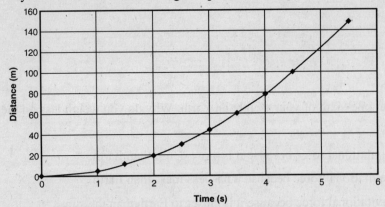

Explain how the graph could be used to determine the skydiver's AVERAGE SPEED for the first 5.5 seconds.

_____

_____

Describe the FORCES acting on the skydiver during the first 4.5 seconds.

_____

_____

Are the forces acting on the skydiver from T= 4.5 seconds to T = 5.5 seconds balanced or unbalanced? How do you know?

_____

_____

The skydiver opens her parachute after 5.5 seconds. Describe how the forces acting on the skydiver change, and what effect the change has on her motion.

_____

_____

_____

Motion and Forces

Key Concepts

Choose the letter of the best answer.

1. Which is an example of centripetal acceleration?

   A. an object at rest

   B. an object moving in a circle at 20 m/s

   C. an object moving at 20 m/s backward, then 20 m/s to the right

   D. an object moving in a straight line at a steady speed of 20 m/s forward

2. Matthew is trying to push a large box across the gym. Although Matthew is exerting a force, the box does not move. In the following picture, the arrow represents the force Matthew exerts on the box.

   What keeps the box from moving even though Matthew is pushing on it?

   A. The inertia of the box is less than Matthew's force.

   B. A greater vertical force is opposed to the force exerted by Matthew.

   C. An equal and opposite force prevents the box from moving.

   D. The force exerted by Matthew on the box is not in the right direction to move the box.

3. The following pictures show the positions and directions of a ball at intervals of 1 s. Which picture shows acceleration due to a change in speed?

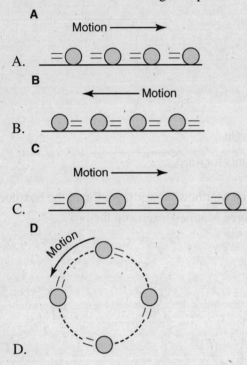

A.

B.

C.

D.

4. If you were orbiting Earth, you would weigh less than you do standing on Earth. Why would your weight in orbit be lower than your weight on Earth's surface?

A. There would be too great a distance between you and Earth for gravity to have any effect.

B. There would be a greater distance between you and Earth, and gravity is related to distance.

C. You would have more mass in orbit, and gravity is related to mass.

D. The gravities of satellites and other objects in orbit around Earth would contribute to your weight while you were in orbit.

5. Rita measured distances that a small boat traveled over 30 s. She wants to create a distance-time graph to show her data. Which of the following should Rita put on the vertical axis?

A. time

B. speed

C. velocity

D. distance

6. A cup of water is left on the roof of a car. When the car begins to move, the cup does not move forward with the car. Instead, it falls off. What happened to the cup of water?

   A. The cup accelerated backward as the car accelerated forward, so the cup fell off the car.

   B. An unbalanced force caused the cup to move with the car, but gravity caused it to fall.

   C. The upward force on the cup increased as the car moved forward, so the cup fell.

   D. Inertia kept the cup from moving while the car moved forward.

7. Masato is practicing his serve for a tennis match. His coach measures the speed of the ball just after Masato hits it. What does the speed indicate?

   A. how fast the ball is moving

   B. what direction the ball moves

   C. what distance the ball has traveled

   D. how long the ball takes to reach the net

8. Which of the following forces can act between two objects that are not touching?

   A. friction force

   B. applied force

   C. spring force

   D. electrical force

9. Every force can be represented as a vector. A vector has two aspects. Which of the following pairs describes a force?

   A. rate and time

   B. rate and size

   C. size and direction

   D. motion and direction

10. Anne and Juan rolled four different objects down a ramp. They measured the distance each object rolled and the time until each object came to a stop. They plotted each point and connected it with a line from origin of the graph.

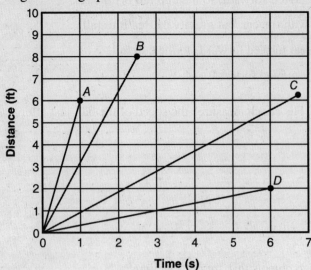

Which object had the **greatest** average speed?

A. object *A*

B. object *B*

C. object *C*

D. object *D*

11. A box of books is on the floor. The following picture shows a push and a pull acting on the box.

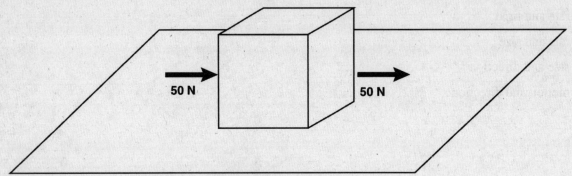

What is the net force toward the right on the box?

A. 0 N

B. 50 N

C. 100 N

D. 2,500 N

12. A model car races down a straight track. The car's speed increases by 2 m/s with each passing second. What is the car's average acceleration after 5 s?

   A. 10 m/s^2

   B. 2 m/s^2

   C. 1 m/s^2

   D. 0 m/s^2

Constructed Response

13. The following diagram shows the forces acting on a box.

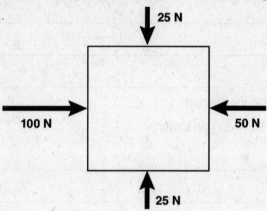

What do the length and the direction of the arrows in the diagram represent?

_____

_____

Are any of the forces acting on the box **balanced**? How do you know?

_____

_____

Are any of the forces acting on the box **unbalanced**? How do you know?

_____

_____

Describe the motion of the box as a result of the forces acting on it.

_____

_____

Extended Response

14. Chandra holds a magnet in each hand, as shown in the illustration below. She holds them still without any movement.

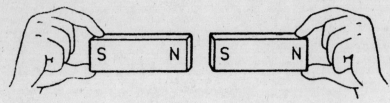

Describe three different forces that are acting on the magnets.

1) _____

2) _____

3) _____

Draw arrows showing the direction of the forces acting on the magnets.

Are the forces on the magnets balanced or unbalanced? How do you know?

_____

_____

Describe **two** things that might happen if Chandra released the magnets. Explain the actions in terms of forces.

1) _____

_____

2) _____

_____

Motion and Forces

Key Concepts

Choose the letter of the best answer.

1. Bao and Andrew are investigating forces. The following picture shows forces acting on a sneaker.

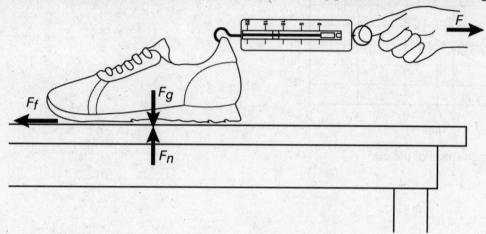

   If the sneaker remains motionless, which statement is **true**?

   A. F_n and F_f have the same strength and F and F_g have the same strength.

   B. F, F_f, F_g, and F_n all have exactly the same strength.

   C. F_f has greater strength than F.

   D. F and F_f have equal strength.

2. Forces act on objects that are either in direct contact or at a distance. Which forces act to keep a book on a table?

   A. mass and magnetic forces

   B. friction and magnetic forces

   C. gravitational and applied forces

   D. velocity and static electric forces

3. The graph below shows the distance a car traveled over 5 seconds while moving on a freeway.

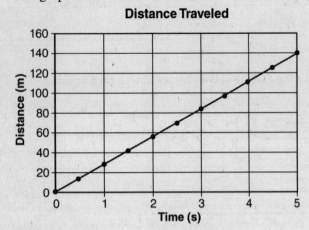

Distance Traveled

What was the average speed of the car?

A. 0 m/s

B. 14 m/s

C. 28 m/s

D. 30 m/s

4. The following pictures show the positions and directions of a particle at intervals of 1 s. Which picture shows acceleration caused by a change in direction?

A.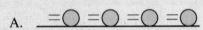

B.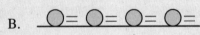

C.

D.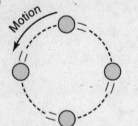

5. During a baseball game, a hitter strikes the ball with a bat. When this happens, the ball and the bat exert a force on each other. Why does the ball accelerate away from the bat more than the bat accelerates away from the ball?

    A. The ball has less mass, so it exerts less force on the bat.

    B. The ball has less mass, so the equal force on the ball and the bat causes greater acceleration on the ball.

    C. The ball has greater velocity before the collision, so force affects the ball more than it affects the bat.

    D. The bat exerts more force than the ball because the batter is exerting a force on the bat as it hits the ball.

6. In science, some quantities are known as vectors. Acceleration is one type of vector. Which of the following is an example of an acceleration vector?

    A. 5 m/s

    B. 5 m/s^2

    C. 5 m/s^2 south

    D. 5 m/s south

7. Melanie watched the path a baseball followed after a pitcher threw it. She noticed that the ball traveled horizontally away from the pitcher, as well as downward toward the ground. What force caused the ball to accelerate in the downward direction when it was thrown?

    A. gravitational force

    B. electrical force

    C. air resistance

    D. applied force

8. A weather station records the wind traveling northeast at 12 km/hr. Which statement explains why northeast at 12 km/h is a vector?

    A. The speed is given in km/h.

    B. The speed is a constant value.

    C. Speed and direction are given.

    D. An average speed is reported.

9. Which picture shows an object accelerating straight upward?

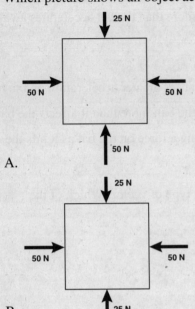

A.

B.

C.

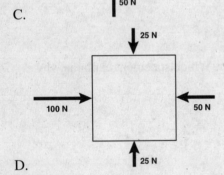

D.

10. Jessica has two balls. One ball has a mass of 1 kg. The other ball has a mass of 2 kg. She pushes each with a force of 100 N. How does the acceleration of the two balls compare?

A. The 1-kg ball accelerates the same as the 2-kg ball.

B. The 1-kg ball accelerates half as much as the 2-kg ball.

C. The 1-kg ball accelerates twice as much as the 2-kg ball.

D. The 1-kg ball accelerates four times as much as the 2-kg ball.

11. Which represents the **greatest** acceleration?

    A. 200 m/s   C. 0.020 km/s^2

    B. 200 m/s^2 D. 0.002 km/s^2

12. Blair and Aaron competed in a 400-m running race. Blair finished the race in 55 s and came in first. Aaron finished the race in 58 s and came in second. Which of the following **must** have been greater for Blair than for Aaron?

    A. maximum speed during the race

    B. average speed for the entire race

    C. speed for the last 100 m of the race

    D. speed for the first 100 m of the race

Constructed Response

13. The diagram below shows forces acting on a box.

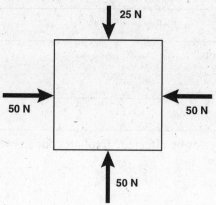

What do the length and the direction of the arrows in the diagram represent?

_____

_____

Are any of the forces acting on the box **balanced**? How do you know?

_____

_____

Are any of the forces acting on the box **unbalanced**? How do you know?

_____

_____

Describe the motion of the box as a result of the forces acting on it.

_____

_____

Extended Response

14. Eddie and Ayana are riding their bicycles down a hill, as shown in the illustration below.

What types of forces are acting on the riders and their bicycles?

_____

_____

What types of forces are Eddie and Ayana exerting on other objects?

_____

_____

If both riders stopped pedaling, how would the motion of the bicycles be affected? Explain your answer in terms of forces.

_____

_____

_____

Describe the balanced and unbalanced forces acting on Ayana's bicycle.

_____

_____

_____

Energy

Choose the letter of the best answer.

1. Chang noticed that it took 2 s for a wave to pass where he was swimming. What property of a wave did he measure?

   A. period

   B. frequency

   C. amplitude

   D. wavelength

2. A boy is riding a bicycle. Why does the bicycle have the ability to do work?

   A. because it has kinetic energy

   B. because it can slow down

   C. because it has gained friction

   D. because it can change direction

3. Fossil fuels are a type of energy source used for generating electricity. Which of the following is **not** an environmental consequence of using fossil fuels?

   A. pollution caused by transportation

   B. radioactive waste products

   C. air pollution

   D. destruction of habitats

4. Feng shines a thin beam of light onto a prism. The light contains wavelengths of red, blue, green, and yellow light. The diagram below shows how the four colors of light exit the prism at different angles.

   Which of the wavelengths is color 1?

   A. red light

   B. blue light

   C. green light

   D. yellow light

5. Which of the following processes is **not** an example of energy being used to do work?

   A. Wind passes through a windmill, turning the blades and producing electricity.

   B. A golfer swings his club and drives his ball down the fairway.

   C. Water passes through a pipe and turns the blades on a turbine, producing electricity.

   D. An athlete uses the energy stored in his muscles as he attempts a bench press, but the barbell does not move.

6. A tennis ball falls off a shelf and bounces several times. Each bounce is lower than the one before. Soon the ball stops. Why doesn't the ball keep bouncing?

   A. The energy becomes stored in the ball.

   B. Some of the energy is changed into mass.

   C. Energy is transferred to the air and ground.

   D. The air and ground slowly destroy the ball's energy.

7. Which describes the speed of a wave?

   A. amplitude × time

   B. period × amplitude

   C. amplitude × wavelength

   D. wavelength × frequency

8. Ebba is in charge of lighting for the school play. When she shines a white light onto one of the props, the prop appears green. What color would the prop appear if she shined a red light onto it?

   A. black

   B. brown

   C. red

   D. white

9. As part of a lab experiment, Tasha drops a metal cube into a beaker of water, as shown in the figure below.

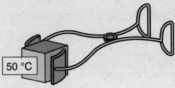

After energy in the form of heat transfers between the substances, what is the final temperature of the water?

   A. The final temperature is 25 °C because there is more water than metal.

   B. The final temperature is 50 °C because the metal warms the water to the temperature of the metal.

   C. The final temperature is between 25 °C and 50 °C because energy is transferred from the metal to the water.

   D. The final temperature is between 25 °C and 50 °C because most of the thermal energy is lost to the air around the substances.

10. A girl uses 60 J of energy to move a box from the floor to a shelf. How much power does she use if it takes her 3 s to move the box?

   A. 15 W

   B. 20 W

   C. 90 W

   D. 180 W

Work, Energy, and Power

Key Concepts
Choose the letter of the best answer.

1. A baseball player used energy to hit a ball out of the park. What is **true** about what took place?

   A. The ball lost energy when it was struck by the bat.

   B. Work was done on the ball through the transfer of energy.

   C. Force was applied in a different direction than motion.

   D. No power was used because the action happened so quickly.

2. Four movers pushed different boxes across a floor for the same distance. The table shows how much force each mover used, the time it took to move the box, and the mass of the box.

Mover	Force (N)	Time (s)	Mass of Box (kg)
Akira	155	5	15
Maddie	120	10	15
Jayden	90	3	18
Hamid	160	10	22

   Which mover did the **most** work moving a box?

   A. Akira

   B. Maddie

   C. Jayden

   D. Hamid

3. A lightbulb uses 2,000 J of energy in 1 min and 20 s. What is the power of the lightbulb?

   A. 25 W

   B. 50 W

   C. 60 W

   D. 100 W

4. A student is planning a camping trip and wants to take a few electronic devices along. Her flexible portable solar panel converts electromagnetic energy from the sun into electrical energy at a rate of 21,600 J/h. Which devices could she charge with it at one time?

Device	Power Needed
Cell phone charger	2 W
PDA charger	5 W
AA/AAA battery charger	7 W

   A. all three devices

   B. the AA/AAA battery charger

   C. the PDA charger or the cell phone charger separately, but not both together

   D. both the cell phone charger and the PDA charger together

5. The table shows different forces and distances that employees in a factory used to lift boxes.

Employee	Force (N)	Distance (m)
Ayanna	24	1.5
Rafael	18	2.5
Cassie	25	1.0
Michael	16	2.0

   Which employee did the **most** work while lifting boxes?

   A. Ayanna

   B. Rafael

   C. Cassie

   D. Michael

Conservation of Energy

Key Concepts
Choose the letter of the best answer.

1. What is the law of conservation of energy?

   A. Energy exists in these forms: mechanical, chemical, thermal, electromagnetic, and nuclear.

   B. Energy is always transferred from the system with the most energy to that with the least.

   C. In an isolated system, matter cannot be created or destroyed.

   D. Energy cannot be created or destroyed; it can only change forms.

2. A spring toy is moving down steps, as shown in the picture.

   What happens to the energy of the toy?

   A. The toy loses energy to the steps.

   B. The toy gains energy as it moves.

   C. The amount and type of energy of the toy stays the same.

   D. The amount of energy the toy has stays the same, but it changes form.

3. What energy transformations take place when a hair dryer is used?

   A. Energy from the sun is transformed to chemical energy.

   B. Electrical energy from the circuit is transformed to electromagnetic energy.

   C. Electrical energy from the circuit is transformed to thermal energy and sound energy.

   D. Electromagnetic energy from the circuit is transformed to thermal energy and sound energy.

4. What is the **most common** explanation for the apparent loss of energy during an energy conversion?

   A. unmeasured forms of energy such as heat or sound

   B. inaccurate measurements of the energy transferred

   C. unnoticed extra energy sources at the beginning of the conversion

   D. electromagnetic energy that is outside of the visible spectrum

5. Four workers at a factory are pushing boxes up ramps. As the workers push the boxes, some energy is transformed to heat due to friction. As a result, the output energy of the workers is less than the input energy. The table shows the input and output energies of each worker.

Worker	Input Energy (J)	Output Energy (J)
Richard	340	270
Molly	310	280
Denzel	280	230
Janice	350	290

   Which worker has the **greatest** efficiency?

   A. Richard

   B. Molly

   C. Denzel

   D. Janice

Thermal Energy and Heat

Key Concepts
Choose the letter of the best answer.

1. These two beakers contain the same liquid substance at the same temperature.

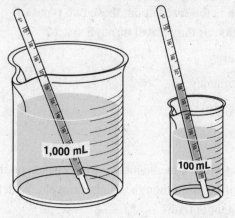

1,000 mL
100 mL

How does the thermal energy of the liquid in the large beaker compare or contrast with the thermal energy of the liquid in the small beaker?

A. The liquid in the large beaker has less thermal energy than the liquid in the small beaker.

B. The liquid in the large beaker has more thermal energy than the liquid in the small beaker.

C. The liquid in the large beaker has the same amount of thermal energy as the liquid in the small beaker.

D. The exact volume of liquid in each beaker must be known to compare the thermal energy of the liquids.

2. When you stand near a campfire, your face and hands feel warm. By which process does **most** energy reach you from a campfire?

A. conduction

B. convection

C. insulation

D. radiation

3. As Warren holds a pan over a fire, the water begins to boil, as shown in the figure below. The metal handle of the pan becomes very hot, causing an uncomfortable sensation in Warren's hand.

What process, indicated by the letter Y, was responsible for transferring energy to Warren's hand?

A. conduction   C. insulation

B. convection   D. radiation

4. The air in a room is warmer near the ceiling than near the floor. The warm air rises through which process?

A. conduction

B. convection

C. insulation

D. radiation

5. If you cook a pizza in a microwave oven, electromagnetic waves warm the pizza, not heat from the surrounding air. Which two types of heat transfer cook a pizza in a microwave oven?

A. convection and insulation

B. convection and conduction

C. radiation and conduction

D. radiation and convection

Waves and Energy

Key Concepts
Choose the letter of the best answer.

1. The diagram below shows a wave pattern.

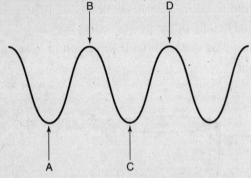

   What part of a wave is represented by B?

   A. crest

   B. trough

   C. amplitude

   D. wavelength

2. Through which of these media do sound waves travel **most** slowly?

   A. iron

   B. wood

   C. water

   D. air

3. What is transferred when a wave disturbs the material through which it travels?

   A. the energy of the wave

   B. the matter in the medium

   C. the medium itself

   D. the amplitude of the wave

4. Visible light and infrared light are two types of electromagnetic waves that radiate from the sun. Which is the **same** about these two types of radiation as they travel through space?

   A. energy

   B. frequency

   C. speed

   D. wavelength

5. The speed of a mechanical wave depends on the type of medium though which it travels. Which statement is **true**?

   A. All waves travel at the same speed through any medium.

   B. All waves travel at the same speed if no medium is present.

   C. Electromagnetic waves require a medium, but mechanical waves do not.

   D. Mechanical waves require a medium, but electromagnetic waves do not.

Interactions of Waves and Matter

Key Concepts
Choose the letter of the best answer.

1. Kana shines a light onto paper. The light contains both blue and red wavelengths of light, as shown in the figure below.

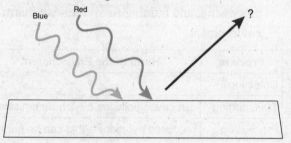

   If the paper were blue, what color (or colors) of light would bounce off the paper?

   A. only red

   B. only blue

   C. both red and blue

   D. neither red nor blue

2. A double-pane window consists of two pieces of glass with air in between. How many times does the light refract as it passes through the window?

   A. 2 times

   B. 3 times

   C. 4 times

   D. 6 times

3. A room contains many objects. Which of these objects would **most** absorb sound waves in a room?

   A. a cloth rug

   B. a metal pan

   C. a wood floor

   D. a glass pitcher

4. A store uses green-colored glass in its windows. What is the **main** reason the glass appears green?

   A. It emits green light.

   B. It absorbs green light.

   C. It reflects green light.

   D. It transmits green light.

5. An overhead light shines onto a sheet of white paper. Which best describes what happens to the light?

   A. It is absorbed.

   B. It is reflected.

   C. It is refracted.

   D. It is transmitted.

Effects of Energy Transfer

Key Concepts

Choose the letter of the best answer.

1. Alternative energy sources that are used to generate electricity have both benefits and drawbacks for the environment. The table shows benefits and drawbacks of energy sources used by four communities.

Community	Benefits	Drawbacks
A	is a renewable energy source	can destroy habitats
B	does not release carbon dioxide	produces waste that is difficult to store
C	is a renewable energy source	can only be used near hot springs or volcanoes
D	is a renewable energy source	releases carbon dioxide

Which community **most likely** uses a hydroelectric power plant to generate most of its electricity?

A. community A   C. community C

B. community B   D. community D

2. Which **best** describes the use of nuclear energy as an energy source when compared to fossil fuels?

A. Nuclear energy produces less harmful waste.

B. Nuclear energy destroys more habitats.

C. Nuclear energy creates more land erosion.

D. Nuclear energy produces less air pollution.

3. How does the use of biomass energy to generate electricity harm the environment the **most**?

A. Biomass energy production can destroy habitats.

B. Biomass energy production can create erosion problems.

C. Biomass energy production can contribute to air pollution.

D. Biomass energy production can generate hazardous waste.

4. A student makes a poster about fossil fuels as energy sources. She includes the table below, which shows how obtaining, transporting, processing, and burning fossil fuels can harm the environment.

Process	Harm to the Environment
Obtaining	?
Transporting	can cause pollution by vehicle emissions
Processing	produces byproducts that can be harmful
Burning	releases greenhouse houses like carbon dioxide

What should she add to the table that explains the **main** way that obtaining fossil fuels harms the environment?

A. destroys habitats

B. emits pollutants

C. disrupts migration patterns

D. releases wastes that must be stored

5. Which method of producing electrical energy can harm the environment by disrupting animal migration patterns?

A. geothermal

B. hydroelectric

C. nuclear

D. solar

Work, Energy, and Power

Climb the Pyramid: *Using Energy*

1. Work on your own, with a partner, or with a small group.

2. Choose one item from each layer of the pyramid. Check your choices.

3. Have your teacher approve your plan.

4. Submit or present your results.

___ Concept Map

Create a concept map that shows how work, energy, and power are related to each other. Make sure that your concept map includes data for force (in newtons), distance (in meters), work (in joules), and the power (in watts). Your concept map should include information on how energy is transferred.

___ Figure It Out!

Three students take turns pulling an object over a distance. Student 1 does 200 joules of work in 5 seconds; student 2 does 250 joules of work in 8 seconds, and student 3 does 300 joules of work in 10 seconds. Figure out the power exerted in each case. Which student exerted the most power?

___ Quiz

Write a quiz for the rest of your class. Assess what students know about work, energy, and power. Make sure your questions are not too complex or difficult. Be sure to include the following topics in your quiz: work, energy, power, force, newtons, joules, watts, energy transfer, formulas for calculating work and power, and anything else you think is important for understanding this lesson.

___ History in Science

The names of many of the units used in physical science come from the names of scientists who studied physics. Watt, Joule, and Newton were physical scientists. Research two of these scientists or two others that contributed to what we now know about work, energy, and power. Explain what you learned in a report or poster.

___ Concentration Cards

Design a concentration game that tests knowledge of work, energy, and power. Jot down information from the lesson, such as a topic and an example of that topic, a topic and the unit it is measured in, a topic and a formula that can be used to calculate it, or any other topic and a detail you think is important. Then separate this information onto two cards—topic on one card, detail, information, or formula on another.

___ Chart

Imagine you have been training for a marathon. Pretend that you weigh about 540 newtons, and keep an imaginary record of your progress. Record how far you ran (in meters) and how long it took you (in seconds) for training sessions that occur over several weeks. Use the information to record how much work you have done and how powerful you are. Be sure to discuss your progress in term of joules and watts.

Conservation of Energy

Take Your Pick: *Energy*
Complete the activities to show what you've learned about energy.

1. Work on your own, with a partner, or with a small group.

2. Choose items below for a total of 10 points. Check your choices.

3. Have your teacher approve your plan.

4. Submit or present your results.

2 Points

_____ **Making a Transformation** Perform a skit in which you identify an instance when one form of energy transforms to another form of energy.

_____ **Energy Observations** Observe your room and note examples of energy. Make a set of diagrams depicting the room. Label and describe at least three examples of energy in the room.

5 Points

_____ **Match the Pairs** Design five cards, one each for *mechanical energy*, *sound energy*, *chemical energy*, *thermal energy*, and *electromagnetic energy*. Design five other cards, each of which pairs with one of the cards you have already made. Then turn the cards face down, and match the pairs.

_____ **Where Did the Energy Go?** Make sketches that show energy transformations. Make sure you account for all of the initial energy. Think about energy that goes into two different forms and the way people use energy. Label the forms of energy in each sketch.

_____ **Puzzling Terms** Design a crossword puzzle using at least four terms about energy conservation and energy conversion. Be sure to include an answer key with your puzzle.

_____ **Be Efficient!** Write a memo to your school superintendent explaining how energy-efficient school buses can save the school district money. Explain what efficiency is, and what qualities should be considered when buying new buses.

8 Points

_____ **Experimenting with Energy** Design an experiment you could conduct that would test the law of conservation of energy. In your design, include the hypothesis you will test and the method you will use to test it. At the beginning of your design, describe the law of conservation of energy.

_____ **What's the Difference?** In recent years, many people have started to use compact fluorescent light bulbs (CFLs) rather than incandescent light bulbs because CFLs use less electricity. Compare the efficiency of CFLs with incandescent lights. How much of the input energy ends up as visible light in each case?

Thermal Energy and Heat

Points of View: *Methods of Thermal Energy Transfer*
Your class will work together to show what you've learned about thermal energy transfer from several different viewpoints.

1. Work in groups as assigned by your teacher. Each group will be assigned to one or two viewpoints.

2. Complete your assignment, and present your perspective to the class.

Methods of Thermal Energy Transfer

 Vocabulary Look up the word *radiation* in the dictionary and write its definition on a sheet of paper. Then look up words that are similar to *radiation*, such as *radiator*, *radiate*, and *radiant*. Write a journal entry in which you compare and contrast the meanings of the related words.

 Examples Make a poster that shows items found indoors and out. On your poster, label at least three examples of objects that make good conductors and at least three examples of objects that make good insulators. Describe the characteristics each has that make it a good conductor or insulator.

 Illustrations Draw a cartoon in which several methods of thermal energy transfer are shown. Include a caption that identifies the methods of transfer and explains how the methods are related.

 Analysis Imagine your friend has just ordered hot cocoa at a restaurant. When she tries to take a sip of the drink, she finds it is too hot. Your friend sets her mug on the table. You notice steam rising from the mug. A few minutes later, your friend can drink her cocoa because it has cooled. Use what you know about energy transfer to explain what has happened.

 Details Develop a PowerPoint presentation in which you explain how convection works by using ocean water as an example. In your presentation, give details about where the water is moving during convection and why it is moving. Describe how water temperature is measured, and how you would measure to show thermal energy transfer.

Waves and Energy

Take Your Pick: *Waves and Energy*
Complete the activities to show what you've learned about waves and energy.

1. Work on your own, with a partner, or with a small group.

2. Choose items below for a total of 10 points. Check your choices.

3. Have your teacher approve your plan.

4. Submit or present your results.

2 Points

_____ **Everyday Waves** Design a poster about a situation in which a wave is involved. Indicate and label the wave featured on your poster, and explain whether the wave is mechanical or electromagnetic.

_____ **Making Waves** Make models of transverse and longitudinal waves. Label your models.

5 Points

_____ **You Ask the Questions** Write five questions about wave speed, amplitude, wavelength, and frequency. On the back of your paper, write the answers to your questions.

_____ **Helping a Friend** Suppose your friend is just about to begin studying waves in his or her science class. Your friend asks you to help explain what a wave is and how a wave is different from its medium. Write a dialogue between you and your friend in which you answer your friend's questions.

_____ **The Wave Game** Play a game in which you identify electromagnetic and mechanical waves. Write the following types of waves on index cards: ocean waves, earthquake waves, sound waves, visible light, ultraviolet light, X-rays, radio waves, and microwaves. Create two columns on the board or on paper and label them "Electromagnetic" and "Mechanical." Shuffle the cards and try to put each type of wave in the correct category.

_____ **Paragraph Paraphrase** Paraphrase what you have learned about amplitude, wavelength, frequency, and wave speed. Be sure to include the most important pieces of information.

8 Points

_____ **Which Wave Are You?** Write and perform a skit in which one actor is a transverse wave and the other actor is a longitudinal wave. Have the actors also act out the way their waves move. Then actors should talk about the similarities and differences between the way they move.

_____ **Compare and Contrast Waves** Make a presentation in which you compare and contrast mechanical waves and electromagnetic waves. Discuss the ways the two types of waves are the same and the ways they are different. Give examples of each type of wave.

Interaction of Waves and Matter

Alternative Assessment

Points of View: *Light and Sound*
**Complete the activities to show what you've learned about
sound waves and light waves and the way they interact with matter.**

1. Work in groups as assigned by your teacher. Each group will be assigned to one or two viewpoints.

2. Complete your assignment, and present your perspective to the class.

 Terms The words *absorb*, *reflect*, *refract*, *media*, and *scatter* all relate to light. Write a short story that tells what happens to a group of light beams that leave the sun, enter Earth's atmosphere, and interact with different media, such as water and grass.

 Examples List examples of three objects that reflect light, three objects that scatter light, and three objects that do not transmit light. Tell the characteristics common to all three objects in each group.

 Analysis Imagine that at a museum, you walk by a display of silhouettes that are lit with ultraviolet light. Your white shirt glows a brilliant purple. Tell why.

 Observations Fill a clear glass with water. Set the glass on a table or desk to look at it from the side. Put a pencil in the water at an angle. What is strange about the way the pencil looks? What is causing the pencil to look this way?

 Details When a sound is made in an otherwise quiet room, the sound can be heard throughout the room. Explain. Tell what happens to the sound when it encounters a metal file cabinet, a pillow, and a window.

Effects of Energy Transfer

Tic-Tac-Toe: *Our Energy Use*

1. Work on your own, with a partner, or with a small group.

2. Choose three quick activities from the game. Check the boxes you plan to complete. They must form a straight line in any direction.

3. Have your teacher approve your plan.

4. Do each activity, and turn in your results.

__ **Be the Teacher**	__ **Collage**	__ **Pro/Con Grid**
Write your own quiz to test how well students have learned the material in this lesson. Make sure your questions cover the lesson's key ideas. Include an answer key. Distribute to students and your teacher and see how well they do.	Cut out images related to energy and the environment from magazines and newspapers. Arrange them to make a collage. Include at least six energy resources in your collage and identify them as renewable or nonrenewable.	Create a grid that organizes the disadvantages and advantages for each of the energy resources described in the lesson. Make sure your grid is neat and includes illustrations or diagrams.
__ **Skit**	__ **Commercial**	__ **Poem**
Write and perform a skit in which characters discuss the issues related to using renewable and nonrenewable resources. The topic you cover should include pollution and cost concerns.	Write and perform a commercial for a real or created product that uses an alternative energy source that highlights the benefits of the energy source. Record a video of your commercial if possible.	Choose a poetry form, such as haiku or acrostic, and write a poem about how human energy use can affect the environment.
__ **Invention**	__ **Puzzle Time**	__ **Web Site**
Design a machine that uses one or more alternative energy sources. Sketch a diagram of your invention and include a description of how it would use alternative energy sources and what effect it would have on the environment.	Make a crossword puzzle that uses words, phrases, and ideas from the lesson as solutions for the clues. The puzzle should use at least ten terms, including *renewable*, *nonrenewable*, and *energy*.	Design a web site that focuses on energy use and its effects on the environment. Include a glossary of key terms, images, and examples. Make sure your web site has at least three pages.

Unit 3 ISTEP+ Review

Choose the letter of the best answer.

1 Calvin shines a thin beam of light onto a material, and the light refracts. Which diagram BEST shows what happens to the light?

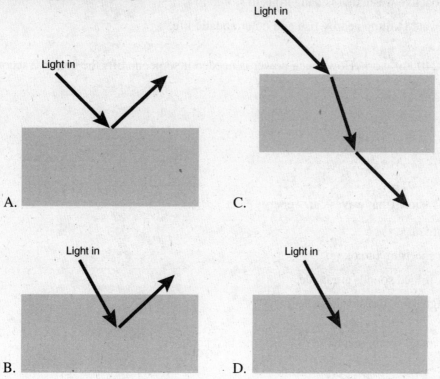

2 A scientist places a block of hot metal in a jar of cool water. Because energy is conserved, what must happen?

A. The sum of the thermal energy of the water and the thermal energy of the metal will increase.

B. The thermal energy of the water and the thermal energy of the metal will remain the same.

C. Some of the metal's thermal energy is transferred to the water as heat, but a small amount changes to mass.

D. The thermal energy of the water will increase by the same amount that the thermal energy of the metal decreases.

3 Water falling from a dam is an energy source used to generate electricity. In what way can a hydroelectric dam be harmful to the environment?

A. It can restrict the movement of migrating fish.

B. It can release gases that cause air pollution.

C. It can generate radioactive waste that is dangerous to store.

D. It can overheat the water, killing nearby fish and other aquatic life.

4 Lifting a box requires 240 J of work. How much power is needed if someone lifts the box in 2 seconds?

A. 120 W

B. 480 W

C. 1200 W

D. 238 W

5 Which statement BEST shows that waves carry energy?

A. Sounds can be recorded.

B. A rainbow shows a spectrum of colors.

C. You feel vibrations if loud sounds are made.

D. Light shining through some trees makes shadows.

6 This diagram shows a metal spoon in a bowl of warm mashed potatoes.

Spoon 20 °C

Mashed potatoes 50 °C

What BEST describes the transfer of energy as heat that is happening in this diagram?

A. Energy moves by radiation from the spoon to the potatoes.

B. Energy moves by radiation from the potatoes to the spoon.

C. Energy moves by conduction from the spoon to the potatoes.

D. Energy moves by conduction from the potatoes to the spoon.

Go On

7 A group of wind turbines operates in an open field. Which statement about the wind turbines is TRUE?

A. The wind turbines cannot do work because they are fixed in one spot.

B. The wind turbines do work by using wind energy to produce electrical energy.

C. The wind turbines do work by producing a movement of air across the open field.

D. The wind turbines do work by transforming electrical energy into electrical power.

8 An ice cube is placed in a glass of warm tea. Later, the ice has melted, and the tea is cooler. What is TRUE about the system now?

A. Thermal energy has been transferred from the ice cube to the warm tea.

B. Thermal energy has been transferred from the tea to the surrounding air and glass.

C. Chemical potential energy of the ice cube has been transferred to the warm tea.

D. Chemical potential energy of the warm tea has been transferred to the surrounding air and glass.

9 What is true of ALL transverse waves and longitudinal waves?

A. They must travel through a medium.

B. They can travel through empty space.

C. They move energy from one place to another.

D. They move particles from one place to another.

10 The table lists the amount of energy that was used and the time it took for 10 students to do various tasks.

Task	Energy (joules)	Time (seconds)
Gina	300	1.5
Jamal	320	2.0
Karen	180	4.0
Richard	540	3.0

Which student did a task that required the MOST power?

A. Gina

B. Jamal

C. Karen

D. Richard

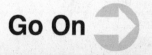

Go On

11 What power system propels a gasoline-burning automobile?

A. wheels

B. axle

C. engine

D. battery

12 The graph below shows the speeds of three types of waves in air and water.

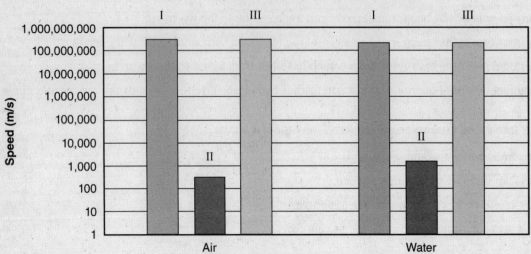

Which wave(s) are electromagnetic waves?

A. II only

B. I, II, and III

C. I and II only

D. I and III only

13 A scientist performed an experiment and measured the energy transferred in each step of her experiment. The total quantity of energy transferred in all of the steps was less than what she had at the beginning. What is the MOST LIKELY explanation for this result?

A. Energy was destroyed during certain steps in the experiment.

B. The steps in the experiment required more energy than was available.

C. The experiment created energy that was then used up at a faster rate.

D. Some energy was transferred into heat energy that was not detected.

Go On

14 Which example illustrates the transfer of energy through RADIATION?

A. feeling warmth when you sit in a sunny place

B. feeling warm air blowing on your neck from a hairdryer

C. feeling the warmth of the bricks around a fireplace by touching them with your hand

D. feeling warmth on the soles of your feet when you walk along a beach on a sunny day

Constructed Response

15 The diagram below shows a light ray moving through air and approaching water.

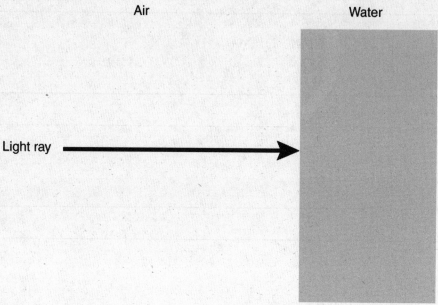

Describe what will happen to the SPEED and DIRECTION of the light ray as it moves into the water. Explain your answer.

_____

_____

Describe what would happen to the SPEED and DIRECTION of the light ray if it were moving, instead, from water into air.

_____

_____

_____

Go On

Extended Response

16 Four alternative energy sources used to generate electrical energy are nuclear energy, energy from burning biomass, solar energy, and hydroelectric energy. Like all energy sources, each of these has both advantages and disadvantages. For each of these four energy sources, describe ONE way that it is either beneficial or harmful to the environment.

Nuclear energy

_____

_____

Energy from burning biomass

_____

_____

Solar energy

_____

_____

Hydroelectric energy

_____

_____

Energy

Key Concepts

Choose the letter of the best answer.

1. Which of these choices **best** describes the thermal energy of a substance?

    A. the sum of the kinetic energy of all of the particles of a substance

    B. the average kinetic energy of the particles that make up a substance

    C. the total kinetic and potential energies of the particles of a substance

    D. the difference between the kinetic energy and potential energy of a substance

2. Waves can be measured in many different ways.

    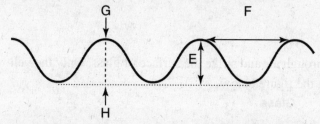

    What property of a wave is measured by F?

    A. period

    B. frequency

    C. amplitude

    D. wavelength

3. Which of these processes is the result of the motion of particles in a gas or liquid?

    A. conduction

    B. convection

    C. insulation

    D. radiation

4. A spaceship is traveling from Earth to Mars. What gives the spaceship the ability to do work?

    A. the kinetic energy of the spaceship

    B. the type of material used to make the spaceship

    C. the aerodynamic shape of the spaceship

    D. the massive size of the spaceship

5. A person walking up a flight of steps changes 1,350 J of energy from one form to another. How much power does the person use if it takes 5 s to walk up the steps?

    A. 54 W

    B. 270 W

    C. 6,750 W

    D. 33,750 W

6. Red light waves and yellow light waves travel through air and strike the surface of glass. Only the yellow light waves travel through the glass, as shown in the figure below.

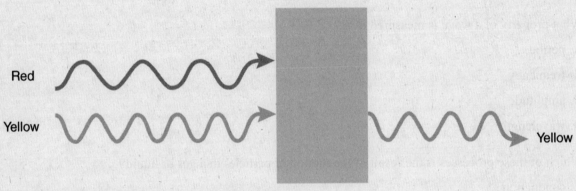

Which of these phrases best describes the glass?

    A. reflective for red light

    B. opaque for yellow light

    C. translucent for red light

    D. transparent for yellow ligh

7. Which of the following best defines energy?

   A. the ability to do work

   B. the resistance to motion

   C. how fast an object moves

   D. amount of force in a given time

8. Which type of power plant uses one of Earth's nonrenewable resources to produce electrical energy?

   A. hydroelectric

   B. nuclear

   C. solar

   D. wind

9. Suppose a mechanical wave is traveling through medium A. When the wave enters medium B, it speeds up. Which of the following statements is true about medium A and medium B?

   A. Medium A is a solid and medium B is a gas.

   B. Medium A is a liquid and medium B is a solid.

   C. Medium A is a gas and medium B is a vacuum.

   D. Medium A is a vacuum and medium B is a liquid.

10. The illustration below shows a device used to do work.

   What provides propulsion for this device?

   A. gears

   B. wind

   C. chemical energy

   D. fossil fuel

11. Kana shines a light onto paper. The light contains both blue and red wavelengths of light, as shown in the figure below.

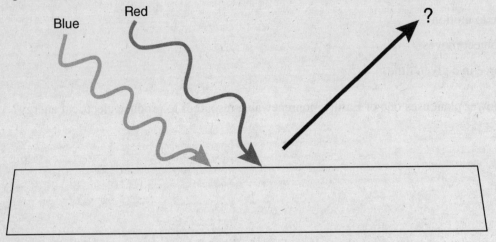

If the paper is white, what color (or colors) of light bounces off the paper?

A. only red

B. only blue

C. both red and blue

D. neither red nor blue

12. A student discovers that the battery in his calculator is no longer working. Which of the following is **true**?

A. The energy from the battery has all been transferred within the system or to another system.

B. The different types of energy in the battery were destroyed over time.

C. The battery needs to be moved by a force over a distance in order to have more energy.

D. The battery must create more energy before it can be used in the calculator.

13. As Wilma holds a pan over a fire, the water begins to boil, as shown in the figure below.

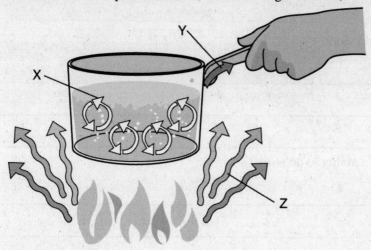

Which process is indicated by the letter X?

A. conduction

B. convection

C. insulation

D. radiation

14. A basketball falls from a hoop and bounces several times. Each bounce transfers some energy to the ground. Which statement is true about the total energy of the ball and ground?

A. The total energy increases because the ball gains energy each time it rises.

B. The total energy decreases because the ball loses energy each time it falls.

C. The total energy does not change the entire time the ball is bouncing.

D. The total energy increases and decreases just until the ball stops bouncing.

15. The following sources are used to generate electricity. Which is **most** likely to contribute to acid rain?

A. geothermal

B. hydroelectric

C. fossil fuels

D. nuclear

Constructed Response

16. A ball is sitting on a desk.

   Explain why the ball has the ability to do work.

   _____

   _____

   _____

   What could you do to increase the ball's ability to do work?

   _____

   _____

   _____

Extended Response

17. The figure below shows a prism with white light shining through one side and different colors of light exiting the other side.

Why does the light change direction?

_____

_____

_____

Why do different colors of light, rather than white light, exit the prism?

_____

_____

_____

Suppose the colors of the light exiting the prism are blue, green, red, and yellow. Identify which is Color 1, which is Color 2, which is Color 3, and which is Color 4.

_____

_____

_____

What would happen if the light shining into the prism were yellow instead of white? Would different colors exit? Why or why not?

_____

_____

_____

Energy

Key Concepts
Choose the letter of the best answer.

1. Lisa has a bottle of water. How can she increase the thermal energy of the water?

   A. She can pour the water into a larger bottle.

   B. She can increase the temperature of the water.

   C. She can place the bottle of water in the refrigerator.

   D. She can divide the water between two identical containers.

2. The diagram below shows four light rays interacting with a material.

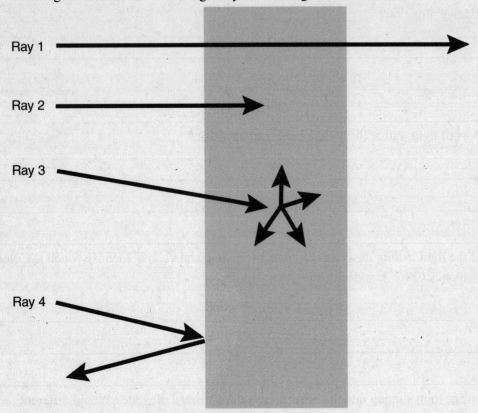

The material is transparent to which light ray?

   A. ray 1

   B. ray 2

   C. ray 3

   D. ray 4

3. There are two types of waves: mechanical and electromagnetic. Microwaves, infrared waves, and radio waves are examples of electromagnetic waves. Which statement is true about the speed of an electromagnetic wave?

   A. It is not affected by a change in medium.

   B. It is slower in a vacuum than in a medium.

   C. In a vacuum, its speed equals half the speed of light.

   D. It slows down when it goes from a vacuum to a medium.

4. A wind turbine can be used to generate electricity. Why is the turbine able to do work?

   A. Electricity keeps the turbine moving.

   B. The turbine is high above the ground.

   C. Wind transfers energy to the blades of the turbine.

   D. The blade direction of the turbine keeps changing.

5. Which of these energy sources used to generate electricity is the **most likely** to contribute to air pollution?

   A. biomass

   B. geothermal

   C. nuclear

   D. solar

6. Ashley warms her hands by placing them on a warm mug of cocoa. How do her hands gain thermal energy?

   A. The mug conducts heat to her hands.

   B. The mug radiates heat to her hands.

   C. The cocoa insulates her hands while the mug conducts heat to it.

   D. The mug convects heats to her hands.

7. Why does placing a battery in an electrical circuit give the circuit the ability to do work?

   A. The battery prevents heat buildup.

   B. The battery provides chemical energy.

   C. The battery provides electrical resistance.

   D. The battery prevents the flow of electrons.

8. A person changes 72 J of chemical energy to kinetic energy by lifting a box onto a shelf. If it takes the person 2 s to move the box, how much power does the person use?

    A. 9 W

    B. 18 W

    C. 36 W

    D. 72 W

9. The amount of light energy put out by an incandescent light bulb is under 10% of the electrical energy the bulb uses. What happens to the remaining 90% of the electrical energy used by the bulb?

    A. The electrical energy is redirected to other electrical appliances in the circuit.

    B. The electrical energy is transformed into thermal energy, so the bulb becomes hot.

    C. The electrical energy is destroyed when it is unused by the bulb.

    D. The electrical energy is captured and 90 J are saved for each bulb.

10. What is a wave?

    A. a disturbance that transfers energy

    B. a disturbance that transfers matter

    C. any type of energy that makes particles move

    D. any type of matter that vibrates back and forth

11. What powers a bicycle?

    A. wheels

    B. gears

    C. chain

    D. rider

12. How far can a 120-N force move an object using 240 J of energy to do the work?

    A. 0.5 m

    B. 2 N·m

    C. 2 m

    D. 10 m

13. Kana shines a light onto paper. The light contains both blue and red wavelengths of light, as shown in the figure below.

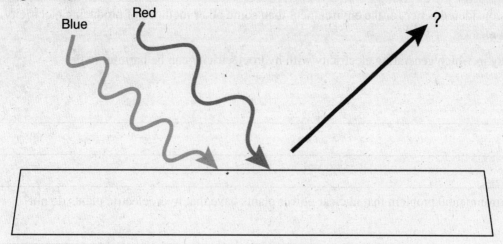

If the paper is green, what color (or colors) of light bounces off the paper?

A. only red

B. only blue

C. both red and blue

D. neither red nor blue

14. How does energy change when a person lifts a box and places it on a shelf?

A. There is an overall increase in the energy of the person and the box.

B. No energy is transferred, but the energy of the box increases.

C. Energy is transferred to the person, but the energy of the box does not change.

D. The energy of the person decreases by the same amount that the energy of the box increases.

15. Which of the following describes a transfer of energy through work?

A. A laboratory burner is used to heat 250 mL of water to boiling.

B. A student carries a heavy backpack one km.

C. A man pushes on a large piece of furniture for 15 min, but it does not move.

D. A woman pushes a luggage cart in an airport over a distance of 100 m.

Constructed Response

16. Hydroelectric power plants use water falling from a dam to generate electricity. Although hydroelectric plants are often considered better for the environment than some other methods of producing electricity, they do have drawbacks.

    Describe **one** way in which generating electricity with hydroelectricity can be harmful to the environment.

    _____

    _____

    _____

    What is **one** environmental problem that nuclear power plants have that hydroelectric plants do not?

    _____

    _____

    _____

    _____

Extended Response

17. A student wants to test heat transfer in different materials. She places four spoons in a bowl of hot water, as shown below. She then makes a data table to record her observations.

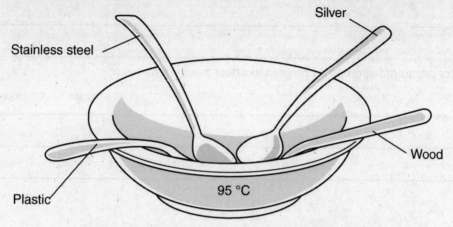

Stainless steel

Silver

Wood

Plastic

95 °C

Material	Observation
plastic	?
stainless steel	?
silver	?
wood	?

Identify and describe the type of heat transfer that occurs between the hot water and the spoons.

_____

_____

After the spoons have been in the water for a couple of minutes, what will the student **most likely** observe about the temperature of each spoon?

_____

_____

_____

Name ______________________________________ Date _________

Classify each of the materials that the student is testing as a conductor or an insulator.

____

____

____

Describe how heat transfer due to radiation could be used to affect this system.

____

____

____

Name _____ Date _____

Earth's Structures

Choose the letter of the best answer.

1. On December 26, 2004, a major tsunami occurred in the Indian Ocean. The tsunami traveled from its point of origin to as far away as Africa—nearly 5,000 km. The map below shows the countries most affected by this tsunami.

December 2004 Tsunami

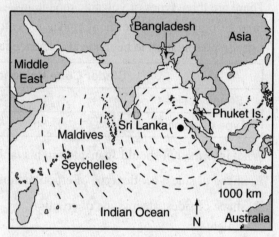

What was the cause of this tsunami?

A. an earthquake beneath the ocean

B. the impact of a large meteorite in the ocean

C. a sudden violent windstorm above the ocean water

D. a typhoon moving from the Indian Ocean toward India

2. What type of instrument is used to detect Earth's magnetic field?

A. a compass

B. a microscope

C. a telescope

D. a calculator

3. Look at the features of the valley in the following picture.

How was this valley formed?

A. A continental glacier retreated, pushing sediment to the side.

B. An alpine glacier flowed down through the valley, causing erosion.

C. An alpine glacier dragged huge blocks of ice that formed kettle lakes.

D. A continental glacier flowed through the valley, depositing glacial drift.

4. Which of the following describes how microorganisms influence soil formation?

A. they add water to soil

B. they dig burrows in the soil

C. they sort rock fragments by size

D. they break down the remains of plants and animals

5. A plate boundary is a place where two tectonic plates meet. There are several types of tectonic plate boundaries. Which statement below shows the correct definition of a tectonic plate boundary?

A. At a divergent boundary, plates separate.

B. At a transform boundary, plates move apart.

C. At a convergent boundary, plates slide past each other.

D. At a divergent boundary, one plate sinks under another plate.

6. Earth has three main compositional layers, one of which is the mantle. Which answer describes the mantle?

A. the thin and solid outermost layer

B. the innermost layer of iron and nickel

C. the hot layer of rock between the crust and the core

D. the liquid layer that encloses a solid ball of iron and nickel

7. The figure below shows a normal fault.

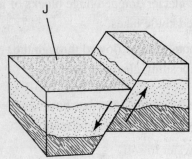

Normal fault

What happens when stress causes a normal fault?

A. The footwall drops down.

B. The hanging wall moves up.

C. The walls move side to side.

D. The hanging wall drops down.

8. Phong is examining samples of quartz, feldspar, and mica. What do all of these samples have in common?

A. They are metals.

B. They are pure elements.

C. They are silicate minerals.

D. They are nonsilicate minerals.

9. There are three types of volcanic mountains. Juan is compiling a table about cinder cones for a group presentation to be made at a science fair.

	Cinder Cone Volcano
Shape of sides	?
Type of eruption	?

What information should Juan enter in his table?

A. shape of sides: gentle; type of eruption: quiet

B. shape of sides: steep; type of eruption: violent

C. shape of sides: steep; type of eruption: alternating quiet and violent

D. shape of sides: gentle; type of eruption: alternating quiet and violent

10. Canyons, caverns, channels, and valleys all form because of erosion by water. Which landform listed is **mainly** formed because of erosion by groundwater?

A. a broad valley

B. a narrow canyon

C. a human-made channel

D. an underground cavern

Minerals

Key Concepts
Choose the letter of the best answer.

1. Diamond is a valuable mineral that is made up of carbon atoms arranged in a repeating pattern. This repeating pattern gives diamonds their hardness. Which of these characteristics do diamonds share with all minerals?

   A. extreme hardness

   B. rarity and high cost

   C. orderly crystal structure

   D. made up of carbon atoms

2. Obsidian is volcanic silicon dioxide glass that forms naturally when lava cools quickly. Because the lava cools so quickly, crystals do not have time to form. Why is obsidian not classified as a mineral?

   A. It contains silicon dioxide.

   B. It does not come from a living thing.

   C. It does not have an orderly internal structure.

   D. It formed from melted rock rather than from sediment.

3. Quartz, feldspar, and mica are silicate minerals. Silicate minerals contain atoms of silicon and oxygen and often other metals bonded together. What must be **true** of silicate minerals?

   A. They are pure elements.

   B. They are made up of compounds.

   C. They are all metallic minerals.

   D. They are made up of only one kind of atom.

4. About 95 percent of Earth's crust is made up of silicate minerals. Which of the following **best** describes silicate minerals?

   A. minerals containing silicon and oxygen

   B. minerals containing only atoms of silicon

   C. minerals containing only atoms of carbon

   D. minerals containing carbon and hydrogen

5. Minerals that contain combinations of carbon and oxygen are examples of which type of mineral?

   A. carbonates

   B. halides

   C. silicates

   D. oxides

The Rock Cycle

Key Concepts

Choose the letter of the best answer.

1. What is the **best** way to describe how subsidence contributes to the rock cycle process?

   A. Earth's crust rises and exposes new rock to the forces of erosion. Over time, erosion wears away rock.

   B. Areas of crust slowly sink forming basins where sediments can collect. Over time, sediments can become sedimentary rock.

   C. When areas of crust subside, earthquakes are common. These uplift and expose new igneous rock to the surface.

   D. Any change in the crust makes volcanoes likely. These can erupt magma, which becomes basalt deposits.

2. Over a long period of time, igneous rock can change into sedimentary rock. What must happen to igneous rock before it can change into sedimentary rock?

   A. It must be broken down into sediment.

   B. It must melt and become magma.

   C. Its minerals must be dissolved in water.

   D. It must be exposed to high pressure and temperature.

3. Rift zones form at the border between tectonic plates. What must happen between tectonic plates to produce a rift zone?

   A. Two oceanic plates move toward each other.

   B. Two continental plates move toward each other.

   C. An oceanic plate collides with a continental plate.

   D. An oceanic plate moves away from another oceanic plate.

4. Coal forms when layers of plant remains are compacted over millions of years. Which type of rock is coal?

   A. intrusive igneous

   B. extrusive igneous

   C. organic sedimentary

   D. clastic sedimentary

5. A compass is used to detect a magnetic field. What type of rock would be **most likely** to affect a compass?

   A. a sedimentary limestone

   B. a metamorphic marble

   C. an igneous basalt

   D. a sedimentary sandstone

Name _____ Date _____

Process that Shape the Land

Key Concepts
Choose the letter of the best answer.

1. Chemical weathering of limestone and groundwater erosion are most likely to create which type of landform?

   A. an arête ridge

   B. an alpine valley

   C. a limestone cave

   D. a cirque formation

2. The alluvial fan shown in the following illustration formed as sediment began to drop out from a stream that could no longer carry all of its sediment.

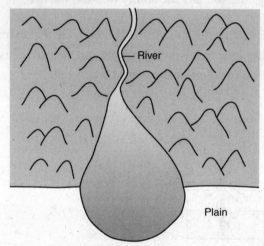

   Which statement **best** explains why the stream could no longer carry all its sediment?

   A. The volume of water was too high.

   B. The slope of the land was too great.

   C. The width of the stream was too small.

   D. The speed of the water was too slow.

3. Examine the drawing of some spelunkers—cave explorers—in a cave. There are several cave formations shown in the illustration.

   Which is the name of the formations that develop and grow up from the cave floor?

   A. stalactites formed by deposition

   B. stalagmites formed by deposition

   C. cirques formed by retreating glaciers

   D. stalagmites formed by groundwater erosion

4. Which of these will **most likely** cause glacial drift to be deposited?

   A. a glacier that is retreating

   B. a glacier that is growing in size

   C. a glacier that is getting thicker

   D. a glacier that is increasing in speed

5. Glaciers form in cold areas with lots of snow. The snow must turn into ice to form a glacier. How does this happen?

   A. The cold wind blows across the top of the snow, turning it into ice.

   B. The snow builds up, and its weight compresses the snow below into ice.

   C. The snow melts as it falls and then freezes once it hits the cold ground.

   D. The temperature on the ground is cold enough to turn the snow into ice.

Soil Formation

Key Concepts
Choose the letter of the best answer.

1. What happens to a rock when it is weathered during the process of soil formation?

   A. It is broken into smaller pieces.

   B. It is moved by wind, air, or water.

   C. It is built up as material is deposited.

   D. It is changed into another type of rock.

2. What can cause granite to break down into soil over time?

   A. rain and wind

   B. soil deposition

   C. heat from magma

   D. pressure underground

3. You have just analyzed a 100 g soil sample. You have organized your findings in the following data table:

Soil Analysis	
Soil Material	Amount (by % volume)
Air	25
Silt	18
Clay	9
Sand	18
Water	25
Organic matter	5

   Which two materials make up at least 50 percent of the composition of your soil sample?

   A. air and silt

   B. silt and sand

   C. air and water

   D. clay and organic matter

4. Gopher tortoises live on dry land. They live in large holes that they dig in the soil. Which statement **best** describes how this behavior aids in soil formation?

   A. It hardens the soil, allowing less water to reach the rocks underground.

   B. It causes weathering of the rocks, as the tortoise breaks the rocks into smaller pieces.

   C. It erodes the soil by moving it from underneath the ground to above ground.

   D. It loosens and mixes the soil, increasing air in the soil and the ability to drain water.

5. Examine the soil profile below. Note that there is a lone tree with deep roots and the surface is filled with ground cover plants.

   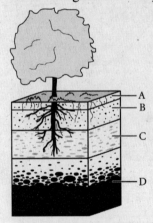

   Which soil horizon is primarily responsible for this soil's fertility?

   A. Horizon A, because it contains humus and other organic nutrients that plants need.

   B. Horizon B, because plant roots can grow down into the smaller rock fragments.

   C. Horizon C, because most of the groundwater is stored in this horizon.

   D. Horizon D, because it is the parent rock that breaks up to form soil.

Earth's Layers

Key Concepts
Choose the letter of the best answer.

1. Which compositional layer of Earth is the thinnest?

   A. the inner core

   B. the outer core

   C. the crust

   D. the mantle

2. Evelyn is making a model of Earth to show how the physical layers correspond to the compositional layers. Which of the following should Evelyn show in her model?

   A. The physical layers exactly match the compositional layers.

   B. The crust is the only compositional layer not included in the physical layers.

   C. The physical layers of the inner core and outer core form a single compositional layer.

   D. The physical layer of the asthenosphere includes the compositional layer of the crust.

3. Earth's physical layers correspond to Earth's compositional layers. Which part of the mantle is also part of the lithosphere?

   A. the fluid, hot part

   B. the rigid upper part

   C. the soft, moving part

   D. the lower stationary part

4. Earth has five layers based on physical properties: the inner core, the outer core, the mesosphere, the asthenosphere, and the lithosphere. Which of these layers do the tectonic plates move on top of?

   A. outer core

   B. lithosphere

   C. mesosphere

   D. asthenosphere

5. The innermost physical layers of Earth are the inner core and outer core. Which two metals are the inner and outer core mostly made of?

   A. lead and iron

   B. iron and nickel

   C. lead and mercury

   D. nickel and mercury

Plate Tectonics

Key Concepts
Choose the letter of the best answer.

1. Which of the following is always found where two plates of lithosphere meet?

   A. convection current

   B. sea-floor spreading

   C. convergent boundary

   D. tectonic plate boundary

2. The Red Sea formed as the African Plate moved apart from the Arabian Plate. Which type of boundary was involved in the formation of the Red Sea?

   A. transform boundary

   B. divergent boundary

   C. stationary boundary

   D. convergent boundary

3. What are the mechanisms that have been proposed to explain the movement of Earth's tectonic plates?

   A. slab pull and sea-floor spreading

   B. mantle convection and continental drift

   C. mantle convection, ridge push, and slab pull

   D. sea-floor spreading and continental drift

4. Scientists think the continents once formed a large, single landmass that broke apart, and the continents slowly drifted to their present locations. What is the name given to this hypothesis?

   A. continental rise

   B. continental drift

   C. continental shelf

   D. continental slope

5. The illustration below shows Earth's tectonic plates. The arrows indicate the direction in which some of these plates are moving.

   According to this map, where can you **infer** that mountains are being formed?

   A. between the Cocos Plate and the Caribbean Plate

   B. between the Philippine Plate and the Pacific Plate

   C. between the South American Plate and the African Plate

   D. between the Indo-Australian Plate and the Scotia Plate

Mountain Building

Key Concepts
Choose the letter of the best answer.

1. Which of these answers **best** describes compression caused by tectonic plate movement?

   A. stress that slides rocks past one another

   B. stress that squeezes rocks

   C. stress that stretches rocks

   D. stress that pulls rocks apart

2. Which of the following can form as a result of tension caused by tectonic plate movement?

   A. a syncline

   B. an anticline

   C. a folded mountain

   D. a fault-block mountain

3. The figure below shows a strike-slip fault.

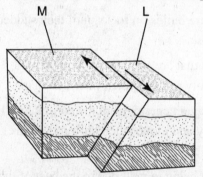

Strike slip fault

   What happens when stress causes a strike-slip fault?

   A. The footwall moves up.

   B. The hanging wall moves up.

   C. The hanging wall drops down.

   D. The walls slide past each other.

4. What is the primary way that folded mountains are formed?

   A. by tension

   B. by shear stress

   C. by compression

   D. by volcanic activity

5. How are volcanic mountains formed?

   A. by tension

   B. by the eruption of melted rock

   C. by shear stress

   D. by compression

Earthquakes

Key Concepts
Choose the letter of the best answer.

1. Which of the following events can produce an earthquake?

   A. the force of tsunamis in the oceans

   B. a sudden release of energy from the mantle

   C. movement of tectonic plates along a fault

   D. the violent shaking of sections of the lithosphere

2. Which type of stress causes deformation that leads to earthquakes at converging plate boundaries?

   A. tension

   B. stretching

   C. shear stress

   D. compression

3. Which of the following causes most of the human injuries during a major earthquake?

   A. car accidents caused by the ground shaking

   B. falling into large cracks that form in the ground

   C. violent winds caused by the rapid movement of the ground

   D. collapsing buildings and other structures caused by the ground shaking

4. Why do most earthquakes take place at tectonic plate boundaries?

   A. The rock in the interior of a tectonic plate is stronger, so it does not deform.

   B. Earthquakes take place where energy is transferred to rock by the motion of tectonic plates.

   C. Earthquakes can only occur at places where magma can reach the surface and transfer energy to rocks.

   D. Earthquakes take place when one plate moves over another plate, which happens only at plate boundaries.

5. The energy released by an earthquake is the result of elastic rebound. How does elastic rebound take place?

   A. Pressure builds on rocks until they suddenly collapse.

   B. Rocks that are stretched or compressed suddenly return to their previous shape.

   C. Rocks gain energy from the constant pull of gravity and move when obstructions are removed.

   D. Rocks begin to melt due to the heat of the mantle and suddenly crystallize when pressure is removed.

Volcanoes

Key Concepts
Choose the letter of the best answer.

1. Molten material flows gently out of a fissure on Earth's surface, then cools and hardens. This process happens again and again over geologic time. Eventually, what will form on the surface?

   A. plate boundary

   B. caldera

   C. magma chamber

   D. volcanic mountain

2. Which volcanic feature forms a relatively small depression around a volcano's vent?

   A. crater

   B. fissure

   C. caldera

   D. lava plateau

3. How does pyroclastic material **differ** from lava?

   A. Unlike lava, pyroclastic material erupts onto Earth's surface.

   B. Unlike lava, pyroclastic material erupts from shield volcanoes.

   C. Unlike lava, pyroclastic material is associated with explosive eruptions.

   D. Unlike lava, pyroclastic material is associated with nonviolent eruptions.

4. A hot spot is a volcanically active area. A volcanic island can form over a hot spot. Which would you expect to find beneath the hot spot?

   A. a convergent boundary

   B. a divergent boundary

   C. a mantle plume

   D. a rift zone

5. Which of these defines magma?

   A. Magma is lava that has cooled to form solid rock.

   B. Magma is melted rock found in underground chambers.

   C. Magma molten rock that flows on Earth's surface.

   D. Magma is any place where gas, ash, or melted rock come out of the ground.

Minerals

Tic-Tac-Toe: *Matter and Minerals*

Complete the activities to show what you've learned about matter and minerals.

1. Work on your own, with a partner, or with a small group.

2. Choose three quick activities from the game. Check the boxes you plan to complete.
    They must form a straight line in any direction.

3. Have your teacher approve your plan.

4. Do each activity, and turn in your results.

__ **You Ask the Questions**	__ **Trading Definitions**	__ **Distinguished Work**
Compose a quiz that contains at least six questions. Write about the ways minerals form. Include different types of questions such as multiple choice, true/false, and short answer.	Design trading cards for the terms *elements*, *atoms*, and *compounds*. Give each term its own card. On each card, draw an example of the item, label it, define the term, and, if appropriate, list a few examples.	Design a collage distinguishing between minerals and nonminerals. Illustrate your collage with pictures from the Internet or old magazines. Include the characteristics of minerals and nonminerals.
__ **Presenting Properties**	__ **You Decide**	__ **Picturing Minerals**
Make a PowerPoint presentation in which you compare and contrast properties of common minerals. Include illustrations or diagrams.	On a small sheet of paper or an index card, answer these questions: *What did you know about minerals before reviewing this lesson? What did you learn about minerals that you did not know before?*	Design a poster that shows minerals and describes their characteristics. Include illustrations or pictures of common minerals. Also list characteristics that all minerals share.
__ **Pair Match Up**	__ **What Am I?**	__ **Guess the Mineral**
Make cards about minerals' physical properties (for example, *color*, *streak*, *luster*, *hardness*, *density*, *cleavage*, and *fracture*). Then make another card that will pair with each property (for example, word definitions, an illustration, and so on). Play a matching game. See who can match the most pairs.	Present a skit in which two actors are different minerals who compare their properties. For example, one actor might be a silicate mineral and another actor a nonsilicate mineral. The actors can talk about their properties and the things that make them different from each other. Then have the class guess who is the silicate mineral and who is the nonsilicate mineral.	Design a game that shows you know the ways to identify minerals. On index cards, write the name of some minerals and how to identify them. To play, draw a card and describe how to identify the mineral. Other players try to guess the mineral.

The Rock Cycle

Mix and Match: *Changes to Rock Types*

Mix and match ideas to show what you've learned about the rock cycle and the ways rock types change.

1. Work on your own, with a partner, or with a small group.

2. Choose two or more choices from Column A, two from Column B, and one from Column C. Check your choices.

3. Have your teacher approve your plan.

4. Do each activity, and turn in your results.

A. Choose Two Rock Types and Processes	B. Choose Two Things to Analyze	C. Choose One Way to Communicate Analysis
___ igneous rock	___ observable properties and characteristics	___ news report or news article
___ sedimentary rock	___ details	___ fictional story or monologue
___ metamorphic rock	___ causes or formation	___ poster or illustration
___ weathering	___ types and variations	___ game
___ erosion		___ questionnaire or worksheet
___ deposition		___ invented dialogue or interview
		___ model or diorama
		___ commercial or video
		___ PowerPoint presentation
		___ a skit or performance

Processes That Shape the Land

Mix and Match: *Pathways of Erosion and Deposition*

Mix and match ideas to show what you've learned about erosion and deposition.

1. Work on your own, with a partner, or with a small group.

2. Choose one information source from Column A, two topics from Column B, and one option from Column C. Check your choices.

3. Have your teacher approve your plan.

4. Submit or present your results.

A. Choose One Information Source	B. Choose Two Things to Analyze	C. Choose One Way to Communicate Analysis
___ photograph of a landform	___ pathway, size, and speed of water	___ diagram or illustration
___ observations of a stream or river	___ origin and destination of material	___ colors, arrows, or symbols marked on a visual, with a key
___ an aerial photograph of an alluvial fan	___ past history	___ model, such as drawings or simulations with sand or clay
___ observations of a local farm	___ future prediction	
___ website describing national parks	___ speed of landform change and why	___ booklet, such as a field guide, travel brochure, playbook, or set of instructions
___ descriptions or photographs of a flood		___ game
___ topographical map		___ story, song, or poem, with supporting details
___ descriptions or photographs of glaciers		___ skit, chant, or dance, with supporting details
___ geological map		___ Multimedia presentation
_____		_____

Soil Formation

Mix and Match: *All About Soil*

Mix and match ideas to show what you've learned about soil and how it forms.

1. Work on your own, with a partner, or with a small group.

2. Choose one information source from Column A, two topics from Column B, and one option from Column C. Check your choices.

3. Have your teacher approve your plan.

4. Submit or present your results.

A. Choose One or More Information Sources	**B. Choose Two or More Things to Analyze**	**C. Choose One Way to Communicate Analysis**
____ direct observations of soil in a natural environment	____ soil horizons	____ realistic illustration
____ direct observation of modified soil, such as from a garden or a potted plant	____ soil characteristics (texture, color, and so on)	____ schematic diagram, with a key
____ observations of soil from a photograph, video, or similar source	____ soil chemistry	____ model
____ records of observations of soil, such as from a naturalist's journal or a geological survey	____ formation, including possible parent rock or transport	____ informational booklet, such as a field guide
_____	____ actions of living things	____ multimedia presentation
		_____

Earth's Layers

Take Your Pick: *Earth's Physical and Compositional Layers*
Complete the activities to show what you've learned about Earth's structure.

1. Work on your own, with a partner, or with a small group.

2. Choose items below for a total of 10 points. Check your choices.

3. Have your teacher approve your plan.

4. Submit or present your results.

2 Points

_____ **Picturing Earth's Layers** Create a poster that shows the solid Earth's compositional layers. On the poster, label and briefly describe the three layers.

_____ **What Are Your Thoughts?** Make a card that answers the following questions: What did you know about Earth's compositional layers before completing this lesson? What was the most interesting thing you learned about Earth's compositional layers during this lesson?

_____ **Down to the Core** Make a Venn diagram in which you compare and contrast Earth's inner and outer cores. Label one circle *Outer Core*, the other circle *Inner Core*, and the overlapping section *Both*. Complete the diagram with details about the cores.

5 Points

_____ **The Layer Quiz** Make a quiz that deals with Earth's physical layers. Write the names of Earth's layers on note cards. Then write some of the properties of the layers on the back of the cards. Shuffle the cards and choose one from the pile. With a partner, take turns quizzing each other about the layers.

_____ **Seeing Inside** How do scientists know about Earth's interior? Find out more about how seismic waves and their speed help scientists learn about the inside of Earth. Present your findings in a visual presentation.

_____ **Your Turn to Teach** Suppose you are a teacher. Your task is to prepare a lesson about the layers of the solid Earth. Gather information from your studies. Present your lesson to another student.

8 Points

_____ **Blast from the Past** Scientific understanding is constantly changing. Find out what scientists thought Earth was made of in the past. Make a timeline showing some past theories about Earth's internal structure.

_____ **What's in a Layer?** Make a multimedia presentation in which you compare and contrast the two ways of looking at Earth's internal structure.

Plate Tectonics

Climb the Pyramid: *Exploring Tectonic Plates*

Complete the activities to show what you have learned about plate tectonics.

1. Work on your own, with a partner, or with a small group.

2. Choose one item from each layer of the pyramid. Check your choices.

3. Have your teacher approve your plan.

4. Submit or present your results.

__ A Puzzling Picture

Create a drawing of the continents as they once fit together. Each continent should be a labeled and drawn in a different color. Carefully cut out each continent to create a puzzle. Then demonstrate the hypothesis of plate tectonics by moving the puzzle pieces and explaining the hypothesis and evidence to support it.

__ Plate Interview

Imagine that you are a newspaper reporter in 1912 who has heard about Alfred Wegener's astonishing new idea called continental drift. You are going to interview the scientist about his theory. List 10 questions to ask Wegener.

__ Sea-floor Spreading

Write a description of the process of sea-floor spreading, using the Mid-Atlantic Ridge as an example. Be sure to tell about how material reaches the surface and why the ridge is higher than the surrounding oceanic plates.

__ Density Differences

Write a poem or song that explains how density differences below Earth's plates causes the plates to move and change shape.

__ Flipbook

Draw a flipbook to show what happens at plate boundaries. Show a convergent boundary, a divergent boundary, and a transform boundary.

__ Collision Diorama

Make a diorama showing convergent boundaries formed between (1) two continental plates, (2) a continental plate and an oceanic plate, or (3) two oceanic plates. Create labels for your diorama.

Mountain Building

Alternative Assessment

Climb the Ladder: *Faults, Folds, and Mountains*

Complete the activities to show what you've learned about mountain building.

1. Work on your own, with a partner, or with a small group.

2. Choose one item from each rung of the ladder. Check your choices.

3. Have your teacher approve your plan.

4. Submit or present your results.

__ **Quiz Cards**	__ **To a Fault**
On three separate cards, write the terms *compression*, *tension*, and *shear stress*. Then write their definitions on three other cards. Finally, mix up the cards and use them to quiz your friends about the terms.	Make a poster that describes the three types of faults. Then draw a sketch of each type under the appropriate heading.
__ **Flipping Forward**	__ **On the Range**
Imagine that one of your classmates needs help understanding how folded mountains form. To help your classmate, create a flipbook that shows the process of a folded mountain forming.	Find out about a famous mountain range located anywhere in the world. Then share with the class what type of mountain range it is and the way it formed.
__ **Plate Talk**	__ **You're the Expert!**
Imagine that you are a tectonic plate that is slowly pushing against another tectonic plate. Present a skit in which you describe what might happen to you and the other plate and why.	Imagine you are a geologist who has examined a syncline fold. Write a report about what you observed in the field. In your report, note where the oldest rock is located in the fold and describe the shape of fold. Also discuss how the syncline occurred.

Earthquakes

Climb the Ladder: *Earthquake Exercises*

Complete the activities to show what you've learned about earthquakes.

1. Work on your own, with a partner, or with a small group.
2. Choose one item from each rung of the ladder. Check your choices.
3. Have your teacher approve your plan.
4. Submit or present your results.

__ Earthquake Poster Make a poster that shows how an earthquake occurs. Label the focus, epicenter, and fault. Show how elastic deformation can take place.	**__ Word Swap** Choose one vocabulary word from this lesson. Write it at the bottom of a sheet of paper. Number each letter. Above the word, write a paragraph that tells something about the word. Then underline letters in your paragraph that are used in the word. Number these letters. Give your puzzle to partner. Have the partner use the numbers to figure out the word.
__ Earthquake Events Create a flipchart that animates the sequence of events that causes an earthquake. Arrange you images into a book, so that when you flip the pages of the book, the earthquake causes the ground to move.	**__ Earthquake Article** Suppose you are a reporter who experiences an earthquake. Write a magazine article about your experience. Describe what caused the quake, when it hit, what the aftermath was like, and how people's lives were affected.
__ Shaky Story Write a short story in which an earthquake occurs. What do your characters do? How do they react? What caused the earthquake?	**__ Boundary Action** Make models of a divergent boundary, a convergent boundary, and a transform plate boundary. Label the direction of plate movement.

Volcanoes

Points of View: *Volcanoes and Volcanic Activity*

Your class will work together to show what you've learned about volcanoes from several different viewpoints.

1. Work in groups as assigned by your teacher. Each group will be assigned to one or two viewpoints.

2. Complete your assignment, and present your perspective to the class.

 Vocabulary Look up the root of the word *volcano*. Then find other words in the lesson that contain the same root. List these words, and write a definition for each.

 Illustrations Design trading cards for each type of volcano. On the cards draw images of and label all the types of volcanoes. Then describe how each type is different from or similar to other types of volcanoes.

 Analysis When volcanoes erupt, they release a number of different materials and change the landforms around them. Volcanoes can also change landforms by collapsing or exploding. How might Earth's surface be different if volcanoes did not exist? Which landforms and landmasses might not exist if it weren't for volcanoes? Create a PowerPoint presentation in which you describe your answers and ideas.

 Details Imagine that you have just watched a news report that stated that all volcanoes form at the boundaries of tectonic plates. Write a letter to the news station explaining that volcanoes can also form in other areas. Describe the other areas in which volcanoes form and explain how these volcanoes occur.

 Models Make a model of a shield volcano. Label the vent, the lava flow, and the magma chamber. Describe how a shield volcano is different from and similar to other types of volcanoes.

Name _____ Date _____

Unit 4 ISTEP+ Review

Choose the letter of the best answer.

1   The diagram below shows a rift zone between two oceanic plates.

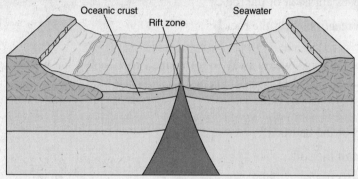

Which of these processes is shown just BELOW the center of the rift zone?

A. subduction

B. magma flowing up

C. lava becoming solid

D. continental crust melting

2   The map below shows the North American plate boundaries.

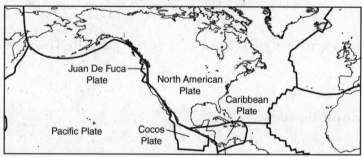

Which statement BEST explains why the risk of earthquakes is very high along the California coast, but very low along the Florida coast?

A. Earthquakes move from west to east due to Earth's rotation, so they do not reach the east coast of the continent.

B. The North American plate is moving toward the west, so there is much more stress at the western boundary.

C. The mountains near the west coast reflect the energy of earthquakes, but the mountains in the east are smaller and do not.

D. There is a plate boundary beneath the west coast of the continent, but the plate extends beyond the east coast of the continent.

Go On

3 What can result when acids in groundwater erode limestone rock underground?

A. Caves can form as the acids dissolve rock over time.

B. Metamorphic rock can form where the limestone was.

C. Sand can build up as the water causes abrasion of the rock.

D. Molten rock can form as chemical reactions heat the rock.

4 Susan rubs two rocks together. One of the rocks wears away to form small particles. What would MOST LIKELY happen if this rock continues to break into small pieces after Susan puts the rocks back on the ground?

A. The small pieces may become part of the bedrock.

B. The small pieces may become part of the soil.

C. The small pieces may become part of the ice wedging process.

D. The small pieces may become part of the organic matter in the soil.

5 How would you describe the landscape made by alpine glaciers compared to the landscape made by continental glaciers?

A. Alpine glaciers create U-shaped valleys, and continental glaciers create V-shaped valleys.

B. Alpine glaciers produce smooth landscapes, and continental glaciers produce hilly landscapes.

C. Alpine glaciers form rugged landscapes, and continental glaciers form flat landscapes.

D. Alpine glaciers make flattened landscapes, and continental glaciers make uneven landscapes.

6 The San Andreas Fault in California is a strike-slip fault. Which of these statements BEST describes a strike-slip fault?

A. One fault block moves up relative to the other.

B. One fault block moves down relative to the other.

C. Two fault blocks move in the same direction.

D. Two fault blocks move past each other horizontally.

7 A sample of igneous rock contains crystals of the iron mineral magnetite. The crystals are all aligned in the same direction. What is the MOST LIKELY explanation for this alignment?

A. As the rock formed, the crystals aligned with Earth's gravity.

B. After the rock formed, the crystals aligned with Earth's gravity.

C. As the rock formed, the crystals aligned with Earth's magnetic field.

D. After the rock formed, the crystals aligned with Earth's magnetic field.

Go On

8 Scientists study different parts of earthquakes and how they are related. This illustration shows a cross section of the lithosphere when an earthquake is taking place.

Cross Section of Lithosphere during an Earthquake

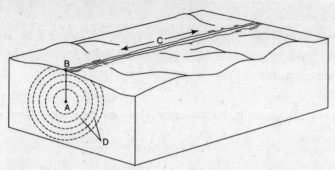

Where is the EPICENTER of this earthquake located?

A. point A

B. point B

C. along the line labeled C.

D. along the line between points A and B

9 How are FAULT-BLOCK MOUNTAINS formed?

A. by tension

B. by shear stress

C. by compression

D. by volcanic activity

10 When glaciers retreat, they can leave behind huge blocks of ice. When these ice blocks melt, they can form kettle lakes. Why is it necessary for sediment to build up around the ice blocks in order for kettle lakes to form?

A. Without the sediment, the water in the lake would dry up.

B. Without the sediment, the water would not stay contained.

C. Without the sediment, vegetation would not be able to grow.

D. Without the sediment, the ice blocks would not warm enough to melt.

11 Imagine that you could travel in a straight line through Earth from a point on one side and come out on the other side. What COMPOSITIONAL LAYER would you travel through in the exact center of Earth?

A. core

B. crust

C. lithosphere

D. mesosphere

Go On

12 The forces of volcanic eruptions vary. Some eruptions explode violently, and others are slow and quiet. Which type of eruption is MOST LIKELY to be associated with the release of pyroclastic materials?

A. a quiet eruption

B. a violent eruption

C. a moderate eruption

D. quiet eruptions alternating with moderate eruptions

13 Earth can be divided into three layers: the core, the mantle, and the crust. How are these three layers identified?

A. by their plate tectonics

B. by their structural features

C. by their physical properties

D. by their chemical composition

14 When a volcano erupts, ash can enter Earth's atmosphere. The ash later falls back down to Earth's surface. Which term describes the falling of volcanic ash to Earth?

A. deposition

B. erosion

C. subsidence

D. weathering

15 Volcanoes often form at convergent plate boundaries. Which set of arrows represents a convergent plate boundary?

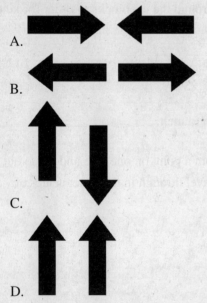

A.

B.

C.

D.

Go On

Name _____ Date _____

Constructed Response

16 The drawing below shows a typical soil profile. The drawing includes a layer of leaf debris and organic matter on the surface, three soil horizons, and parent rock at the bottom.

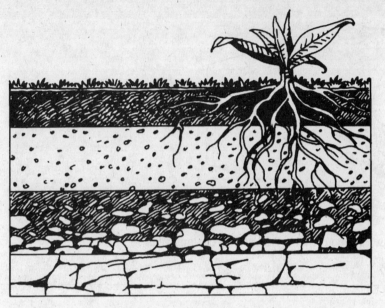

Explain why the UPPERMOST soil horizon is dark in color.

_____

_____

Describe one way in which living things influence the process of soil formation.

_____

_____

Go On

Extended Response

17 The figure below shows mountains and shows the rock layers that make up part of the lithosphere beneath the surface.

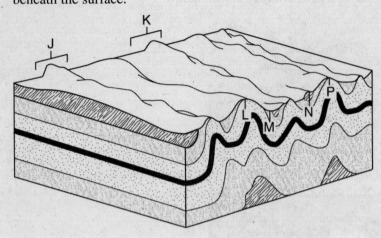

What kind of mountains are shown in the drawing? Explain your answer.

_____

_____

_____

What type of stress formed the mountains? Draw labels on the diagram to show the direction in which the stress was pushing on the lithosphere when these mountains formed.

_____

STOP

Earth's Structures

Key Concepts
Choose the letter of the best answer.

1. Over time, repeated cycles of heating and cooling can cause a rock to crack. The rock may then break into smaller pieces. What is this process called?

   A. deposition

   B. erosion

   C. subsidence

   D. weathering

2. Slate is a metamorphic rock that forms from shale, which is a sedimentary rock. Which of the following would be needed for slate to form from shale?

   A. weathering

   B. erosion and deposition

   C. melting and solidification

   D. heat and pressure

3. The three compositional layers of Earth are the core, the mantle, and the crust. Which phrase **best** describes the crust?

   A. the innermost layer of Earth's interior below the mantle

   B. the thin and solid outermost layer of Earth

   C. the hot, slow-flowing layer of Earth's interior above the core

   D. the layer of Earth on which the tectonic plates move

4. The roof of a cave eroded and became thinner over time. The roof then collapsed, and the landform shown in the following figure formed.

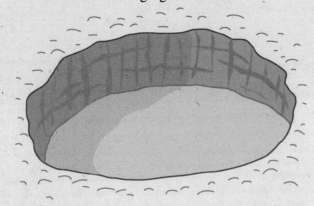

What is the correct term for the landform shown?

A. canyon

B. cavern

C. channel

D. sinkhole

5. The image below shows a scientist testing a mineral.

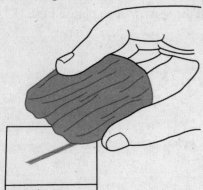

What property is the scientist observing?

A. cleavage

B. color

C. luster

D. streak

6. Which of the following is the source of humus found in soil?

   A. bedrock

   B. horizon B

   C. parent rock

   D. plants and animals

7. Scientists study earthquakes and how energy is transferred as waves through Earth. This figure shows a cross section of the lithosphere when an earthquake is taking place.

   Cross Section of Lithosphere during an Earthquake

   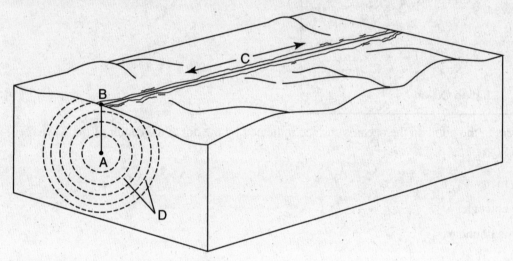

   Where is the focus of the earthquake located?

   A. point A

   B. point B

   C. along the line labeled C

   D. along the series of circles labeled D

8. Countries shown in a light color on the map below were affected by a tsunami on December 26, 2004. The dashed lines on the map indicate the path of the wave, which was caused by a major earthquake.

December 2004 Tsunami

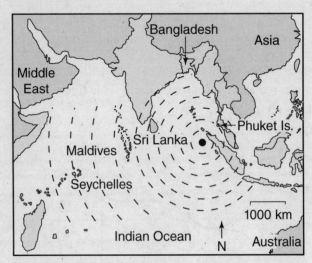

What term refers to the point on the ocean's surface indicated by the dot at the center of the waves?

A. fault boundary

B. earthquake focus

C. earthquake epicenter

D. tectonic plate boundary

9. Volcanoes have different shapes and erupt differently. Which type of volcano has gently sloping sides and erupts nonexplosively?

A. shield volcano

B. composite volcano

C. pyroclastic volcano

D. cinder cone volcano

10. Which of the following **best** describes the layer of Earth that tectonic plates are part of?

A. part of Earth's core

B. part of Earth's mantle

C. part of Earth's lithosphere

D. part of Earth's asthenosphere

11. What is the name of the landform shown in the picture?

A. alpine glacier   C. glacial cirques

B. glacial drift   D. continental glacier

12. The figure below shows three kinds of faults: normal faults, reverse faults, and strike-slip faults.

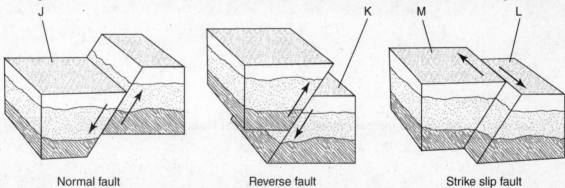

Which letter in the figure points to a hanging wall that has moved down in relation to a footwall?

A. *J*   C. *L*

B. *K*   D. *M*

13. Which statement describes one way in which a divergent boundary is **different** from a transform boundary?

A. At a divergent boundary, tectonic plates collide with each other.

B. At a transform boundary, tectonic plates move away from each other.

C. Plates slide past each other at a divergent boundary.

D. Plates slide past each other at a transform boundary.

14. What is magma?

    A. ice blocks

    B. solid rock

    C. molten rock

    D. volcanic ash

15. Which of the following **best** describes a model of Earth's magnetic field?

    A. a bar magnet with two north poles

    B. a bar magnet with a north and south pole

    C. a convection current flowing in Earth's mantle

    D. seismic waves traveling outward from an earthquake's focus

Constructed Response

16. The illustration below represents a simple graphic cross-section of Earth. Each circle, including the center, represents a different compositional layer.

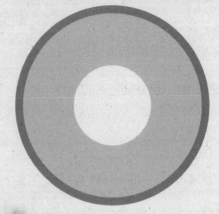

    Identify and describe each of the three compositional layers that is shown in the illustration:

    The outermost layer:

    _____

    _____

    The middle layer:

    _____

    _____

    The innermost layer:

    _____

    _____

Name _____ Date _____

Extended Response

17. Different properties are used to identify minerals. Two properties that are used to identify a mineral are color and luster.

Color and Luster of Some Minerals		
	Color	**Luster**
copper	brown	metallic
diamond	range from colorless to black	brilliant
gold	yellow	metallic
malachite	green	silky
talc	white	pearly

Define color as applied to a mineral.

_____

_____

Define luster as applied to a mineral.

_____

_____

Which of the minerals above is the most reflective? Explain.

_____

_____

Describe the color and luster of gold.

_____

_____

Earth's Structures

Key Concepts

Choose the letter of the best answer.

1. Erosion is a process that slowly changes rocks. Which of the following most likely causes pebbles in a stream to erode?

   A. flowing water

   B. force of gravity

   C. movement of ice

   D. freezing and thawing

2. Zane and his class have been collecting fossils and minerals on a field trip. They have gotten turned around in the woods. Zane uses his compass to figure out which way they should go to get back to the campsite. What direction will the compass needle point toward?

   A. south

   B. east

   C. north

   D. west

3. Earth can be divided into layers based on chemical composition. The three compositional layers of Earth are the core, the mantle, and the crust. Which of these answers **best** describes the core?

   A. the innermost part of Earth below the mantle

   B. the solid outer layer of Earth above the mantle

   C. the hot, slow-flowing layer of material beneath the crust

   D. the layer of Earth on which the tectonic plates move

4. Earth can be divided into five layers: the lithosphere, the asthenosphere, the mesosphere, the outer core, and the inner core. Which properties do scientists use to make these divisions?

   A. compositional properties

   B. physical properties

   C. chemical properties

   D. elemental properties

5. Leaves release acids into the soil as they decay. How could decaying leaves affect rock in the soil beneath them?

A. They could expose the rock to wind and water.

B. They could decrease the amount of weathering that occurs within the soil.

C. They could increase the amount of chemical weathering of rock and soil formation.

D. They could decrease the amount of chemical weathering and slow down the rate of soil formation.

6. The following diagram shows the site of a sinkhole.

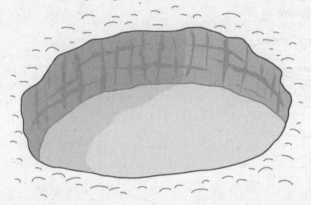

Which landform was **most likely** present before the sinkhole formed?

A. a canyon

B. a shallow pond

C. a deep river valley

D. a cave

7. The table below lists the masses and volumes of four mineral samples.

Mineral	Mass (g)	Volume (mL)
Feldspar	16	6.2
Galena	9	1.2
Garnet	12	3.0
Quartz	10	3.7

Which mineral has the **greatest** density?

A. feldspar

B. galena

C. garnet

D. quartz

8. How can acid be used to identify a mineral?

    A. Minerals that scratch acidic minerals are themselves acidic minerals.

    B. Minerals that produce bubbles when wet with an acid are carbonates.

    C. Minerals that have the same density as hydrochloric acid are carbonates.

    D. Minerals that produce bubbles when wet with an acid are acidic minerals.

9. This figure shows a cross section of the lithosphere where an earthquake is taking place. Point *A* is the focus (origin) of the earthquake.

    Cross Section of Lithosphere during an Earthquake

    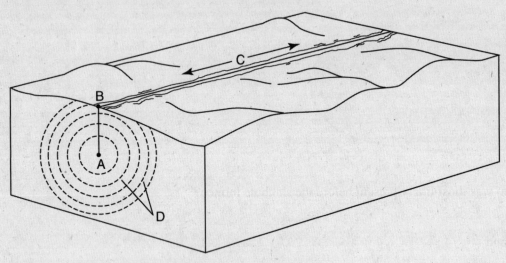

    What do the circles (D) around the focus represent?

    A. the epicenter of the earthquake

    B. rocks collapsing inward toward the focus

    C. the fault on which the earthquake is taking place

    D. waves of energy released by the earthquake traveling outward

10. During the year 2003, a greater number of earthquakes took place than is usually recorded per year. The map below shows the locations of some major earthquakes of 2003.

Locations of Major Earthquakes in 2003

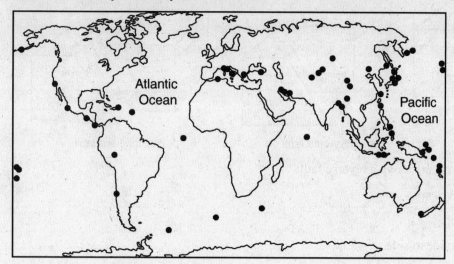

What is the **most likely** reason that there were no major earthquakes recorded in the interior of the continent of Africa?

A. The plate boundary inside Africa is too small to form earthquakes.

B. The landmass of Africa is too great to be affected by earthquakes.

C. There are no faults in Africa.

D. The entire continent of Africa is located on a single continental tectonic plate.

11. Amir's teacher asked him to present a model of a volcanic landform to the class. How could Amir visually show a lava plateau?

A. Glue a sheet of paper into a cone shape.

B. Put a cardboard box upside down on a table.

C. Make a depression in a piece of modeling clay.

D. Make a deep cut down the center of a piece of modeling clay.

12. Volcanic islands can form over hot spots. The Hawaiian Islands started forming over a hot spot in the Pacific Ocean millions of years ago. What process causes the hot, solid rock to rise through the mantle at these locations?

A. condensation

B. conduction

C. convection

D. radiation

13. The figure below shows three kinds of faults: normal faults, reverse faults, and strike-slip faults.

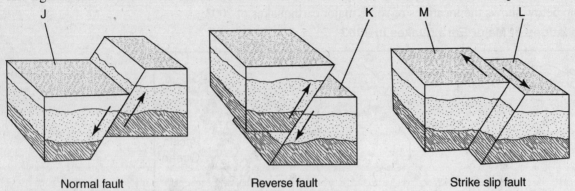

Normal fault   Reverse fault   Strike slip fault

What kind of movement occurs along a reverse fault?

A. The hanging wall moves up.

B. The footwall moves up.

C. The walls move from side to side.

D. The hanging wall drops down.

14. The landform shown in the following picture can be found on every continent; they are even found in Africa.

What conditions are necessary for this landform to form?

A. It must be below freezing and very dry.

B. It must be cold, and more snow must fall than melts.

C. It must be mild, and there must be lots of precipitation.

D. It must be below freezing, and more snow must melt than falls.

15. Tectonic plates can be made of continental crust or oceanic crust, or a combination of the two. Besides their location, how else are these two kinds of crust **different**?

   A. Tectonic plates made of continental crust are larger than plates made of oceanic crust.

   B. Continental crust is thinner than oceanic crust.

   C. Continental crust is thicker than oceanic plates.

   D. Tectonic plates made of continental crust are smaller than plates made of oceanic crust.

Constructed Response

16. The table below provides data about the formation of six mountains in the United States.

Mountain Formation			
Name of mountain	Elevation above sea level	Location of mountain	How the mountain was formed
Clingman's Dome	6,643 feet	Tennessee	sedimentary rock
Long's Peak	14,239 feet	Colorado	glacier
Mauna Kea	13,796 feet	Hawaii	volcano
Mt. Greylock	3, 487 feet	Massachusetts	fault
Mt. McKinley	20,320 feet	Alaska	fault
Mt. Rainier	14,411 feet	Washington	volcano

Can you infer from the data table that faults always produce the highest mountains? Explain.

_____

_____

_____

Which two mountains were formed by faults? How do they differ in elevation above sea level?

_____

Are you able to say that all the mountains listed in the table are on the boundaries of the same tectonic plate? Why or why not?

_____

_____

_____

Name _____ Date _____

Extended Response

17. The three diagrams below illustrate one way that rock begins to break down in the early stages of soil formation.

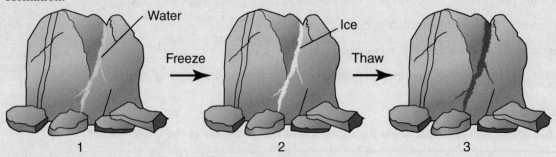

Explain how rock is broken down in the process shown.

_____

_____

_____

What is the physical property of water that is at work in this process?

_____

How can this process increase the rate at which rock is broken down in the process of soil formation?

_____

_____

Name _____ Date _____

The Changing Earth

Choose the letter of the best answer.

1. In 1897, a British scientist proposed that Earth was between 20 and 400 million years old. Based on radiometric dating, scientists now propose a different age for Earth. How old do they think Earth is?

   A. 40 billion years old

   B. 20 billion years old

   C. 4.6 billion years old

   D. 4.6 million years old

2. Which of the following objects is a fossil?

   A. a sinkhole formed by a retreating glacier

   B. a sedimentary rock that formed a long time ago

   C. a crystal formation suspended from the ceiling of a cave

   D. the remains of an organism preserved in limestone

3. Earth's history is immense. What do scientists use to arrange Earth's history into distinct divisions?

   A. the geologic time scale

   B. relative dating

   C. absolute dating

   D. the law of superposition

4. The chart below describes some important events in Earth's geologic history.

Event	How Long Ago Event Occurred
Earth formed.	4.6 billion years ago
The first primitive life forms appeared in the fossil record.	about 3.5 billion years ago
The Paleozoic era began.	about 542 million years ago
The first fish appeared in the fossil record.	about 500 million years ago
The Mesozoic era began.	about 251 million years ago
The first birds appeared in the fossil record.	about 160 million years ago
The Cenozoic era began.	about 65 million years ago
Modern humans appeared in the fossil record.	about 200,000 years ago

   What can you infer from the chart?

   A. Modern humans have existed since the beginning of geologic time.

   B. An era is a division of geologic time.

   C. Earth is about 3.5 billion years old.

   D. Birds evolved before fish.

5. An igneous intrusion cuts through three layers of sedimentary rock. Which rock is the youngest?

   A. the igneous intrusion

   B. the top layer of sedimentary rock

   C. the middle layer of sedimentary rock

   D. the bottom layer of sedimentary rock

6. Your local museum has a fossil of an animal that once lived in your area. The evidence suggests that the animal lived only in seashore environments. Your area is hundreds of miles from the sea. What is the **most likely** conclusion you can draw?

A. Your area was once farther from the ocean than it is now.

B. Your area was once more mountainous that it is now.

C. Your area was once a seashore environment.

D. The climate in your area has changed.

7. The table below shows the age ranges of several index fossils.

Age Ranges of Index Fossils	
Index Fossil	Age Range
Fossil A	540 to 511 million years
Fossil B	494 to 450 million years
Fossil C	425 to 470million years
Fossil D	230 to 208 million years

A scientist is studying a rock layer that contains fossil B. What can she infer?

A. The rock layer is older than rock layers containing fossils A, C, and D.

B. The rock layer is younger than rock layers containing fossils C and D.

C. The rock layer is older than a rock layers containing fossils C and D.

D. The rock layer is older than a rock layer containing fossil D.

8. What portion of Earth's geologic history is made up of Precambrian time?

A. 10 percent

B. 30 percent

C. 60 percent

D. 90 percent

9. The figure below shows one type of physical evidence that scientists use to understand how Earth's climate has changed in the past.

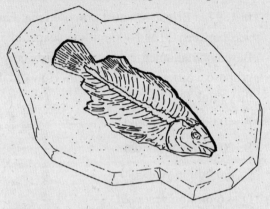

What type of physical evidence is shown in this figure?

A. coprolite

B. fossil

C. ice core

D. tree rings

10. Which of these statements describes what happens during radioactive decay?

A. A stable isotope interacts with an unstable isotope.

B. A stable isotope breaks down and becomes unstable.

C. An unstable isotope breaks down into a stable isotope.

D. An unstable isotope interacts with another unstable isotope.

Fossils and Changing Environments

Key Concepts
Choose the letter of the best answer.

1. Sometimes a fossil is formed as a result of the movement of an organism in soft sediment. What type of fossil is this called?

   A. bone fossil

   B. trace fossil

   C. frozen fossil

   D. petrified fossil

2. Imagine that you found this fossil on a mountaintop.

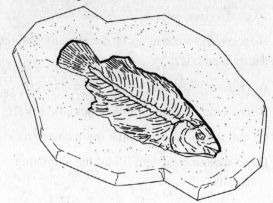

   What could you conclude from your discovery?

   A. This organism is now extinct.

   B. This trace fossil is older than the mountaintop.

   C. The mountaintop is made of metamorphic rock.

   D. The rocks on this mountaintop were once at the bottom of an ocean.

3. A fossil of an ancient seashell is found in the Rocky Mountains. What living organism would you expect to find in that region now?

   A. tropical plant

   B. shark

   C. grizzly bear

   D. penguin

4. Over millions of years, landmasses can break up and move apart. What could you do to determine if two separate areas were once part of a single landmass?

   A. compare the types of fossils found in the two areas

   B. compare the types of living things found in the two areas

   C. analyze the ages of trees in the two areas

   D. calculate the number of different fossils found in the two areas

5. Suppose the climate where you live is cool and dry. What could you infer about the ancient climate of your area if you found a fossil of a tropical fern?

   A. The area was once covered in ice.

   B. The area was once humid and warm.

   C. The area was once part of a large, single landmass.

   D. The area has always had a cool, dry climate.

Relative Dating and Absolute Dating

Key Concepts
Choose the letter of the best answer.

1. Which of these choices is an example of the way a geologist would use relative dating?

    A. determining the minerals that make up rocks

    B. placing rock layers in order of oldest to youngest

    C. classifying rocks as igneous, sedimentary, or metamorphic

    D. using radioactive isotopes to determine the exact ages of rock samples

2. Which property of fossils allows scientists to determine the relative ages of rock layers?

    A. Fossils form from the remains of living organisms.

    B. Fossils are usually found only in sedimentary rock.

    C. Fossils show how organisms change over time.

    D. Fossils can be analyzed to determine their exact ages.

3. Fossils are the preserved remains or traces of plants and animals that have lived on Earth throughout Earth's history. How does the fossil record of animals compare to animals that exist today?

    A. Animals in the fossil record are usually more complex than animals that exist today.

    B. Animals in the fossil record are the same as animals that exist today.

    C. Animals in the fossil record have no similarities to animals that exist today.

    D. Animals in the fossil record are ancestors of animals that exist today.

4. Ammonites are an example of an index fossil. The drawing below shows fossil ammonites in a layer of sedimentary rock in between two layers of igneous rock.

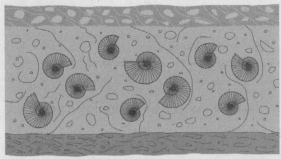

How can the ammonites be dated using absolute dating methods?

    A. radiometric dating of the igneous layers

    B. radiometric dating of the ammonite fossils

    C. radiometric dating of the sedimentary rock

    D. determining the half life of the ammonite fossils

5. Basalt is a gray or black igneous rock. Pilar uses an absolute dating method to study a sample of basalt. What will the method help her learn about the basalt sample?

    A. the age of the sample

    B. the composition of the sample

    C. the physical structure of the sample

    D. the geographic distribution of the sample

Geologic Change Over Time

Key Concepts

Choose the letter of the best answer.

1. Fossils of the same plants and animals have been found on continents that are separated by the Atlantic Ocean. Which of the following statements does this observation support?

   A. The animals and plants crossed the Atlantic Ocean.

   B. The Atlantic Ocean was once a large body of freshwater.

   C. The continents now separated by the Atlantic Ocean once formed a single landmass.

   D. The continents now separated by the Atlantic Ocean have the same kinds of organisms today as they did millions of years ago.

2. Earth's history is divided into time units in the geologic time scale. Put the following time divisions in proper order from largest to smallest: era, period, epoch, eon.

   A. epoch, period, era, and eon

   B. eon, era, period, and epoch

   C. era, period, epoch, and eon

   D. period, eon, era, and epoch

3. If you looked closely at a sedimentary rock, you might be able to tell how the rock was formed. Which of the following would provide the **best** evidence of how the rock was formed?

   A. the rock's age

   B. the rock's color

   C. the rock's texture

   D. the rock's fossil content

4. Fossils can provide clues to Earth's geologic past. Which of these is a fossil that could **best** provide information about climate changes in a particular area over time

   A. imprint of a fish in sandstone

   B. bone embedded in rock

   C. a large tree with many thick rings

   D. mammoth frozen in ice

5. The geologic time scale divides Earth's geologic history into time units. Which era do you live in?

   A. Precambrian

   B. Paleozoic

   C. Mesozoic

   D. Cenozoic

Fossils and Changing Environments

Climb the Ladder: *Fossil Hunters*

You are a member of a local fossil-hunting club that enjoys searching for different types of fossils.

1. Work on your own, with a partner, or with a small group.

2. Choose one item from each rung of the ladder. Check your choices.

3. Have your teacher approve your plan.

4. Submit or present your results.

__ **Fossil Club**	__ **Club Pamphlet**
Design a Web page for the fossil-hunting club. The page should summarize the five ways fossils form. Include at least one picture of each type of fossil on your page.	Design an information pamphlet for your fossil-hunting club members. The pamphlet should describe the five ways that fossils are formed. Each description should include a picture to help members identify the fossil type.
__ **Climate Quiz**	__ **Climate Clues**
Compose a quiz to test your club members' knowledge about Earth's climates and the changes they have undergone. Include at least five questions on your quiz. The answers can be multiple-choice, short answer, or true/false.	Imagine that members of your club found fossils. Many of the fossils are of palm fronds and ferns. Present a news report about the findings. In your report, explain what these fossils might indicate about the climate in the past.
__ **Not a Trace**	__ **Fossil Television**
Imagine that your club has been invited to a museum to help new paleontology students identify trace fossils. Write a lecture about trace fossils. In your lecture, define trace fossils, provide examples, and explain how to distinguish them from other fossils.	Imagine your club is going to perform a fun science segment about trace fossils on television. Write the script and perform the segment. Include the definition of trace fossils and show how scientists use them to learn about animals.

Relative Dating and Absolute Dating

Tic-Tac-Toe: *Create a Museum Exhibit*

Suppose you are an expert in the age of rocks, and you have offered to help a local museum create an exhibit about Earth's age.

1. Work on your own, with a partner, or with a small group.

2. Choose three quick activities from the game. Check the boxes you plan to complete. They must form a straight line in any direction.

3. Have your teacher approve your plan.

4. Do each activity, and turn in your results.

__ **Half-Life Breakdown**	__ **You Ask the Questions**	__ **Relative Brochure**
Create a poster or display for the museum exhibit that explains what half-life is. The poster should also discuss how scientists use half-life in radiometric dating.	The exhibit you're creating will have an interactive quiz for visitors to take. Write a quiz that contains at least four questions about index fossils and the ways scientists use them.	The museum's director asks you to create a brochure comparing disturbed and undisturbed sedimentary rock layers. The brochure should also explain how the laws of superposition and crosscutting are used to order disturbed and undisturbed rock layers. Use diagrams in your brochure.
__ **Dating Description**	__ **Decay Drama**	__ **Fossil Persuasion**
Create a multimedia presentation that lists and describes the different methods of relative dating. Include information about dating rock layers that are undisturbed and disturbed.	Develop and put on a skit to show visitors how radioactive decay makes it possible for scientists to date objects.	Museum donors are unsure whether they want to pay you to develop the exhibit. They do not understand what index fossils are. Give a persuasive speech in which you explain what index fossils are and why they are needed in the exhibit.
__ **Meeting the Requirements**	__ **Come on Down!**	__ **Old Rock and Roll?**
Design a Web page that will help bring people to the new exhibit. On the page, discuss the requirements fossils must meet to be considered index fossils.	To encourage press coverage of the exhibit, you must write a press release. Write a press release that explains what relative dating is and why people should visit the exhibit.	Create and perform a song that will play at the new museum exhibit. In your song, describe how scientists use absolute dating to determine the ages of rocks.

Geologic Change over Time

Alternative Assessment

Choose Your Meal: *Geologic Dinner Time*
Complete the activities to show what you've learned about relative dating.

1. Work on your own, with a partner, or with a small group.

2. Choose one item from each section of the menu, with an optional dessert. Check your choices.

3. Have your teacher approve your plan.

4. Submit or present your results.

Appetizers

_____ **Sedimentary CSI** Imagine that you are a geologic "crime scene" investigator. Write and produce a short video or web clip that shows how the composition of sedimentary rock provides evidence of the environment in which the rock formed. Include explanations and visuals (pictures or examples) of composition and texture.

_____ **Functional Fossils** Make a model of a plant or animal fossil. Include information about how the fossil provides clues about changing climates and how organisms have changed over time.

Main Dish

_____ **Continental Breakfast** Write a poem or a song about the theory of continental drift. In your work, summarize the evidence that supports the changing positions of the landmasses.

_____ **A Scientist's Story** Write a short story about a scientist who is researching how landforms have changed over time in a particular area. The story should explain how Earth's features indicate slow changes over time.

_____ **This Just In!** Present a news report in which you describe the theory of continental drift. Include information about the evidence that supports the changing positions of the landmasses.

Side Dishes

_____ **Climatic Conference** Imagine you are a scientist at a conference. Present a speech in which you explain the evidence that supports the theory that Earth's climates have changed in the past. In your speech include information about tree rings, sea-floor sediments, and ice cores.

_____ **Post the Evidence** Design a poster about the different evidence that suggests Earth's climates have changed in the past. Include information about tree rings, sea-floor sediments, and ice cores.

Desserts (optional)

_____ **Tipping the Scale** Imagine you are putting together a museum exhibit on the geologic time scale. Make a plan or a model of the exhibit. Include the eons, eras, periods, and epochs.

Unit 5 ISTEP+ Review

Choose the letter of the best answer.

1 Tiny fossils provide evidence that life on Earth began about 3.5 billion years ago. About how old was Earth when life first appeared on the planet?

A. 4.6 billion years

B. 3.5 billion years

C. 2.3 billion years

D. 1.1 billion years

2 Which type of evidence acts as a record of changes in organisms over time AND indicates major changes in Earth's surface and climate?

A. fossil record

B. continental drift

C. climatic changes

D. composition of ice core samples

3 The geologic time scale divides Earth's geologic history into time units. Which of these geologic time units is SMALLEST?

A. eon

B. era

C. period

D. epoch

4 Index fossils are used to date rock strata that would otherwise be very hard to date. Which of these statements describes a KEY CHARACTERISTIC of index fossils?

A. They existed in a unique location.

B. They are present in very small numbers.

C. They existed for a short span of time.

D. They are similar to other fossils.

Go On

5 This table shows some important events in Earth's geologic history. What can you infer from the table?

Event	How Long Ago Event Occurred
Earth forms.	about 4.6 billion years ago
First primitive life forms appear in fossil record.	about 3.5 billion years ago
Paleozoic era begins.	about 543 million years ago
First fish appear in fossil record.	about 500 million years ago
Mesozoic era begins.	about 250 million years ago
First birds appear in fossil record.	about 160 million years ago
Cenozoic era begins.	about 65 million years ago
Modern humans appear in the fossil record.	about 200,000 years ago

A. The Mesozoic era came before the Cenozoic era.

B. Reptiles evolved after humans.

C. The Paleozoic era lasted about 4 billion years.

D. Earth's geologic history spans a few million years.

6 The table below shows the ages of several fossils.

Ages of Fossils

Fossil	Age
Fossil A	511 million years
Fossil B	494 million years
Fossil C	2.5 million years
Fossil D	500,000 years

A scientist finds a rock layer that contains fossils A and B. What can she conclude about the rock layer?

A. It formed between 500,000 years and 2.5 million years ago.

B. It formed between 490 million years and 515 million years ago.

C. Its age is 494 million years.

D. Its age is 511 million years.

7. Why did scientists develop the geologic time scale?

A. to better understand the arrangement of rock layers

B. to better determine the absolute ages of rocks

C. to better classify index fossils

D. to better study Earth's immense history

Go On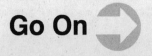

8 Two rock layers on different continents contain the same type of index fossil. What can you infer about these two rock layers?

    A. They formed at about the same time.

    B. They formed at different times.

    C. They were not disturbed by geologic processes.

    D. They contain unconformities.

Constructed Response

9 A fossil similar to the one shown below was found in an undisturbed rock layer. Above this layer, another undisturbed rock layer contained evidence that showed that this upper layer had been covered by an ice sheet.

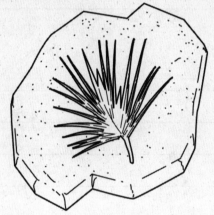

Based on this information, what can you conclude about a change in the climate in this area?

_____

_____

Scientists might use relative dating or absolute dating to date these rock layers. Explain the DIFFERENCE between these two methods of dating.

_____

_____

_____

Go On

Extended Response

10 What is an index fossil?

_____

_____

_____

What are TWO characteristics of an index fossil?

1) _____

2) _____

How can an index fossil be used to learn more about a rock layer?

_____

_____

_____

_____

The Changing Earth

Key Concepts
Choose the letter of the best answer.

1. Which sequence below shows the proper order of time units in the geologic time scale, from smallest to largest?

   A. eon, era, period, epoch

   B. period, epoch, eon, era

   C. epoch, period, era, eon

   D. era, eon, epoch, period

2. What can you learn when you compare a fern fossil found in the area in which you live to the cactus plants that currently grows in the same area?

   A. how the climate has changed over time

   B. how ice core samples have changed over time

   C. how the atmosphere has changed over time

   D. the absolute age of the rock in which the fossil was found

3. The diagram below shows rock layers that have shifted due to a fault.

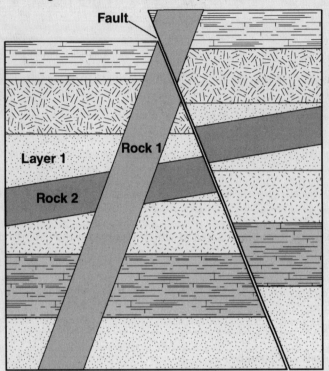

According to the law of crosscutting relationships, which of the following is the oldest?

A. fault

B. rock 1

C. rock 2

D. layer 1

4. According to the rock record, Earth's geologic history covers what amount of time?

A. 2.5 million years

B. 8.8 million years

C. 4.6 billion years

D. 7.3 billion years

5. Which of the following is known as the "Age of Mammals"?

A. the Paleozoic

B. the Cenozoic

C. the Precambrian

D. the Mesozoic

6. Rock *A* contains a fossil of an organism similar to organisms alive today. Rock *B* contains a fossil of an organism not similar to any organisms alive today. What conclusion can you draw?

A. Rock *A* is younger than Rock *B*.

B. Rock *B* is younger than Rock *A*.

C. Rocks *A* and *B* are the same age.

D. Fossils do not provide information about the ages of rocks.

7. Ricardo was doing a laboratory exercise on geologic changes over time. The figure below shows what he was doing.

What was Ricardo doing?

A. modeling fossil formation

B. modeling ice core formation

C. modeling an unconformity

D. modeling a geologic column

8. Which of the following is at type of fossil that would be **most** helpful in estimating the age of a rock layer?

   A. bone fossil

   B. trapped fossil

   C. trace fossil

   D. index fossil

9. Lina is studying different isotopes. She drew the diagram below to show a relationship between carbon-14 and nitrogen-14.

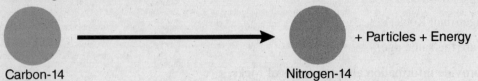

Carbon-14   Nitrogen-14

   What is the correct term for the process shown above?

   A. absolute decay

   B. radioactive decay

   C. relative dating

   D. unconformity

10. During which time in Earth's history would you expect to find the **least** fossil information about life forms?

   A. Cenozoic era

   B. Paleozoic era

   C. Precambrian time

   D. Mesozoic era

11. You want to know how modern humans differ from Earth's earliest humans. You would study fossils from which time?

   A. Mesozoic era

   B. Paleozoic era

   C. Precambrian time

   D. Cenozoic era

12. What is **true** of eras?

   A. They are the largest time units of the geologic time scale.

   B. They are divided into periods.

   C. They are divided into eons.

   D. They are the smallest units of the geologic time scale.

Constructed Response

13. The figure below shows one type of physical evidence that scientists use to understand Earth's past.

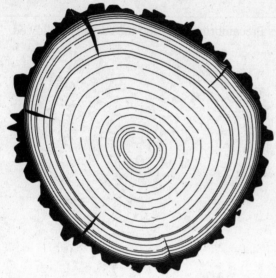

   What type of physical evidence is shown in this figure?

   _____

   What can scientists learn from this evidence?

   _____

   _____

Extended Response

14. What is the geologic time scale?

_____

_____

What kinds of events in Earth's geologic history are used to distinguish one time unit from another?

_____

_____

In the space below, draw and label a timeline that shows Precambrian time and the eras that followed.

Write **one** detail about each time unit next to its label on your timeline.

The Changing Earth

Key Concepts
Choose the letter of the best answer.

1. A fossil of a tropical fern in an arctic region would indicate that the region was once located where?

   A. in high latitudes

   B. near the equator

   C. in mid-latitudes

   D. near the poles

2. Which of the following could be an index fossil?

   A. a fossil that represents a species that was common and geographically limited

   B. a fossil that is trapped in amber and representative of a species that existed for a long time

   C. a fossil that represents a species that was common and widespread

   D. a fossil that is trapped in ice and well-preserved

Name _____ Date _____

3. By analyzing ice cores, scientists can learn how Earth's climate has changed in the past. Other ways of learning about the history of Earth's climate include analyses of tree rings, lake sediments, mountain glaciers, and ocean sediments. The figure below shows a timeline.

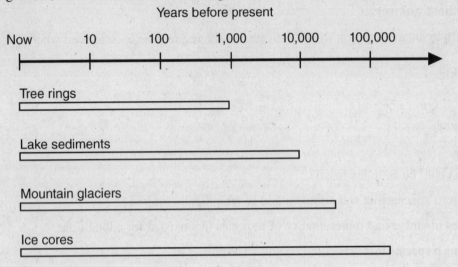

What can you conclude from this figure?

A. Ice cores provide climate information that goes back the furthest in time.

B. Ice cores provide climate information that goes back only to 1,000 years ago.

C. Ice cores provide climate information that goes back more than 100,000 years.

D. Ice cores provide climate information that cannot be obtained from other sources.

4. What biological information could you learn by studying fossils?

A. how climates have changed over time

B. how organisms have changed over time

C. the absolute ages of rocks

D. the relative ages of rocks

5. Imagine that you are searching for fossils. Which of the following is the **best** place to visit for finding fossils?

    A. Petrified Forest National Park, Arizona

    B. Pennsylvania Avenue, Washington D.C.

    C. Bronx Zoo, New York

    D. Mariana Trench, Pacific Ocean

6. Consider an area that was covered by an ocean throughout most of its history, but today is dry land. If you were to study this area's sedimentary rocks, which fossils would you **least likely** find?

    A. fossils of pine trees

    B. fossils of fish

    C. fossils of seashells

    D. fossils of sharks

7. How do epochs differ from eras?

    A. Epochs are shorter time units than eras.

    B. Epochs describe recent geologic time and eras describe ancient geologic time.

    C. Epochs are characterized by mass extinctions.

    D. Epochs are shorter than eons and eras are longer than eons.

8. How could you **best** use a fossil to learn about a geologic process?

    A. You could use a fossil to determine the past climate of an area.

    B. You could compare the DNA of two fossils trapped in amber.

    C. You could compare frozen fossils from the Northern and Southern Hemispheres.

    D. You could estimate the age of a rock layer in which a fossil formed.

9. Scientists have discovered dinosaur fossils that have evidence of feathers. Some scientists think the feathers might have kept the dinosaurs warm. If so, in what type of environment did these dinosaurs probably live?

   A. desert

   B. tropical rain forest

   C. region near the equator

   D. area with cold seasonal temperatures

10. What is often used to distinguish one era from another in the geologic time scale?

   A. rates of weathering and erosion

   B. location of poles

   C. mass extinctions

   D. earthquakes

11. Why do so few fossils exist from Precambrian time?

   A. Organisms did not exist during Precambrian time.

   B. Organisms with hard body parts did not exist during Precambrian time.

   C. Precambrian time did not last long enough for fossil formation to occur.

   D. Rock layers from Precambrian time no longer exist.

12. You find a fossil of a dinosaur. During which time did the fossil **most likely** form?

   A. Mesozoic

   B. Cenozoic

   C. Precambrian

   D. Paleozoic

Name _____ Date _____

Constructed Response

13. Look at this diagram of rock layers.

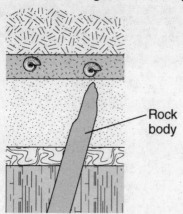

Rock body

What is the relative age of the igneous intrusion compared to the bottom layer of rock shown in this diagram?

_____

_____

State the geologic law that you used to determine your answer.

_____

_____

Extended Response

14. Michael was studying absolute dating. He drew the diagram below.

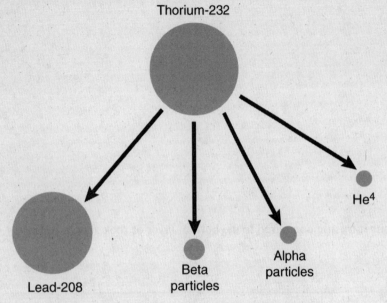

Thorium-232

Lead-208

Beta particles

Alpha particles

He⁴

What process does Michael's drawing represent?

_____

Identify the parent isotope and the daughter isotope.

_____

_____

Explain what happens during the decay process.

_____

_____

Explain why Lead-208 does not decay.

_____

_____

The Cell

Choose the letter of the best answer.

1. Emily knows that an organism must be able to perform all the functions necessary for life. Which of the following is an organism?

    A. DNA

    B. nucleus

    C. cytoplasm

    D. prokaryote

2. Luis is making a chart of compounds found in the human body. Which of these is the most important compound in the human body?

    A. water

    B. salt

    C. carbon dioxide

    D. sodium bicarbonate

3. Jorge looks through a microscope and concludes that the cells he observes are eukaryotic cells. Which of the following structures did Jorge **most likely** observe before making his conclusion?

    A. nucleus

    B. cytoplasm

    C. cell membrane

    D. genetic material

4. During photosynthesis, plant cells use sunlight as an energy source. Animal cells do not use photosynthesis. What organelle in plant cells makes it possible for plants to carry out photosynthesis?

    A. cell wall

    B. chloroplast

    C. lysosome

    D. nucleus

5. When you eat an apple, you are eating a type of tissue that stores nutrients in plants. Which type of tissue stores nutrients in plants?

    A. connective tissue

    B. ground tissue

    C. protective tissue

    D. transport tissue

6. Janine drew the following diagram to show a cell process. Notice that this process includes four stages, represented by labels G1, S, G2, and M. Label M indicates when mitosis happens during the process.

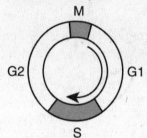

    What process is illustrated in Janine's diagram?

    A. endocytosis

    B. exocytosis

    C. the cell cycle

    D. cellular respiration

7. According to cell theory, which one of the following is the basic unit of life?

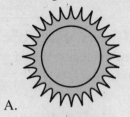

A.

B.

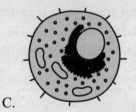

C.

D.

8. Cells exchange materials with the environment around them. What is the main reason for this?

A. to replace damaged and dying cells

B. to keep the cell membrane functioning

C. to release energy into the environment

D. to get rid of wastes and take in nutrients

9. What is a difference between eukaryotic cells and prokaryotic cells?

A. Only prokaryotic cells have cytoplasm.

B. Only eukaryotic cells have a cell membrane.

C. Only prokaryotic cells have genetic material.

D. Only eukaryotic cells have membrane-bound organelles.

10. Which statement is **true**?

A. Tissues are made up of organs.

B. Organs are made up of organisms.

C. Cells are made up of organ systems.

D. Organ systems are made up of organs.

Name _____ Date _____

The Characteristics of Cells

Key Concepts
Choose the letter of the best answer.

1. Which of the following characteristics do all unicellular organisms share?

   A. All unicellular organisms reproduce.

   B. All unicellular organisms have nuclei.

   C. All unicellular organisms are eukaryotes.

   D. All unicellular organisms are prokaryotes.

2. What observation led Rudolf Virchow to conclude that all cells come from other cells?

   A. Cells divide.

   B. Cells have nuclei.

   C. Cells move around.

   D. Cells have cell membranes.

3. Which term describes "one or more cells that carries out all of the processes needed to sustain life"?

   A. DNA

   B. organism

   C. organelles

   D. cytoplasm

4. DNA is genetic material that provides instructions for all cell processes. Where is the DNA located in prokaryotes?

   A. in the nucleus

   B. in the cytoplasm

   C. in the flagella

   D. in membrane-bound organelles

5. One part of the cell theory states that cells come from other cells. Which statement below **best** explains this part of cell theory?

   A. The cells of all organisms excrete waste.

   B. The cells of all organisms have cytoplasm.

   C. The cells of all organisms divide to make more cells.

   D. The cells of all organisms take in nutrients from their environment.

Chemistry of Life

Key Concepts
Choose the letter of the best answer.

1. Which of the following is a compound that is important for life processes in cells?

   A. gold

   B. water

   C. nitrogen

   D. hydrogen peroxide

2. Some dog foods contain corn and wheat that provide the dog with carbohydrates. Why are carbohydrates important to cells?

   A. They are a source of energy.

   B. They make amino acids.

   C. They form cell membranes.

   D. They help chemical processes happen.

3. Nutritionists know that lipids are vital nutrients that help keep cells working properly. What is one way cells in our bodies use lipids?

   A. to make amino acids

   B. to repair broken bones

   C. to form cell membranes

   D. to carry information in the cell

4. Animals produce enzymes that help chemical processes happen in the cells of their bodies. In which category do enzymes belong?

   A. lipids

   B. proteins

   C. nucleic acids

   D. carbohydrates

5. A cell must work to maintain a stable internal environment. It is also important for environment around the cell to be stable. What happens when the concentration of water inside a cell is lower than the concentration of water outside the cell?

   A. The cell takes in salt.

   B. The cell divides into two new cells.

   C. Water moves out of the cell.

   D. Water moves into the cell.

Name _____ Date _____

Cell Structure and Function

Key Concepts
Choose the letter of the best answer.

1. Which of the following describes the cytoskeleton?

   A. a web of proteins that gives shape and support to the cell

   B. a membrane-bound organelle that contains genetic material

   C. the outer covering of a cell that separates it from the environment

   D. the structure that contains the information about how to make a cell's proteins

2. Which of the following correctly pairs a structure in a eukaryotic cell with its description?

   A. nucleus; supports the cell's shape

   B. DNA; found in the cytoplasm

   C. cell membrane; separates the cell from its environment

   D. cytoskeleton; consists of all genetic information needed by the cell

3. Hanna is growing two different types of eukaryotic cells in her lab. Both types are found in the same multicellular organism, but one cell type produces many proteins, and the other does not. What would Hanna be **most likely** to observe about these cells?

   A. The cells that make fewer proteins have smaller nuclei than the other cells.

   B. The cells that make many proteins have more ribosomes than the other cells.

   C. The cells that make fewer proteins have fewer mitochondria than the other cells.

   D. The cells that make many proteins have thicker cell membranes than the other cells.

4. Which cellular organelle is responsible for digestion and for the breakdown of damaged organelles inside an animal cell, but not in a plant cell?

   A. Golgi complex

   B. lysosome

   C. ribosome

   D. rough endoplasmic reticulum

5. Latoya adds sugar molecules to the cells she is studying. The cells transport the sugar to the organelles that will use it to make ATP. Latoya traces the movement of the sugar inside the cells. Toward which organelle is Latoya likely to find the sugar molecules moving?

   A. chloroplast

   B. lysosome

   C. mitochondrion

   D. nucleus

Homeostasis and Cell Processes

Key Concepts
Choose the letter of the best answer.

1. What do tissues and organs of the cardiovascular system in animals have in common with xylem and phloem in plants?

    A. Both function in reproduction.

    B. Both function by sending messages throughout the organism.

    C. Both function in the transport of materials throughout the organism.

    D. Both function in providing structure and support to the organism.

2. Which of the following explains one main reason why some cells in multicellular organisms repeatedly divide?

    A. to make more cells so the organism can grow

    B. to make more cells in order to remove wastes

    C. to make more cells that take in and use oxygen

    D. to make more cells in order to produce more food

3. In one type of cell division, a single cell forms two new cells. This process is called mitosis. What is a reason that human skin cells frequently undergo mitosis?

    A. to get energy for the body

    B. to replace dead or damaged skin cells

    C. to prevent bruises on the body

    D. to replace dead or damaged muscle cells

4. Cells need to move water, materials for energy, waste materials, and other molecules across the cell membrane to help maintain homeostasis. Molecules move across cell membranes by active transport or by passive transport. How are these two processes different?

    A. Passive transport requires energy, and active transport does not.

    B. Active transport requires energy, and passive transport does not.

    C. Active transport includes diffusion, and passive transport does not.

    D. Passive transport includes exocytosis, and active transport does not.

5. Organisms must respond to changes in their environment in order to survive. Which of the following is an example of a **physical** response to an environmental change?

    A. a bat hibernating in winter

    B. a bird migrating when the season changes

    C. a dolphin performing tricks for food at an aquarium

    D. a plant turning so that its leaves face the sunlight

Levels of Cellular Organization

Key Concepts
Choose the letter of the best answer.

1. Which of the following choices lists the processes involved in the development of specialized tissues in the correct order?

   A. fertilization, cell division, embryo develops, specialization

   B. cell division, fertilization, embryo develops, specialization

   C. fertilization, embryo develops, specialization, cell division

   D. embryo develops, specialization, fertilization, cell division

2. Which of the following is a plant organ responsible for trapping light energy to make food?

   A. fruit

   B. leaf

   C. petal

   D. root

3. Kevin is making a class display about different types of tissue. To illustrate one type of tissue, he draws a mail truck moving along a system of roads. His display explains how the truck carries messages from one place to another. Which type of tissue is Kevin **most likely** comparing to a mail truck carrying messages?

   A. ground tissue

   B. muscle tissue

   C. nerve tissue

   D. protective tissue

4. Which comparison of multicellular and unicellular organisms is **true**?

   A. Both are made up of more than one cell.

   B. Unicellular organisms can live longer than multicellular organisms.

   C. The cells of multicellular organisms perform all of the functions necessary for life, and the cells of unicellular organisms do not.

   D. Multicellular organisms develop tissues and organs, and unicellular organisms do not.

5. Which cells carry oxygen and carbon dioxide throughout the body?

   A. skin cells

   B. blood cells

   C. nerve cells

   D. muscle cells

The Characteristics of Cells

Tic-Tac-Toe: *The Basic Form of Life*

1. Work on your own, with a partner, or with a small group.

2. Choose three quick activities from the game. Check the boxes you plan to complete. They must form a straight line in any direction.

3. Have your teacher approve your plan.

4. Do each activity, and turn in your results.

__ **Historical Cell Fiction**	__ **Something in Common**	__ **A Great Adventure**
Research information on the three scientists who developed the cell theory. Write about the conversations that may have happened in developing the cell theory.	Make a drawing of a eukaryotic cell and label its major parts. Make a drawing of a prokaryotic cell and label its major parts. Place the drawings side by side and use string or yarn to connect the common parts.	Pretend you are running an amusement park. All of the rides are built to resemble structures found within a eukaryotic cell. Write a guidebook describing each ride and what it does. Include a color-coded map of the amusement park.
__ **A Simple Cell**	__ **How It Works**	__ **Time Capsule**
Write a poem about being a prokaryotic cell. Select a type of bacteria or archaea. Include facts about this organism in the poem.	Write a persuasive essay about why it is a good thing to be small. Include information about why a cell must be small, and why it cannot survive if it is too large.	Write a journal entry from the point of view of Theodor Schwann. Describe the three things he concluded about cells.
__ **A Model of a Cell**	__ **Public Service Announcement**	__ **A New Report**
Make a 3-dimensional model of a eukaryotic cell using art supplies. Each organelle must be labeled and be a different color. Include a key that identifies each organelle.	Create an advertising campaign to tell people about the importance of the cell theory. Include a drawing to help convey your message.	Write a news report about a one-celled organism that lives inside your body. Include what this bacterium is, what it does, and where it can be found.

Chemistry of Life

Points of View: *Exploring Atoms and Molecules*
**Your class will work together to show what you've learned
about the building blocks of organisms.**

1. Work in groups as assigned by your teacher. Each group will be assigned to one or two viewpoints.

2. Complete your assignment, and present your perspective to the class.

 Vocabulary Define the terms *compound, nutrients, proteins,* and *elements.* Then write down a dictionary or textbook definition. Use each term in a sentence that describes how it relates to molecules.

 Details Describe how sugars and starches are related to carbohydrates. Then describe how amino acids are related to proteins. Finally, describe how DNA and nucleotides are related to nucleic acids.

 Illustrations Draw pictures of an atom, a molecule, and a compound such as a water molecule. Finally, draw an illustration depicting how atoms, molecules, and compounds relate to cells.

 Analysis Create a diagram that explains how molecules, atoms, elements, and compounds relate to each other.

 Models Find a way to model the cell membrane. Make sure your model shows how the phospholipid molecules form this membrane.

Cell Structure and Function

Alternative Assessment

Mix and Match: *Structure and Function of Cell Organelles*
Mix and match ideas to show what you've learned about the structure and function of cells.

1. Work on your own, with a partner, or with a small group.

2. Choose one information source from Column A, two topics from Column B, and one option from Column C. Check your choices.

3. Have your teacher approve your plan.

4. Submit or present your results.

A. Choose Two Information Source	B. Choose Two Things to Analyze	C. Choose One Way to Communicate Analysis
____ observations of cells with a microscope	____ the difference between prokaryotes and eukaryotes	____ diagram or illustration
____ photographs of prokaryotic and eukaryotic cells	____ the general characteristics of the eukaryotic cell	____ colors, symbols, and/or arrows marked on a visual, with a key
____ photographs of cell organelles	____ how mitochondria function	____ model, such as drawings or descriptions showing differences or relationships
____ illustrations of cells and the types of organelles	____ how the ribosomes, ER, and the Golgi complex work together	____ field guide describing structures found in eukaryotic cells
____ video that includes the structure and function of various cell organelles engaged in life processes	____ Differences and similarities between the cell wall and the large central vacuole of plants	____ game
____ print or audio description that includes the life processes of a cell	____ the differences between chloroplasts found in plant cells and the lysosomes found in animal cells	____ story, song, or poem, with supporting details
____ digital simulation of cell organelles and the life processes		____ skit, chant, or dance, with supporting details
		____ multimedia presentation
____ _____		____ _____

Homeostasis and Cell Processes

Climb the Ladder: *Maintaining Homeostasis*

Select an idea from each rung of the ladder to show what you've learned about the different ways organisms maintain homeostasis.

1. Work on your own, with a partner, or with a small group.

2. Choose one item from each rung of the ladder. Check your choices.

3. Have your teacher approve your plan.

4. Submit or present your results.

__ Illustrate a Poster Make a poster illustrating photosynthesis and cellular respiration. You can illustrate the starting materials and end products with drawings or photographs. Include an explanation of why these processes are essential for cells' survival. Give an oral explanation of how the two processes relate.	**__ Build a Model** Make a 3-D model of photosynthesis and cellular respiration. Use materials such as clay, marshmallows, or pipe cleaners to represent the starting materials and end products. Label your model and give an oral explanation of photosynthesis, cellular respiration, and why they are essential to cells' survival.
__ Write a Picture Book Write a picture book that shows the different stages of the cell cycle. Label the nucleus, chromosomes, and chromatids. Write one sentence on each page that explains what is happening at that stage of the cycle.	**__ Be a Broadcaster** Look at the photographs of the plant and animal cell dividing. Imagine that you are a news broadcaster and these photographs are being shown behind you. Describe in detail what is happening as if it were breaking news. You can write or record your broadcast.
__ Write a Skit Write a skit that describes passive and active transport. Assign roles to the different type of materials that need to pass through a membrane. Include information on how these methods of transport help cells maintain balance.	**__ Create an Animation** Use a computer program to create an animation to demonstrate passive and active transport. Include a spoken description of both types of transport and how these help the cell maintain balance.

Name _____ Date _____

Levels of Cellular Organization

Alternative Assessment

Tic-Tac-Toe: *Design Artificial Organs*

Imagine that you are on a committee that is considering whether or not to create artificial tissues, organs, or cells. Investigate cells, tissues, organs, organ systems, bacteria, and multicellular organisms and how these are organized in order to gather information for your committee.

1.   Work on your own, with a partner, or with a small group.

2.   Choose three quick activities from the game. Check the boxes you plan to complete. They must form a straight line in any direction.

3.   Have your teacher approve your plan.

4.   Do each activity, and turn in your results.

__ **Structure and Function**	__ **Diagram**	__ **Organ Journal**
Every organ has a structure directly related to its function. Describe two organs and explain how each structure helps it to function. Pick one organ and describe what type of structure you think would be ideal for its function, and why.	Choose two or more organ systems and draw a diagram showing how they work together keep an organism healthy. You can choose either plant or animal systems.	Write a journal entry describing two organs you would like to create. Include a diagram of these organs.
__ **Human Cell Types**	__ **Building a System**	__ **Instruction Booklet**
Look up different kinds of human cell types. There are more than 200! Briefly describe the function of 10 human body cells. Pick one type you would want to create and tell why, or discuss why this type of cell could never be created artificially.	The four levels of organization for cells, tissues, organs, and organ systems are nearly the same for all multicellular organisms. Write a skit describing how these four levels make up an organism.	Pick an organ system. Research the names of the organs that make up this system. Design an instruction booklet on the use of this system.
__ **Designer Cell**	__ **Life in a Pond**	__ **Which Tissue?**
Design and sketch an imaginary specialized cell that could be part of your artificial organ. Describe the function of this cell that makes it unique.	Write a poem comparing a single-celled paramecium and a multicellular sunfish living in the same freshwater pond. Explore ways in which each organism is adapted for survival.	Describe the functions of the four types of tissues found in humans. Decide which type you think might be the most useful to manufacture, and compose a speech to convince others of the value of this type of tissue.

Unit 6 ISTEP+ Review

Choose the letter of the best answer.

1 What is the function of a cell's nucleus?

A. to hold DNA

B. to hold organelles

C. to hold cytoplasm

D. to hold the cell membrane

2 The basic tissues of an embryo develop to form all the specialized tissues and organs of a multicellular organism. Which statement BEST describes this type of specialization that occurs in most multicellular organisms?

A. Each cell has many levels of organization.

B. Each cell can perform all functions necessary for life.

C. Tissues and organs have specific functions and can work together.

D. Tissues and organs have similar functions and work independently.

3 The following diagrams show a prokaryotic cell and a eukaryotic cell.

A 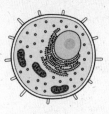   B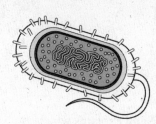

Which statement correctly IDENTIFIES the eukaryotic cell and then EXPLAINS how to identify the eukaryotic cell?

A. Cell B is eukaryotic, because there is DNA in its cytoplasm.

B. Cell B is eukaryotic, because there is cytoplasm filling the cell.

C. Cell A is eukaryotic, because a cell membrane surrounds the cell.

D. Cell A is eukaryotic, because it has a nucleus in the middle of the cell.

4 Ling is looking at a normal healthy plant cell using a microscope. About what fraction of the cell's mass is made of water?

A. one-third

B. two-thirds

C. one-fourth

D. two-fourths

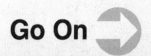

Go On

5 Which of the following is a TRUE statement about unicellular organisms?

A. Unicellular organisms live longer than multicellular organisms.

B. Unicellular organisms are smaller than multicellular organisms.

C. Unicellular organisms are made of more than one cell.

D. Unicellular organisms have cells that work together.

6 This diagram shows a living cell.

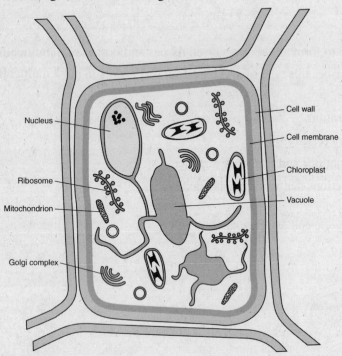

Which statement correctly identifies the cell type and explains why?

A. This is a plant cell; the evidence is the cell wall.

B. This is a plant cell; the evidence is the nucleus.

C. This is an animal cell; the evidence is the mitochondria.

D. This is an animal cell; the evidence is the cell membrane.

7 Some cells in multicellular organisms are constantly dividing. What is ONE reason why cells divide?

A. so that an organism can eliminate wastes

B. so that an organism can grow by adding new cells

C. so that an organism can obtain the energy that it needs

D. so that an organism can exchange materials with its environment

Go On

8 Which of the following lists correctly orders the levels of cellular organization from SMALLEST TO LARGEST?

A. cells, tissues, organ systems, organisms, organs

B. cells, tissues, organs, organ systems, organisms

C. tissues, cells, organ systems, organs, organisms

D. tissues, cells, organs, organisms, organ systems

9 Maria observes that the cells of an organism have lysosomes but not cell walls. What type of organism has Maria MOST LIKELY found?

A. a plant

B. a fungus

C. an animal

D. a prokaryote

10 A student draws a diagram showing the movement of water and nutrients through a plant. What system in people is MOST similar to the diagram?

A. nervous

B. skeletal

C. circulatory

D. respiratory

Constructed Response

11 This diagram shows parts of a plant.

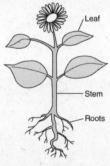

Identify one organ, one organ system, and one organism shown here.

_____

_____

For the organ that you identified above, describe how it helps to meet the needs of the organism.

_____

_____

_____

Go On

Extended Response

12 Complete the data table to compare prokaryotic and eukaryotic cells. Write *Yes* if the cell has the structure. Write *No* if the cell does not have the structure.

Structure	Prokaryotic Cell	Eukaryotic Cell
cell membrane		
cytoplasm		
nucleus		

Describe the function of ONE of the cell structures listed above.

_____

_____

Describe ONE difference between prokaryotes and eukaryotes that is NOT indicated by the table.

_____

_____

_____

_____

The Cell

Key Concepts
Choose the letter of the best answer.

1. The following picture shows a unicellular organism.

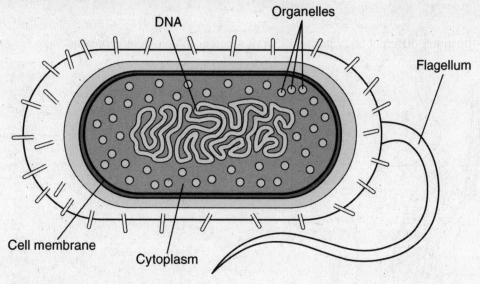

What type of a cell is shown?

A. organelle

B. membrane

C. eukaryotic

D. prokaryotic

2. What is the main function of chloroplasts in a plant cell?

A. They produce proteins.

B. They store water and food.

C. They perform photosynthesis.

D. They protect cells from the surrounding environment.

3. Which statement is **true** of a multicellular organism?

A. Each cell in a multicellular organism performs all special functions.

B. All cells in a multicellular organism perform the same special function.

C. Different types of cells in a multicellular organism perform special functions.

D. Different organelles of a multicellular organism's cells perform all special functions.

4. Which of these is one of the six **most** common elements found in the human body?

   A. iron

   B. oxygen

   C. helium

   D. water

5. The diagram below illustrates different body parts that work together to help people breathe.

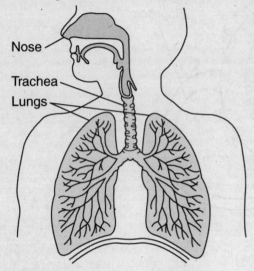

   Which term **best** describes a lung?

   A. organ

   B. tissue

   C. organism

   D. organ system

6. Pedro examines a tissue sample under a high-powered microscope. He makes a sketch in his lab notebook of one of the cells he observes. His sketch is shown below.

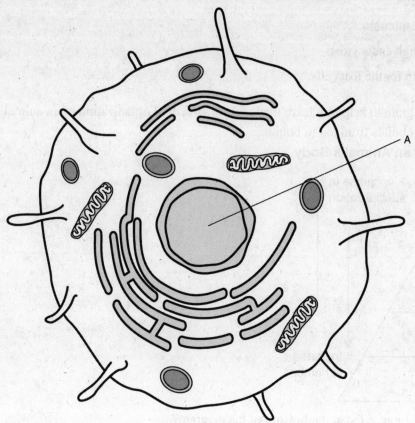

Which label should Pedro use for structure A?

A. cytoskeleton

B. lysosome

C. mitochondrion

D. nucleus

7. Which of the following have cell walls?

A. animal cells and plant cells

B. fungal cells and animal cells

C. plant cells

D. plant cells, animal cells, and fungal cells

8. Cells can die or become damaged. What cell process replaces dead or damaged cells?

   A. Cells divide to make new cells.

   B. Cells multiply by cellular respiration.

   C. Cells take in new cells through endocytosis.

   D. Cells grow larger to make up for the lost cells.

9. Eugene drew the following diagram to help him learn the levels of structural organization of an animal's body. The level of organization builds from top to bottom.

   Levels of Organization of an Animal's Body

   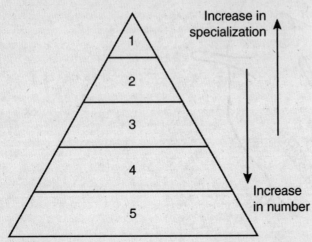

   Which of the following should Eugene list at the **bottom** of his diagram?

   A. organ

   B. tissue

   C. organism

   D. organ system

10. Which of the following structures surround cells?

    A. cell wall and nucleus

    B. cell membrane and cell wall

    C. cytoplasm and cytoskeleton

    D. cell membrane and cytoplasm

11. Cells must be able to perform certain functions in order to survive. Which of the following must all cells do to survive?

    A. obtain energy

    B. use oxygen

    C. absorb wastes

    D. continue growing

12. The following picture shows a microscopic view of blood. Blood is made of different types of cells that work together.

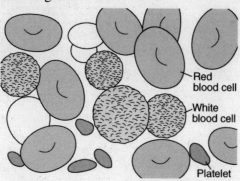

Which term expresses the concept that each type of cell plays a different role?

A. function   C. organization

B. structure   D. specialization

Constructed Response

13. The diagram below shows the two main parts of the human body's central nervous system.

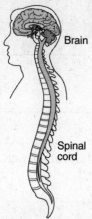

Identify **three** levels of organization associated with the body parts shown, and give **one** example for each.

1) _____

2) _____

3) _____

Identify the level of organization associated with these body parts that is **least** specialized.

_____

Describe its function.

_____

_____

Extended Response

14. The following diagram shows a single cell.

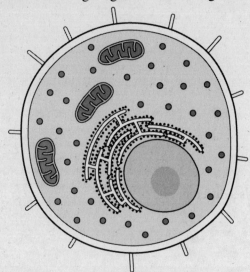

Identify **two** structures of this cell, and describe the function of each.

1) _____

2) _____

Is this cell from a prokaryote or a eukaryote? Justify your answer.

_____

_____

Identify the kind of organism that this cell comes from: bacteria, plant, or animal. Justify your answer.

_____

_____

The Cell

Key Concepts
Choose the letter of the best answer.

1. Eukaryotic cells and prokaryotic cells have some parts that are different. Which of the following would you find **only** in a eukaryotic cell?

   A. membrane-bound organelles and a nucleus

   B. a nucleus and organelles without membranes

   C. a cell membrane and organelles without membranes

   D. membrane-bound organelles and DNA in cytoplasm

2. Eugene drew the following diagram to help him learn the levels of structural organization of an animal's body. The level of organization builds from top to bottom.

   Levels of Organization of an Animal's Body

   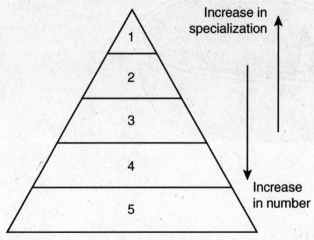

   Which of the following should he put in **level 5** on the diagram?

   A. organ

   B. tissue

   C. organism

   D. organ system

3. Some organisms consist of one cell. Other organisms consist of multiple cells. Which of the following is **true** of cells in a multicellular organism?

   A. Different types of cells have the same function.

   B. Different types of cells have different functions.

   C. Every cell has a different function.

   D. All cells have the same function.

4. What are the four main types of molecules found in the cells of living things?

   A. water, hydrogen, oxygen, and various salts

   B. carbohydrates, lipids, nucleic acids, and proteins

   C. lipids, nutrients, nucleic acids, and carbon dioxide

   D. atoms, molecules, chemical compounds, and carbohydrates

5. Eukaryotic cells undergo mitosis as part of the cell cycle. What does a cell produce as a result of mitosis?

   A. two cells with identical genetic information

   B. two cells that are larger than the original cell

   C. two cells with genetic material that is different from the original cell

   D. two cells that no longer participate in the stages of the cell cycle

6. Tina looks at a diagram of a cellular organelle in her science book. The diagram is shown below.

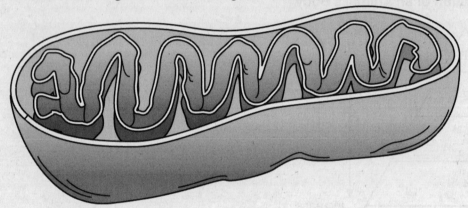

   Which cellular structure is Tina observing?

   A. cytoskeleton

   B. DNA

   C. mitochondrion

   D. ribosome

7. The diagram below shows parts of the human body that work together to help the body digest food.

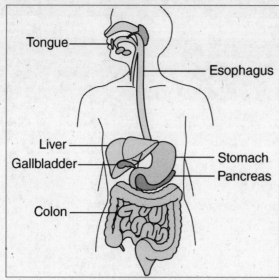

What can you conclude about the tongue from this diagram?

A. It is made of just one type of cell.

B. It is made of just one type of organ system.

C. It is made of two or more types of tissue that work together to perform a function.

D. It is made of two or more types of organs that work together to perform a function.

8. What is the function of the large central vacuole in a plant cell?

A. water storage and support

B. protein production and digestion

C. cellular respiration and photosynthesis

D. waste disposal and storage of the genetic material

9. The survival of a cell depends on the cell maintaining homeostasis. What is **most likely** to happen to a cell if homeostasis is not maintained?

A. The cell will immediately divide.

B. Cell processes will continue unchanged.

C. The cell will eliminate wastes more efficiently.

D. Many chemical reactions in the cell will slow down or even stop.

10. Jana drew the plant shown in the following illustration. She labeled parts of the plant.

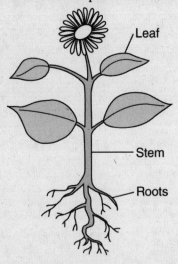

Leaf

Stem

Roots

What is **true** of the roots of the plant?

A. The roots are made of just one type of cell.

B. The roots are made of just one type of organ system.

C. The roots are made of a group of tissues that work together to perform a function.

D. The roots are made of two or more types of organs that work together to perform a function.

11. Jun Ming puts a slide of a eukaryotic cell under a microscope. The following diagram represents what Jun Ming observes.

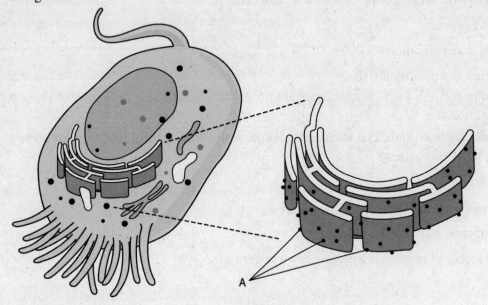

A

Which of the following choices **best** describes the structures labeled A?

A. These structures transport substances throughout the cell.

B. These structures contain DNA and have a folded inner membrane.

C. These structures produce energy for the cell in the form of ATP.

D. These structures are the cell's smallest organelles and do not have membranes.

12. Which of the following choices includes two structures that are in plant cells, but not in animal cells?

   A. cell wall, nucleus

   B. chloroplasts, ribosomes

   C. lysosomes, mitochondria

   D. cell wall, large central vacuole

Constructed Response

13. The following picture shows a microscopic view of blood.

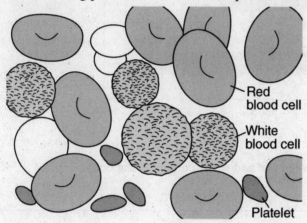

Identify **three** levels of organization associated with blood, and give **one** example for each.

1) _____

2) _____

3) _____

Identify the level of organization associated with blood that is **most** specialized. Describe its function.

_____

_____

Extended Response

14. The following graph shows the percentage of water content in human bodies at different ages.

Average Water Content Found in Humans

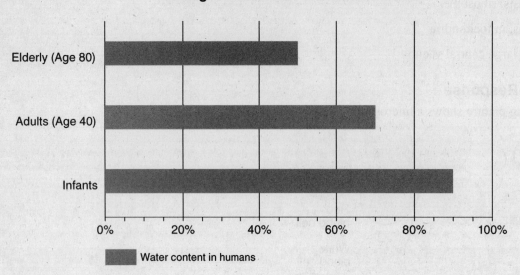

Based on the graph, describe the relationship between age and water content in the body.

_____

_____

What does the graph suggest about the water content of individual cells in the body?

_____

_____

Suppose you are an athletic trainer, and an adult athlete comes to you for advice. She has experienced a decline in the water content of her body. The percentage has dropped to below 70 percent. What advice do you give her?

_____

_____

Why is water important to the body?

_____

_____

_____

Name _____ Date _____

Design Process Test

1. Selena is going camping soon, and she wants to bring some board games to play in the evening. However, some of her board games are in bulky boxes which are hard to pack in her camping bag.

    What is another problem that Selena might face if she brings traditional board games on a camping trip?

    _____

    _____

    Select a traditional board game and describe how the board and pieces can be modified to solve both problems.

    _____

    _____

    _____

    Selena decides to make a prototype of a modified board game to address the problems. Use the space below to draw the prototype and label its modifications.

2. People are using some natural resources, such as fossil fuels, faster than these resources can be replenished. There are many possible solutions to the problem of too much fossil fuel use. For example, an engineer wants to design a new vehicle that can travel at least 10 more miles per gallon of fuel, compared to similar-sized vehicles.

How is the engineer's plan a solution to the problem of too much fossil fuel use?

_____

_____

The engineer designs and makes a prototype of her new vehicle, Car A. She then tests it against several other vehicles, Cars B, C, and D. The data she collects are shown in the table below.

Vehicle	Gallons of fuel	Miles travelled
Car A	7	364
Car B	8	304
Car C	9	396
Car D	6	246

How many miles does each vehicle travel per gallon of fuel used?

Car A _____   Car C _____

Car B _____   Car D _____

Complete the bar graph below to show a comparison of miles per gallon (mpg) for each vehicle.

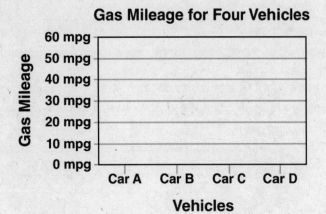

Gas Mileage for Four Vehicles

Does the engineer's prototype Car A meet her goal? Use data to explain your answer.

_____

_____

_____

3. Caleb's science class recently got an aquarium with several fish. Caleb is helping his teacher design a process for cleaning the aquarium. The process will be displayed on a flowchart for other students to follow. Caleb comes up with the following list of tasks that must be done as part of the clean-up:

A. Place the rinsed gravel and artificial plants back in the empty aquarium.

B. Remove the fish and place them in safe, temporary containers.

C. Fill the aquarium with clean water.

D. Rinse the dirty gravel and artificial plants in fresh water.

E. Allow the clean water to adjust to the appropriate temperature in the aquarium.

F. Remove dirty water, gravel, and artificial plants from aquarium.

G. Place the fish back in the aquarium.

Organize these tasks into logical order in the flowchart.

_____ →

_____ →

_____ →

_____ →

_____ →

_____

Caleb shows his flowchart to his teacher. The teacher explains that fish might not survive in fresh tap water, so the students will need to test the water and add chemicals before the fish can be added safely. How can Caleb adjust the flowchart to include these steps?

_____

_____

4. While organizing supplies in his science classroom, Dion finds rope, yarn, and sewing thread. All three of these materials can be used to tie or bind things.

   Explain a circumstance in which Dion would use rope, but not yarn or sewing thread.

   _____

   _____

   _____

   Dion also finds many types of paper, including graph paper, toilet tissue, and poster board.

   Select the type of paper that would be most appropriate for drawing a model of the classroom and explain your reasoning.

   _____

   _____

   _____

   Dion finds many measuring devices in the room, including thermometers, tape measures, balances, graduated cylinders, metersticks, and spring scales.

   Which measuring device(s) can be used for measuring the volume of a liquid? _____

   Which measuring device(s) can be used for measuring mass? _____

   Dion designs and builds a sturdy wooden box to store a fragile piece of laboratory equipment. Explain the kinds of measurements Dion should take to make sure the box meets the storage needs.

   _____

   _____

   _____

ISTEP+ Practice Test 1

Choose the letter of the best answer.

1   Which of the following is an example of energy being used to do work?

A. A boy holds a fishing pole over the water.

B. A girl climbs a ladder holding a paint can.

C. A woman sits on the edge of a bench.

D. A soccer ball rests at the top of a hill.

2   Which example illustrates the transfer of energy through RADIATION?

A. feeling warmth when you sit in a sunny place

B. feeling warm air while standing in front of the blower from a heating system

C. feeling the warmth of the bricks around a fireplace when you touch them with your hand

D. feeling warmth on the soles of your feet when you walk along a beach on a sunny day

3   Two groups of students were challenged to make their own compasses by floating identical small corks in a bowl of water and laying identical needles on top of the cork. For group A, no matter how they turned the bowl, the needle pointed north. For group B, the needle just pointed in random directions. Why did results of the two groups differ?

A. Group B was not located in Earth's magnetic field.

B. Group A was located in Earth's magnetic field.

C. Group A first rubbed the needle on a magnet, magnetizing it.

D. Group B placed the needle too close to the edge of the cork.

Go On

4 An earthquake sends out mechanical waves in all directions. The waves change speed, direction, and shape as they move through the different materials that make up Earth. In answering the following question, assume that the four labeled waves in the illustration all have the same energy when they leave the earthquake source.

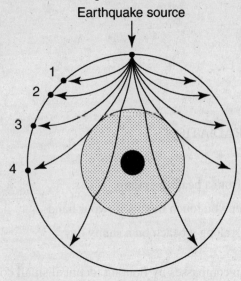

Earthquake source

Which wave has the LEAST effect on Earth's surface?

A. wave 1

B. wave 2

C. wave 3

D. wave 4

5 Some forces act at a distance. Other forces act only when two objects are in direct contact. Which force can act ACROSS A DISTANCE?

A. the force of friction

B. a normal force

C. a mechanical force

D. the magnetic force

6 Which is an explanation of POWER?

A. the time it takes for energy to be transferred from one object to another

B. the rate at which energy is transformed from one form to another

C. one joule of energy transferred in one second

D. work divided by time

Go On

7 A student made a table to help her understand units of geologic time. She ordered the units alphabetically.

Units of geologic time	Length of a unit
Age	shorter than an epoch
Eon	longer than an era
Epoch	shorter than a period
Era	longer than an period
Period	longer than an epoch

Which unit of geologic time is the LONGEST?

A. age

B. epoch

C. eon

D. era

8 The following picture shows forces acting on a sneaker. Suppose that the sneaker is moving toward the spring scale.

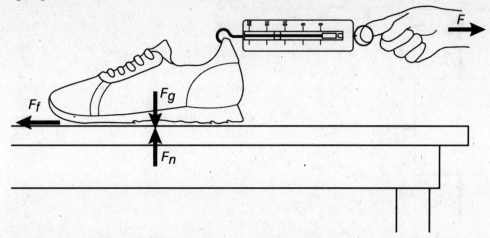

In which direction is the NET FORCE (the sum of all forces) acting?

A. The net force is acting in an upward direction.

B. The net force is acting in a downward direction.

C. The net force is acting to the left.

D. era The net force is acting to the right.

Go On

9 A group of four students used spring scales to measure the forces applied to the sides of a box. During each trial, they changed the forces, observed the results, and sketched a diagram showing the applied forces. Which picture shows the box with NO NET FORCE?

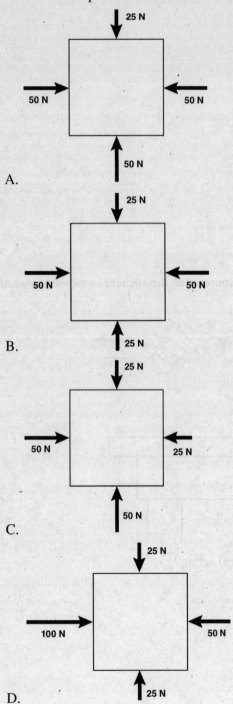

A.

B.

C.

D.

Go On

10 Which happens when energy is transferred from one system to another?

A. New energy is created.

B. Some energy is destroyed.

C. The energy changes forms.

D. The energy changes into mass.

11 Scientists divide Earth into three main layers. Each layer has a different chemical composition. Which is the INNERMOST layer of Earth?

A. Earth's innermost layer is the core.

B. Earth's innermost layer is the asthenosphere.

C. Earth's innermost layer is the lithosphere.

D. Earth's innermost layer is the mantle.

12 Ryan's young sister has back problems and cannot use standard swings on playgrounds. Ryan designs and makes a swing that will support her back. However, he notices that the swing is too high for her to climb into on her own. What step of the design process should Ryan use now?

A. identify the problem

B. create a prototype

C. redesign for improvement

D. test and evaluate

13 The flow chart below shows how a metamorphic rock can change into a sedimentary rock.

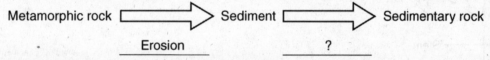

Metamorphic rock ⟹ Sediment ⟹ Sedimentary rock

Erosion   ?

Which term should replace the question mark?

A. cooling

B. melting

C. pressure

D. weathering

14 Which did Matthias Schleiden and Theodor Schwann identify as the basic unit of all living things?

A. the cell

B. the nucleus

C. the organelle

D. the organism

Go On

15 Laura is trying to make a scale model of a cell using a shoebox and other materials found in the classroom. Which of the following is the MOST IMPORTANT factor to consider when she chooses the materials to make her cell model?

A. the texture of each material

B. the size of each material

C. the color of each material

D. the attractiveness of each material

16 Lisa and Vinay notice a structure in the cells they are observing under a microscope. Lisa predicts that the structure is the rough endoplasmic reticulum. Vinay predicts that it is the Golgi complex. Which choice describes a way to support one of their predictions?

A. Lisa's prediction would be supported if they observed that the structure contained DNA.

B. Lisa's prediction would be supported if they observed ribosomes on the structure.

C. Vinay's prediction would be supported if they observed that the structure produced ATP molecules.

D. Vinay's prediction would be supported if they observed that the structure carried out photosynthesis.

17 Jana is studying the structure and function of different parts of a flowering plant. She drew and labeled the plant shown in the following illustration.

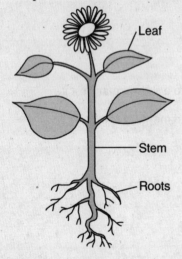

Which statement describes a FUNCTION OF THE ROOTS?

A. The roots are connected to the stem.

B. The roots have tiny root hairs on them.

C. The roots are about 15 cm long.

D. The roots take in nutrients from the soil.

Go On

18 Maria's class was investigating how the soil around their school was affected by the animals that live in the soil. They observed the soil and the animals within its layers, and they recorded their observations in their science journals. Then, Maria made a poster to show what she learned. What kind of an investigation did Maria conduct?

A. survey

B. controlled experiment

C. field observation

D. laboratory experiment

19 Cells age and eventually die. What happens to ensure an adequate supply of healthy cells in a multicellular organism?

A. Living cells near the dead cells grow larger.

B. Living cells pass nutrients to the dead cells, restoring them.

C. Living cells divide, making new cells.

D. Living cells in other tissue take on the functions of the dead cells.

20 Most U.S. energy needs are met by fossil fuels. The table below describes ways in which obtaining, transporting, converting, and using fossil fuels can affect the environment.

Human action	Ways in which the environment is affected
1	can produce harmful byproducts
2	can destroy habitats and pollute water and soil by drilling and mining
3	can produce air pollution, such as carbon dioxide, a greenhouse gas
4	can create spills, which cause pollution and harm organisms

Which human action BEST fits in the table cell numbered 3?

A. obtaining fossil fuels

B. transporting fossil fuels

C. converting fossil fuels to usable forms

D. using fossil fuels

Go On

Constructed Response

21 Fossils can help scientists determine the relative ages of rocks. The diagram below shows fossils of animals that existed at different periods of Earth's history.

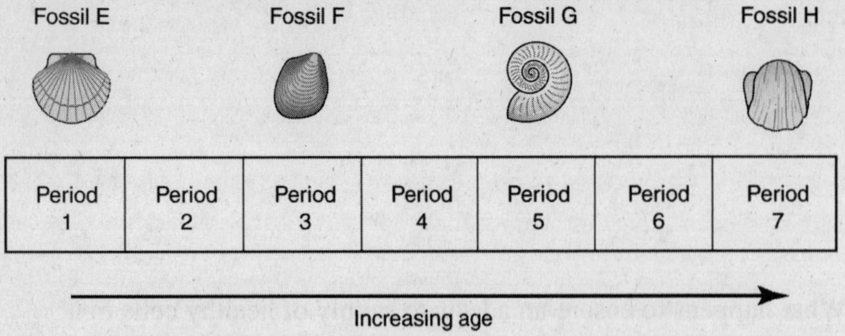

Fossil E   Fossil F   Fossil G   Fossil H

Period 1	Period 2	Period 3	Period 4	Period 5	Period 6	Period 7

Increasing age

How do rock layers containing fossil H differ in age from rock layers containing fossil F?

_____

_____

_____

How can scientists use fossils to learn how species evolve?

_____

_____

_____

22 Energy can be harnessed to do work using many processes.

How can energy from wind be used to generate electrical energy? Describe the energy transformations that occur in this process.

_____

_____

_____

How can energy from water be used to generate electrical energy? Describe the energy transformations that occur in this process.

_____

_____

_____

Go On

23 Many multicellular organisms reproduce through sexual reproduction.

Describe FERTILIZATION, the first step in the process of sexual reproduction.

_____

_____

Describe what happens after fertilization to produce a complete multicellular organism. Include at least THREE levels of structural organization in your description.

_____

_____

_____

_____

Extended Response

24 Water is necessary for life. A cell must have water in order to function.

Approximately how much of the MASS of living cells is made up of water?

_____

Explain the role that phospholipids have in the regulation of water in a cell.

_____

_____

_____

Describe what happens to a cell that has TOO MUCH WATER.

_____

_____

What happens when a cell has TOO LITTLE WATER?

_____

_____

Go On

25 A glacier is a large mass of moving ice. Glaciers are found where it is cold enough for ice to remain frozen all year.

What FORCE causes a glacier to move?

_____

Why does a glacier change the land it moves over?

_____

_____

_____

What is the DIFFERENCE between an alpine glacier and a continental glacier?

_____

_____

Compare ways that alpine glaciers and continental glaciers shape the land. Include at least TWO features formed by each type of glacier.

_____

_____

_____

_____

ISTEP+ Practice Test 2

Choose the letter of the best answer.

1 Willa holds a pan over a campfire, as shown in the figure below. She feels warmth from the fire.

Most of the warmth Willa feels comes from the process represented by letter Z. What is this process?

A. conduction

B. convection

C. mutualism

D. radiation

2 A student made a table to show relative sizes of units of geologic time.

Units of geologic time	Length of a unit
Era	longer than an period
Age	shorter than an epoch
Eon	longer than an era
Epoch	shorter than a period
Period	longer than an epoch

Which of the following shows the correct sequence of the units of geologic time, FROM SHORTEST TO LONGEST?

A. eon, era, period, epoch, age

B. age, epoch, period, era, eon

C. era, epoch, period, age, eon

D. age, era, period, epoch, eon

3 Waves move energy from one place to another. Which statement is TRUE about how waves move energy?

A. A wave traveling through a medium transfers energy but not matter.

B. A wave traveling through a medium transfers both matter and energy.

C. A longitudinal wave transfers energy in a direction perpendicular to the direction of vibration.

D. A transverse wave transfers energy in the direction of vibration.

Go On

4   It can take a long time for soil to form. Which are the PRIMARY factors that affect soil formation?

A. rainfall, temperature, wind, time, and plants

B. parent rock, sunshine, plants, animals, and bacteria

C. climate, parent rock, topography, living things, and time

D. time, climate, topography, plants, and animals

5   Forces act on objects either by direct contact or over a distance. Which forces act to keep a cup on a shelf?

A. mass force and magnetic force

B. normal force and magnetic force

C. gravitational force and normal force

D. velocity force and gravitational force

6   The forces acting on an object are added to determine the net force on the object. Students are using spring scales to measure the forces they apply to the sides of a box. They then draw pictures showing the applied forces. Which picture shows a box with a net force that is UP and to the RIGHT?

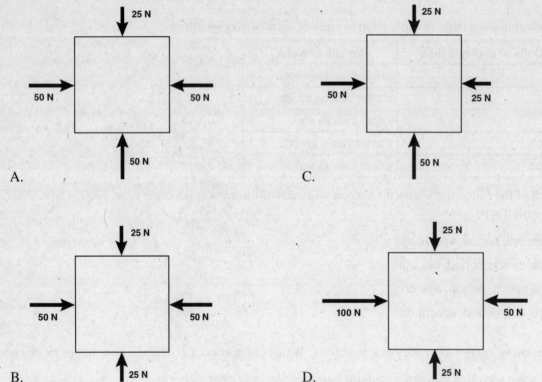

Go On

7 A class wanted to put three salt-water plants into an aquarium. To find out how much salt the plants could tolerate, they did an experiment. First, they used a microscope to observe cells from the plants. Then, they placed each plant in identical volumes of solutions containing different amounts of salt. The next day, the students again observed cells of the plants. They recorded their observations in the following data table.

Amount of Salt in 50 mL water	Observations		
	Plant1	Plant 2	Plant 3
0g	cells slightly larger than usual	cells much larger than usual	cells larger than usual
3 g t	cells normal size	cells normal size	cells normal size
6 g	cells shrunken and small	cells shriveled and small	cells shriveled and small

What can the students infer about how salt affects the cells of the plants?

A. The cells of the plants are not dependent on water, so they can live in water with any salt concentration.

B. As more salt is added to the water, more water is present in the cells.

C. As more salt is added to the water, less water is present in the cells.

D. The amount of salt added to the water has no affect on the amount of water in the cells.

8 Michelle finds that there are three routes to get from her home to school. She travels each route on foot, on a bicycle, and in a car, and she times her trips. She created the data table below to show her results.

Route	Time, on foot (min)	Time, by bicycle (min)	Time, by car (min)
1	15	9	7
2	17	11	8
3	14	7	7

How much time does Michelle save by taking Route 2 on her bicycle instead of walking Route 1?

A. 2 minutes

B. 4 minutes

C. 6 minutes

D. 8 minutes

Go On

9 A rocket sitting on a launch pad is at rest. When a rocket burns fuel to create hot gases that explode violently out of the rocket engine, the explosion creates thrust. Thrust is a force that changes the motion of the rocket by pushing it upward. What force must thrust OVERCOME in order for the rocket to move?

A. gravity acting on the rocket

B. gravity acting on the exploding gases

C. friction between the rocket and the ground

D. friction between the rocket and the exploding gases

10 New ocean floor is most likely to form as movement occurs at which type of plate boundary?

A. a divergent boundary

B. a transform boundary

C. a subducting boundary

D. a convergent boundary

11 The cross section below shows layers of Earth. The crust includes the tectonic plates.

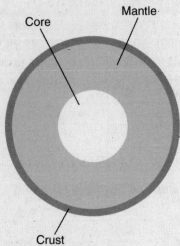

The layers are divided according to their chemical compositions. . Based on the diagram, which of these statements is CORRECT?

A. The mantle has more volume than the crust has.

B. The crust has the greatest mass of any of the layers.

C. The core is located between the crust and the mantle.

D. The crust is denser than either the core or the mantle.

Go On →

12 Energy is the ability to do work. In which of these examples does using energy cause work to be done?

    A. A boy holds a suitcase by his side.

    B. A girl kicks a ball across a field.

    C. A pitcher holds a ball in his glove.

    D. A woman reads instructions for assembling her bicycle.

13 The following steps are part of a laboratory exercise that sixth-grade students are doing in their science class.

Step	Procedure
1	Obtain an ice cube that has been darkly colored with food coloring.
2	Use tongs to place the ice cube in a beaker containing warm water. Be sure to lower the ice cube slowly to keep the water as still as possible.
3	Observe the ice cube and water mixture for at least five minutes.

What are these students modeling?

    A. plate boundary

    B. continental drift

    C. movement of tectonic plates

    D. convection currents in the mantle

14 How do scientists use fossils to determine the relative ages of rock layers?

    A. by determining the positions of fossils in many different rock layers

    B. by locating other areas of the world where the same fossils are found

    C. by comparing all the fossils in one rock layer

    D. by comparing fossils in many different rock layers

15 What term describes the SMALLEST unit that can perform all of the functions necessary for life?

    A. a single cell

    B. a cell nucleus

    C. a cell membrane

    D. a multicellular organism

16 Which of the following describes the relationship between chloroplasts and mitochondria?

    A. Mitochondria produce sugar, and chloroplasts use this sugar to make ATP.

    B. Chloroplasts produce sugar, and mitochondria use this sugar to make ATP.

    C. Mitochondria produce the enzymes that chloroplasts need to carry out photosynthesis.

    D. Chloroplasts produce the proteins that mitochondria need to perform cellular respiration.

Go On

17 Terrell uses a microscope to observe and compare cells from the leaves and roots of the same plant. What does Terrell most likely observe?

A. The cells are identical.

B. The leaf cells contain nuclei, whereas the root cells do not.

C. The leaf cells have cell walls, whereas the root cells have cell membranes.

D. The leaf cells contain many more chloroplasts than the root cells do.

18 The diagram shows different body parts that work together to help you breathe. These parts form the respiratory system.

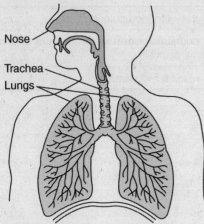

Which statement is TRUE about how the respiratory system works with the circulatory system to supply the needs of cells?

A. Both the circulatory system and the respiratory system remove cellular wastes from the body.

B. Both the circulatory system and the respiratory system carry nutrients and water to cells.

C. The circulatory system removes cellular wastes from the body, and the respiratory system carries nutrients and water to cells.

D. The circulatory system carries nutrients and water to cells, and the respiratory system removes cellular wastes from the body.

19 What process do cells undergo to make more cells for growth and repair?

A. meiosis

B. fertilization

C. mitosis

D. asexual reproduction

20 Dr. Hernandez and Dr. Osman measure the power of a new type of lightbulb. Both researchers find the energy measurement as 90 J for a time of 30 s. However, Dr. Hernandez determines that the power is 3 J/s, and Dr. Osman says that the power is 2700 J•s. Why do the results differ?

A. Dr. Hernandez has the correct numerical value but an incorrect unit.

B. Dr. Osman has an incorrect numerical value but a correct unit.

C. The units are correct for Dr. Hernandez's results but Dr. Osman multiplied the units instead of dividing them.

D. The units are correct for Dr. Osman's results but Dr. Hernandez divided the units instead of multiplying them.

Constructed Response

21 The rock cycle describes how rocks change over time. The flow chart below shows one way that igneous rock can change to metamorphic rock.

Igneous rock → Sediment → Sedimentary Rock → Metamorphic rock

Explain the process by which igneous rock becomes sedimentary rock.

_____

_____

Explain the process by which sedimentary rock becomes metamorphic rock.

_____

_____

Go On

22 Teams of students are competing in orienteering. Orienteering involves using a compass and a set of instructions or a map to reach a goal. Each team must make and record accurate measurements of both distance and direction.

What units should the students use when recording the distance they travel? Explain your answer.

_____

_____

What must the students know about a compass before they can use it to determine direction?

_____

_____

Explain how and why a compass works.

_____

_____

_____

23 Forces of nature shape Earth's surface, but they also shape areas of Earth's crust beneath the surface.

What is karst topography and in what type of rock does it occur?

_____

_____

_____

What is a sinkhole, and how does a sinkhole form?

_____

_____

_____

Go On ➡

Extended Response

24 Depending on the number of cells they contain, organisms are either unicellular or multicellular.

What are TWO general characteristics of a multicellular organism?

1) _____

2) _____

Many multicellular organisms reproduce using sexual reproduction. Explain fertilization and its significance to heredity.

_____

_____

_____

_____

What structure forms when a small cluster of cells divides after fertilization?

_____

Discuss the process by which a multicellular organism develops. Include at least THREE levels of structural organization.

_____

_____

Go On

25 Energy can be used to do work using many processes. Complete the chart by identifying the energy conversion or conversions that take place for each example given. The first example is done for you.

Example	Energy conversion(s)
You get energy when you eat and digest food.	Chemical energy from food is converted to mechanical energy you can use to do work.
Energy from a battery runs a CD player.	
Energy from a windmill lights a lamp.	
Differences in temperatures cause wind.	
A loud noise makes the windows rattle.	

Name _____ Date _____

PLEASE NOTE

- Use only a no. 2 pencil
- Example: Ⓐ ● Ⓒ Ⓓ
- Erase changes COMPLETELY.

Indiana ISTEP+ Practice Test
Mark one answer for each question.

1 Ⓐ Ⓑ Ⓒ Ⓓ   8 Ⓐ Ⓑ Ⓒ Ⓓ   15 Ⓐ Ⓑ Ⓒ Ⓓ

2 Ⓐ Ⓑ Ⓒ Ⓓ   9 Ⓐ Ⓑ Ⓒ Ⓓ   16 Ⓐ Ⓑ Ⓒ Ⓓ

3 Ⓐ Ⓑ Ⓒ Ⓓ   10 Ⓐ Ⓑ Ⓒ Ⓓ   17 Ⓐ Ⓑ Ⓒ Ⓓ

4 Ⓐ Ⓑ Ⓒ Ⓓ   11 Ⓐ Ⓑ Ⓒ Ⓓ   18 Ⓐ Ⓑ Ⓒ Ⓓ

5 Ⓐ Ⓑ Ⓒ Ⓓ   12 Ⓐ Ⓑ Ⓒ Ⓓ   19 Ⓐ Ⓑ Ⓒ Ⓓ

6 Ⓐ Ⓑ Ⓒ Ⓓ   13 Ⓐ Ⓑ Ⓒ Ⓓ   20 Ⓐ Ⓑ Ⓒ Ⓓ

7 Ⓐ Ⓑ Ⓒ Ⓓ   14 Ⓐ Ⓑ Ⓒ Ⓓ

Test Doctor

Unit 1 Nature of Science
Unit Pretest

1. C	5. A	9. A
2. D	6. B	10. C
3. B	7. A	
4. D	8. C	

1. C

A is incorrect because microscopes are useful for examining things that are too small to see with the naked eye, and a variety of liquids and stain repellant could be used in an experiment about stain removal, but not necessarily an experiment about which liquid absorbs the most.

B is incorrect because, though the experiment about which fabric absorbs the most will require a variety of fabrics, this experiment will not require a thermometer or heat source.

C is correct because an experiment about which fabric is most absorbent will require testing multiple fabrics to see which absorbs the most volume of the same liquid.

D is incorrect because, though the experiment will require a graduated cylinder to measure the amount of liquid that can be absorbed, it will not require stain repellant or a hand lens.

2. D

A is incorrect because, though mathematics are often involved in the data analysis step that follows an experiment, mathematical analysis is not an appropriate description of an experiment.

B is incorrect because observation of the natural world is most often part of fieldwork, not experiments, which are often performed in laboratories.

C is incorrect because an experiment occurs under controlled conditions.

D is correct because an experiment involves an organized procedure, controlled conditions, and dependent and independent variables.

3. B

A is incorrect because a balance is used to measure mass.

B is correct because a graduated cylinder is used to measure volume of liquids.

C is incorrect because a ruler is used to measure length. Volume of solids often can be calculated based on length measurements.

D is incorrect because a thermometer is used to measure temperature.

4. D

A is incorrect because DNA does exist and is found in all living things.

B is incorrect because DNA is very small, not large, as indicated by the scale shown on the model.

C is incorrect because DNA is found in all living things, and therefore not rare.

D is correct because DNA is a microscopic molecule, as indicated by the scale shown on the model. Computer models make it easier to study DNA because the models can be enlarged.

5. A

A is correct because both laws and theories are based on evidence collected through scientific investigation.

B is incorrect because only theories explain natural phenomena; scientific laws describe, but do not explain, phenomena.

C is incorrect because both scientific laws and theories are based on evidence, not opinions.

D is incorrect because both laws and theories can be modified as new evidence becomes available.

6. B

A is incorrect because the dependent variable is not controlled, but rather is measured to gather results.

B is correct because this defines the dependent variable.

C is incorrect because this describes any variable, not necessarily the dependent variable.

D is incorrect because this defines the independent variable, not the dependent variable.

7. A

A is correct because a person's sense of taste can detect sourness, which is a property of vinegar and other acids.

B is incorrect because determining pH requires scientific equipment.

C is incorrect because determining density requires scientific equipment.

D is incorrect because testing for electrical conductivity requires scientific equipment.

8. C

A is incorrect because the data table includes all the labels that are required.

B is incorrect because the data table includes all the units that are required.

C is correct because the data table includes units, labels, and values, but does not include a title.

D is incorrect because the data table includes all the values that were recorded.

9. A

A is correct because the data table shows a larger population each year for 4 consecutive years.

B is incorrect because the data table shows an increase in the population of Greenwood from 2005 to 2008.

C is incorrect because the data table shows that the population increases by about 4,000 people each year, not four people.

D is incorrect because the data stops in 2008, so no conclusion can be drawn about the most recent years.

10. C

A is incorrect because the value is given in units of °F instead of °C. 100.4 °F is the equivalent of 38.0 °C.

B is incorrect because 102.6 °C is not as close to the known standard for the boiling point of water as 100.4 °C is, so it is not as accurate.

C is correct because this measurement most closely matches 100 °C, the known standard for the boiling point of water, and is therefore the most accurate.

D is incorrect because the value is given in units of °F instead of °C. 102.6 °F is the equivalent of 39.2 °C.

Lesson 1 Quiz

1. C 4. B
2. A 5. B
3. A

1. C

A is incorrect because both theories and law require evidence.

B is incorrect because theories and laws are based on both experimentation and observation.

C is correct because theories explain phenomena whereas laws describe them.

D is incorrect because both laws and theories can be modified as new evidence becomes available.

2. A

A is correct because scientific ideas may change as new evidence is found.

B is incorrect because although scientific ideas may be based on extensive evidence, they can always change as new evidence emerges.

C is incorrect because there is no hierarchical progression of idea to theory to law. Theories and laws are different concepts.

D is incorrect because scientific ideas change as a result of empirical evidence, not opinion.

3. A

A is correct because controlled experiments most often take place in a laboratory because a laboratory is a controlled setting.

B is incorrect because the experiment described needs to be controlled, which is hard to do in the field.

C is incorrect because surveys collect information through interviews and polls, which are not the same as controlled experiments.

D is incorrect because scientific laws are descriptions of phenomena, but are not a means of studying chemical reactions or conducting experiments.

4. B

A is incorrect because the three drawings clearly show that atomic models have varied over time.

B is correct because as scientists learned more about atoms through experimentation and observation, they

modified the atomic model to match their discoveries.

C is incorrect because the dates on the models indicate that they show a progression of the atomic models.

D is incorrect because the dates on the models indicate that they show a progression of the atomic models.

5. B

A is incorrect because chemists are less likely to be in the field observing organisms.

B is correct because some biologists frequently work in the field to observe organisms.

C is incorrect because physicists are less likely to be in the field observing organisms.

D is incorrect because mathematicians rarely perform fieldwork to gather information. They use computers, surveys, and calculations.

Lesson 2 Quiz

1. B 4. A
2. C 5. D
3. C

1. B

A is incorrect because a balance is used to measure mass.

B is correct because a ruler is used to measure length.

C is incorrect because a graduated cylinder is used to measure volume.

D is incorrect because a thermometer is used to measure temperature.

2. C

A is incorrect because collecting and organizing data typically happens after defining a problem and planning an experimental procedure to investigate the problem.

B is incorrect because a scientist must define the problem before planning the experiment.

C is correct because once a scientist defines the problem, this information helps to plan all other steps.

D is incorrect because a scientist usually defines the problem, plans the procedure, and collects and organizes data before drawing and defending conclusions.

3. C

A is incorrect because a 2 kg object requires more force than a 1kg object does. Therefore, an object that requires 0.10 N of force should have a mass of 0.5 kg.

B is incorrect because a 2 kg object requires about 2 times more force than a 1kg object does. Therefore, an object that requires 1.20 N of force should have a mass of 6 kg.

C is correct because a 2 kg object requires about 2 times more force than a 1kg object does. Therefore, an 8 kg object requires about 2 times more force than a 4 kg object does.

D is incorrect because a 2 kg object requires about 2 times more force than a 1kg object does. Therefore, an object that requires 2.00 N of force should have a mass of 10 kg.

4. A

A is correct because the act of counting birds does not include variables.

B is incorrect because temperature is the independent variable and reproduction rate is the dependent variable in the investigation described.

C is incorrect because mass is the independent variable and speed is the dependent variable in the investigation described.

D is incorrect because wind speed is the independent variable and air flow resistance is the dependent variable in the investigation described.

5. D

A is incorrect because the graph would show a straight, horizontal line if the amount of stretch stayed the same.

B is incorrect because the change in y would have increased as x increased, but the graph shows that the change in y decreased as x increased.

C is incorrect because the graph would show a straight, horizontal line if the amount of stretch was unaffected by weight

D is correct because the change in y decreased as x increased.

Lesson 3 Quiz

1. D   4. C
2. A   5. D
3. C

1. D

A is incorrect because a camera would record qualitative characteristics, such as shape and color, but would not record the quantitative measurements of length, height, and mass.

B is incorrect because drawings would be records of qualitative characteristics, such as shape, but the drawings are not recordings of length, height, and mass.

C is incorrect because graphs are constructed after the data has been recorded in a table and analyzed.

D is correct because data tables provide a place to record and organize both quantitative and qualitative data.

2. A

A is correct because the sample is the same length regardless of the side on which the measurement begins and ends.

B is incorrect because rulers are rigid and will not bend around the rock sample whereas measuring tapes are not rigid and will conform to the shape of the rock. These two pieces of equipment could give different length measurements.

C is incorrect because using different units of measurement changes the precision of the measurements. This could be a reason that the lengths are different.

D is incorrect because measuring technique could cause differences in measurements.

3. C

A is incorrect because it is inappropriate to omit or delete data just because it doesn't fit expectations.

B is incorrect because using a different ball changes variables within the investigation. The data collected using one ball may be different than the data collected using another ball.

C is correct because increasing the number of trials will allow for more data to be collected, and it will improve the accuracy of the investigation.

D is incorrect because changing the settings on the machine changes variables within the investigation. The data collected using one machine setting may be different than the data collected using another machine setting.

4. C

A is incorrect because models can be used to predict things, though the predictions aren't always correct.

B is incorrect because the ability to predict weather events in advance is a benefit of using models, not a limitation.

C is correct because a model cannot take into account how every variable that affects the path of a hurricane will change. Real hurricanes are more complex and have more variables than models.

D is incorrect because models can be used to show both physical structures and events.

5. D

A is incorrect because this value does not take into account that the units are thousands, and it uses the value for 2006, not 2007.

B is incorrect because this value does not take into account that the units are thousands.

C is incorrect because this number uses the value for 2006 instead of 2007.

D is correct because the value for 2007 is 217 and the units are in thousands. Therefore, the population in 2007 was 217,000.

Lesson 1 Alternative Assessment

Take Your Pick: Science and Scientific Knowledge

Gathering Evidence: Sketch shows one way a chemist can collect empirical evidence about pollutants in a river.

What Do You Think?: Cards describe the most interesting fact learned in this lesson and how the lesson changed the way the student felt or thought about learning science.

You Ask the Questions: Quizzes contain at least five questions or activities that deal with scientific theories and laws, and include an answer key.

A Scientific Skit: Skits compare a scientific theory with the use of the word *theory* in a detective or mystery story.

Defending Review: Speech explains why the group of scientists should not be upset because another group of scientists has criticized the findings. Speech describes how peer review and discussion is important to establishing scientific knowledge.

An Empirical Essay: Essays define, describe, and give examples of empirical evidence. Essays also include introductions, bodies, and conclusions.

What's Your Theory?: Commercials explain what a scientific theory is and the how it is formed. Commercials also promote a specific scientific theory.

Lesson 2 Alternative Assessment

Points of View: Learning Through Investigations

Vocabulary: Writing includes the terms and their definitions, as well as descriptions that help to explain the terms.

Examples: Students print articles about science experiments and underline sections that tell about the scientific methods the scientists used.

Analysis: Answers correctly identify the independent variable and one dependent variable. Students decide whether the independent variable can be changed without changing the entire experiment, whether the dependent variable can be changed without changing the entire experiment, other ways the experiment could be conducted, and what the new experiment might test.

Observations: Notes describe the processes that the scientists used and the order in which they were used. A poster shows the processes the scientist used.

Details: Diagrams correctly identify characteristics of experiments and characteristics of other scientific observations. A summation uses these details to give an overview of the two types of investigations.

Lesson 3 Alternative Assessment

Climb the ladder: Showing Your Data

Make a Model: Models shows an object likely to be studied in science class. Presentation describes the model's uses and limitations.

Analyze a Model: Students show the model and describe how the model is used, its advantages, and limitations.

Develop a Line Graph: Graph uses data from a data table on the bottom rung of the ladder. Graph includes all labels, numbers, and units a line graph needs.

Gather Data and Make a Graph: Scatter plot shows average monthly temperature over a one-year period, and includes all the labels, numbers, and units a scatter plot needs.

Make a Data Table from a Direct Data Source: Table organizes the numerical data in a correctly constructed data table.

Organize Data in a Table: Table organizes the information from the survey in a correctly constructed data table.

Indiana ISTEP+ Review

Key Concepts

1. D
2. B
3. C
4. A
5. A
6. A
7. B
8. D

1. D See Unit 1, Lesson 3

A is incorrect because black holes do exist but are too far away to study directly.

B is incorrect because black holes are too far away to observe directly.

C is incorrect because the color of black holes is not the reason they are studied using models.

D is correct because black holes are too far away to study directly and are better studied using a computer model.

2. B See Unit 1, Lesson 2

A is incorrect because good experiments are conducted under controlled conditions.

B is correct because good experiments are most valid if results can be replicated by others.

C is incorrect because a small sample size is less likely to be accurate.

D is incorrect because good experiments follow organized procedures that can be repeated the same way each time.

3. C See Unit 1, Lesson 2

A is incorrect because publication is a key component of a good scientific investigation.

B is incorrect because multiple trials increase the sample size of the data, which is a characteristic of a good investigation.

C is correct because reliable scientific results depend on accuracy and precision.

D is incorrect because the use of sophisticated equipment does not, by itself, lead to good results.

4. A See Unit 1, Lesson 3

A is correct because the chemical equation summarizes the multiple steps of photosynthesis.

B is incorrect because the model simplifies the process, making it easier to study.

C is incorrect because a chemical formula is one of the easiest and most useful ways to study a metabolic reaction that takes place at the cellular level.

D is incorrect because additional steps can be added to the equation to show a more detailed picture.

5. A See Unit 1, Lesson 2

A is correct because scientists draw conclusions based on the data collected.

B is incorrect because scientists form hypotheses before they collect data.

C is incorrect because scientists make a plan before they collect data.

D is incorrect because scientists follow procedures during data collection.

6. A See Unit 1, Lesson 3

A is correct because the data shows that grew to be 31 cm while the plants in part shade only grew to be 25 cm.

B is incorrect because the study was only on tomato plants, not all plants.

C is incorrect because this was not measured in the experiment.

D is incorrect because the plants in part shade still grew taller, just not as quickly as those in the sun.

7. B See Unit 1, Lesson 3

A is incorrect because the existing title is a correct title for the table.

B is correct because mass and time should have units.

C is incorrect because there is no evidence to suggest that the values included are incorrect.

D is incorrect because there are no extra rows in this table.

8. D See Unit 1, Lesson 2

A is incorrect because the amount of gas stays the same inside the balloon.

B is incorrect because the amount of gas stays the same inside the balloon.

C is incorrect because this is not consistent with the kinetic theory of matter.

D is correct because this prediction takes into account the kinetic theory and is consistent with the data in the diagram.

Constructed Response

9. See Unit 1, Lesson 2
Key elements:

• Both of the following: the gender of the student and the types of programs watched (e.g., *the name of each television program watched; the genre of the program (comedy, drama, game show, news; etc.);, etc.*)

AND

• an understanding of appropriate collection methods, such as surveys (e.g., *Jill should give each classmate a record sheet to write down the name and/or genre of the shows he or she watches each day for a week. After a week, she should collect the record sheets and use the information to make a data tables of the television programs and the frequency that her classmates watched different programs by gender; etc.*)

Rubric:
2 points Two key elements
1 point One key element
0 points Other

Extended Response

10. See Unit 1, Lesson 2

Key elements:

- the independent and dependent variables (e.g., *Independent variable: type of soil; Dependent variable: plant height that is measured*; etc.)

AND

- comparison of the results and the prediction based on observations (e.g., *Greg's prediction was incorrect because the plant in soil A grew to about 23 cm while the plant in soil B only grew to 18 cm. The plant in soil B was not taller than the plant in soil A*; etc.)

AND

- a new testable question to investigate (e.g., *How does the type of soil affect the number of leaves a plant grows?; How does the amount of compost affect the health of the leaves on a plant?* etc.)

AND

- at least three steps in an experimental plan to investigate the new question (e.g., *1. Plant three of the same type and same size plant in two pots. In each pot, use soil with different amounts of compost. 2. Place the pots in the same sunny location, water at equal time intervals and in equal amounts for 12 weeks. 3. Every two weeks, record the number of leaves on each plant and make observations about the plants' health. For example, note any insects, brown spots, or dead or damaged leaves*, etc.)

Rubric:

4 points Four key elements
3 points Three key elements
2 points Two key elements
1 point One key element
0 points Other

Unit Test A

Key Concepts

1.	A	5.	C	9.	D
2.	D	6.	A	10.	B
3.	C	7.	B	11.	C
4.	A	8.	B	12.	D

1. A

A is correct because empirical evidence is the cumulative body of explanations of a natural phenomenon.

B is incorrect because empirical evidence is not based on opinion.

C is incorrect because these are subjective, not objective like empirical evidence is.

D is incorrect because scientists cannot make up evidence to support a scientific investigation.

2. D

A is incorrect because the results of an experiment are the data collected during the experiment.

B is incorrect because the dependence on scientific tools does not determine whether a factor is a dependent variable or not.

C is incorrect because this is a variable, but not necessarily an independent variable.

D is correct because the dependent variable is dependent on the independent variable.

3. C

A is incorrect because an experiment is a procedure, not a diagram.

B is incorrect because the diagram is not an observation of an actual water molecule.

C is correct because the diagram is a visual model of a water molecule.

D is incorrect because the diagram is a model, but it is not a mathematical model.

4. A

A is correct because repetition, or multiple trials, increases the data sample size, thus providing more data for more complete analysis of what is being tested.

B is incorrect because repeating calculations based on one set of data does not increase the data sample size and so would not improve accuracy or reliability.

C is incorrect because experiments must follow the same procedure to ensure reproducibility.

D is incorrect because for best reproducibility, multiple trials must follow the same procedure. This includes using the same equipment.

5. C

A is incorrect because teaching a concept does not generate new empirical evidence to modify a scientific idea.

B is incorrect because the scientists' results support the existing empirical evidence for the idea.

C is correct because finding new evidence may lead to the modification of a scientific idea.

D is incorrect because the experiment is flawed due to contamination.

6. A

A is correct because the graph is missing a key that shows which line represents the plant watered with tap water and which line represents the plant watered with plant feed.

B is incorrect because the x-axis on the graph is present and shows the time in weeks.

C is incorrect because the graph has the title *Plant Growth*.

D is incorrect because the graph has the correct units.

7. B

A is incorrect because although Monday had the lowest temperature, the least difference between the low and high temperature was not on this day.

B is correct because the difference between the low and high temperature was 3 °C, which is the least difference.

C is incorrect because the difference between the low and high temperature was 9 °C, which is the greatest difference.

D is incorrect because the difference between the low and high temperature was 6 °C, which is greater than the difference of 3 °C on Tuesday.

8. B

A is incorrect because the force is constant, as stated in the question.

B is correct because the distance depends on the angle at which the ball is thrown. Distance changes as a result of the angle of the throw, making it the dependent variable.

C is incorrect because the angle of the throw is the independent variable that Jim changes in each trial.

D is incorrect because it is not part of this experiment.

9. D

A is incorrect because a prediction is often an if-then statement that is formulated before an experiment is conducted.

B is incorrect because good experiments must include controlled conditions.

C is incorrect because a testable statement is a hypothesis, and a hypothesis is what is tested through the experiment.

D is correct because controlled conditions and an organized procedure characterize a scientific experiment.

10. B

A is incorrect because these terms do not give accurate details on the time that the temperature was measured.

B is correct because these values indicate specific times that the temperatures were recorded.

C is incorrect because these values do not indicate at what time the temperatures were recorded.

D is incorrect because these terms do not give accurate details on the time that the temperatures were measured.

11. C

A is incorrect because milliliters are units of volume, not tools for measurement.

B is incorrect because beakers can be used to hold liquid, but they are not accurate tools for measurement.

C is correct because graduated cylinders measure liquid volume.

D is incorrect because cubic centimeters are units of volume, not tools for measuring volume.

12. D

A is incorrect because more trials using the same procedures and materials will not change the results.

B is incorrect because it is unethical to alter data to fit a hypothesis and it reduces the validity of the results.

C is incorrect because others will be unable to replicate the experiment if this is done.

D is correct because the researcher can use information from the first experiment as she develops the new hypothesis to test.

Constructed Response

13. Key elements:

- Any two of the following: verified through repetition and replication, communicated to others, peer review, open to critique and questioning (e.g., *It can be replicated and it includes multiple trials of the same experiment; It has a large sample size and its processes and results are communicated to others;* etc.)

AND

- valid explanation of how a characteristic increases the accuracy or precision of an experiment (e.g., *An experiment that can be replicated by other scientists is more precise because many scientists can get the same results, making them more reliable; by doing multiple trials and recording all the results, a scientist increases the sample size of the data. More data means the data is more accurate. It can also increase the consistency of the data;* etc.)

Rubric:
2 points Two key elements
1 point One key element
0 points Other

Extended Response

14. Key Elements:

- a prediction that relates water temperature and freezing time (e.g., *If hot water and cool water are placed outside when it's freezing, then the hot water will freeze faster than the cool water;* etc.)

AND

- independent variable: temperature of water at the beginning of the trial

- dependent variable: time it takes to freeze

AND

- a reasonable plan for the experimental procedure outlined in three steps (e.g., 1. *I would measure two equal samples of cool water. I would heat one sample until it is hot, but not boiling. 2. Next, I would fill an ice cube tray with cool water and an identical tray with the hot water. Then I would put the trays outside in the same location. 3. I would record how long it took for each tray to freeze. Then I would see if the data supports the hypothesis;* etc.)

AND

- an understanding of how the results will or will not support the prediction (e.g., *If the water in the cool tray freezes before the hot tray, then I would know the prediction was not correct;* etc.)

Rubric:
4 points Four key elements
3 points Three key elements
2 points Two key elements
1 point One key element
0 points Other

Unit Test B
Key Concepts

1.	A	5.	A	9.	D
2.	D	6.	B	10.	C
3.	B	7.	D	11.	C
4.	A	8.	B	12.	C

1. A

A is correct because scientists add to empirical evidence by making new observations.

B is incorrect because debate may lead to idea modification, but it does not really add to empirical evidence.

C is incorrect because real observations, not opinions, are not part of empirical evidence.

D is incorrect because laws result from extensive empirical evidence. They do not produce more empirical evidence.

2. D

A is incorrect because the independent variable is purposely changed to determine the affects on the dependent variable. Typically, the dependent variable does change as a result of the independent variable.

B is incorrect because the independent variable is purposely changed, and the dependent variable often changes as a result of the independent variable.

C is incorrect because the dependent variable changes based on the independent variable; it is not a controlled variable. The independent variable is what is changed, so that it can be tested.

D is correct because the independent variable is the factor that is purposely changed, and the dependent variable changes due to the change in the independent variable.

3. B

A is incorrect because more data from multiple trials takes more time and effort to analyze.

B is correct because a larger sample size means more data will be gathered and more data improves experimental accuracy.

C is incorrect because sample size concerns how many samples are used in each experiment, not how many times the experiment is repeated.

D is incorrect because experimental procedure should be consistent from one trial to the next, so experiments can be replicated.

4. A

A is correct because the hinge is used as a model to show the movement of the elbow joint.

B is incorrect because the movement of the hinge shows the function, whereas the width of the hinge model is not as important.

C is incorrect because the color of the hinge has nothing to do with the way it functions.

D is incorrect because how the hinge moves is more important to function than what the hinge model is made of.

5. A

A is correct because scientists debate and discuss conflicting ideas to come to a consensus about a scientific idea.

B is incorrect because keeping silent will not produce confirming evidence.

C is incorrect because discussing ideas with others who agree probably will not lead to a solution to the problem.

D is incorrect because, while remaining friends is nice, it probably will not lead to a solution to the problem.

6. B

A is incorrect because the title tells the purpose of the graph.

B is correct because the key is necessary for determining which plant is represented by each line.

C is incorrect because the label and units show how often the plants were measured.

D is incorrect because the units are included as part of the labels along each axis.

7. D

A is incorrect because this is the low temperature for Thursday, and the units are incorrect.

B is incorrect because the labels for the table show that the units are °C, not °F.

C is incorrect because this is the low temperature for Thursday.

D is correct because the value for Thursday is 33, and the units are °C.

8. B

A is incorrect because the drawings of her observations do not record that force was measured.

B is correct because the drawing of the observations show how the angle of the shot affects the distance the shot travels.

C is incorrect because drawings of the observations do not show that time in the air was measured.

D is incorrect because drawings of the observations do not show that force was measured.

9. D

A is incorrect because it this is a question that could be investigated through scientific means.

B is incorrect because this is a prediction that can be tested through an experiment..

C is incorrect because this describes a conclusion found after gathering evidence and analyzing it.

D is correct because an observation is data that can be quantitive or qualitative and may be gathered with or without using tools.

10. C

A is incorrect because the title of the table does not indicate that speed was recorded.

B is incorrect because the title of the table does not indicate that mass was recorded.

C is correct because the column label should include both the description of the data and the unit used.

D is incorrect because no unit is given.

11. C

A is incorrect because these terms do not give accurate details about the years that the population was measured.

B is incorrect because these values do not indicate years that the population was recorded.

C is correct because these values show years that the population was measured over a 10-year period.

D is incorrect because these values are years, but they do not indicate that the population was measured over a 10-year period.

12. C

A is incorrect because predictions are made before data is collected, and do not have to be correct.

B is incorrect because it is unethical to alter data to fit a prediction and it reduces the validity of the results.

C is correct because the researchers should use large sample sizes (multiple tide pools) in order to eliminate the effects of localized variables, such as contamination of a tide pool.

D is incorrect because others will be unable to replicate the experiment if this is done.

Constructed Response

13. Key Elements:

• Any two of the following: verified through repetition and replication, communicated to others, peer review, open to critique and questioning (e.g., *It can be replicated and it includes multiple trials of the same experiment; It has a large sample size and its processes and results are communicated to others,* etc.)

AND

• valid explanation of how a characteristic increases the accuracy or precision of an experiment (e.g., *An experiment that can be replicated by other scientists is more precise because many scientists can get the same results, making them more reliable; by doing multiple trials and recording all the results, a scientist increases the sample size of the data. More data means the data is more* accurate. It can also increase the consistency of the data; etc.)

Rubric:
2 points Two key elements
1 point One key element
0 points Other

Extended Response

14. Key Elements:

- a prediction that relates water temperature and freezing time (e.g., *If the same amount of hot water and cool water are placed in a freezer, then the hot water will freeze faster than the cool water;* etc.)

AND

- independent variable: initial temperature of water

- dependent variable: time to freeze

AND

- Any two of the following control variables: the type of water storage tray used, the amount of water in each tray, the location where trays are placed, the time that trays are placed outside, the temperature inside the freezer, or other reasonable answer

AND

- any reasonable plan for the experimental procedure (e.g., *I would measure two equal samples of cool water. I would heat one sample until it is hot, but not boiling. Next, I would fill an ice cube tray with cool water and an identical tray with the hot water. Then I would put the trays outside in the same location. I would record how long it took for each tray to freeze. Then I would see if the data supports the hypothesis;* etc.)

AND

- an understanding of how the results will or will not support the prediction (e.g., *If the water in the cool tray freezes before the hot tray, then I would know the prediction was not correct;* etc.)

Rubric:
4 points Five key elements
3 points Three or four key elements
2 points Two key elements
1 point One key element
0 points Other

Unit 2 Energy Transformations

Unit Pretest

1. C	5. A	9. D
2. C	6. A	10. C
3. C	7. B	
4. D	8. B	

1. C
A is incorrect because forces transfer energy, but they do not affect the mass of an object.

B is incorrect because a force can change an object by moving it or by transferring energy to or from it.

C is correct because forces are pushes or pulls that transfer energy to or from an object.

D is incorrect because weight depends on mass and the force of gravity, so force affects weight only if it affects the force of gravity.

2. C
A is incorrect because there are unbalanced forces in the horizontal direction as well as in the vertical direction.

B is incorrect because there are unbalanced forces in the vertical direction as well as in the horizontal direction.

C is correct because the forces are unbalanced, and the greater forces are directed upward and to the right.

D is incorrect because the unbalanced horizontal forces are directed toward the right, not the left.

3. C
A is incorrect because average speed is determined by dividing total distance by total time, not total time by total distance.

B is incorrect because 1.19 m/s is the average speed of the first half of the race, not the average speed of the entire race.

C is correct because the average speed is determined by dividing the total distance (100 m) by the total time (82 s).

D is incorrect because 1.25 m/s is the average speed of the second half of the race, not the average speed of the entire race.

4. D
A is incorrect because the box's gravitational force down is balanced by the force of the surface pushing up, so there is no motion up or down. The forces are all being applied horizontally.

B is incorrect because the box's gravitational force is balanced by the force of the surface pushing up, so there is no motion up or down. The forces are all being applied horizontally.

C is incorrect because increasing the force to the right would increase the motion of the box.

D is correct because a force of 100 N to the left would balance the total force of 100 N to the right, therefore stopping the motion of the box.

5. A
A is correct because a net force of zero indicates that the motion of the chair is not changing.

B is incorrect because a net force of zero indicates that the motion of the chair is not changing.

C is incorrect because a net force of zero indicates that although the motion of the chair is not changing, the chair is not necessarily stationary.

D is incorrect because a net force of zero indicates that although the motion of the chair is not changing, the chair is not necessarily moving.

6. A
A is correct because speed is a measure of distance over time.

B is incorrect because distance and time, not direction, are needed to determine speed.

C is incorrect because time and distance, not position, are needed to determine speed.

D is incorrect because neither position nor direction is needed to determine speed.

7. B

A is incorrect because gravity is a pulling force, not a pushing force, and there is gravity between objects in space, not just on Earth.

B is correct because gravity exists between any two objects that have mass, including between an object near or on Earth and Earth itself.

C is incorrect because Earth's magnetic field does not affect gravity.

D is incorrect because geothermal energy does not affect gravity.

8. B

A is incorrect because when velocity and acceleration point in the same direction, the object is accelerating.

B is correct because when velocity and acceleration point in the same direction, an object's speed continues to increase.

C is incorrect because speed decreases when acceleration and velocity point in opposite directions.

D is incorrect because an object's speed continues to increase when velocity and acceleration point in the same direction.

9. D

A is incorrect because meters per hour (m/h) are units of speed, not acceleration.

B is incorrect because kilometers per hour (km/h) are units of speed, not acceleration.

C is incorrect because kilometers per second (km/s) are units of speed, not acceleration.

D is correct because acceleration is the rate of change of velocity, and thus the units are kilometers per hour per second (km/h/s).

10. C

A is incorrect because drag from air resistance opposes the forward motion of an airplane; drag is represented by arrow 1.

B is incorrect because thrust is the forward-pushing force provided by an airplane's engines; thrust is represented by arrow 4.

C is correct because Earth's gravity is the force that pulls all objects toward Earth's center, downward.

D is incorrect because lift opposes gravity; lift is represented by arrow 2.

Lesson 1 Quiz

1. D   4. B
2. A   5. C
3. A

1. D

A is incorrect because average speed is not a vector quantity, so the direction the train traveled is not needed to determine its average speed.

B is incorrect because the train traveled to, not from, Union station.

C is incorrect because average speed is determined not by finding the average initial and maximum speeds, but by dividing the total distance by the total time.

D is correct because average speed is calculated by dividing the total distance by the total time, and the arrival time at Union station is needed to determine the total time.

2. A

A is correct because motion is defined as a change in position over time.

B is incorrect because the speed and direction of an object is velocity.

C is incorrect because the length of the path between points is distance.

D is incorrect because a location compared to other locations is a reference point.

3. A

A is correct because the measures given are the speeds of the car at specific points.

B is incorrect because velocity requires not only a measure of speed but also a measure of direction, and direction is not given.

C is incorrect because average speed is the distance traveled over a certain time, and the measures given are the speeds at specific points.

D is incorrect because average velocity is a measure of the rate of change in speed and direction, and changes are not given.

---

4. B

A is incorrect the ball travels farther each second, indicating a change in speed..

B is correct because the line becomes steeper, and a steeper line indicates a greater speed.

C is incorrect because if the speed were decreasing, the slope of the line would be decreasing, not increasing..

D is incorrect because the line rises at an increasing rate and the steepness does not decrease at any point in time.

5. C

A is incorrect because an unplanned stop would not increase the total distance the runner traveled.

B is incorrect because an unplanned stop would not decrease the total distance the runner traveled.

C is correct because the runner's total time increased, which decreased her average speed.

D is incorrect because the runner's time increased, not decreased, when she stopped to tie her shoe.

Lesson 2 Quiz

1. B   4. C
2. A   5. B
3. C

1. B

A is incorrect because acceleration the rate of change in velocity, and not the direction of motion.

B is correct because acceleration is defined as the rate of change of velocity with time.

C is incorrect because an object's mass times its speed is its momentum, not its acceleration.

D is incorrect because the rate at which an object's position changes is velocity, not acceleration.

2. A

A is correct because the can is constant change in direction during circular motion.

B is incorrect because the speed of the can is constant.

C is incorrect because the speed of the can is constant.

D is incorrect because the can accelerates because its direction is always changing.

3. C

A is incorrect because N stands for newtons, which are units of force.

B is incorrect because m/s stands for meters per second, which are units of velocity.

C is correct because m/s^2 stands for meters per second per second, which are units of acceleration.

D is incorrect because kg·m/s stands for kilogram-meters per second, which are units of momentum.

4. C

A is incorrect because the skater accelerates both while she moves in a straight direction and in a curve.

B is incorrect because the skater accelerates both while she moves in a straight direction and in a curve.

C is correct because the skater changes her speed as she skates in a straight line, and also changes her direction when she turns.

D is incorrect because each time the skater's speed increases or decreases or her direction changes, acceleration takes place.

5. B

A is incorrect because 2.0 is the sum of all speeds divided by the time, and the average acceleration is found by dividing the total change in velocity (3 m/s) by the total time it took to reach the final velocity (3 s).

B is correct because the average acceleration is found by dividing the total change in velocity (3 m/s) by the total time it took to reach the final velocity (3 s), yielding 1 m/s^2.

C is incorrect because 1.5 m/s is the average velocity.

D is incorrect because 3 m/s is the final velocity.

Lesson 3 Quiz

1. C   4. B
2. C   5. A
3. B

1. C

A is incorrect because an unbalanced force affects the motion, not the mass, of an object.

B is incorrect because a stationary object shows no change in motion, so it does not provide evidence that an unbalanced force is acting on it.

C is correct because an unbalanced force changes the motion of an object.

D is incorrect because the motion of the object is not changing, so there is no unbalanced force acting on it.

2. C

A is incorrect because acceleration is a change in an object's motion, not a measure of an object's inertia.

B is incorrect because gravity is a force of attraction between two objects, not a property of a single object.

C is correct because an object's inertia increases in proportion to an increase in its mass.

D is incorrect because velocity describes an object's motion; it does not measure an object's inertia.

3. B

A is incorrect because the vector arrow indicates force, not motion.

B is correct because the vector arrow indicates the size of the force as well as the direction in which it is applied.

C is incorrect because force does not necessarily cause motion. The vector arrow describes the size and direction of the force.

D is incorrect because although the vector arrow represents a force applied to the box, there are no other force arrows to indicate whether this force is balanced or unbalanced.

4. B

A is incorrect because the up and down forces are not balanced.

B is correct because the up and down forces are balanced, and the left and right forces are also balanced.

C is incorrect because neither the up and down forces nor the left and right forces are balanced.

D is incorrect because the left and right forces are not balanced.

5. A

A is correct because a stationary object will move only if an unbalanced force acts on it.

B is incorrect because the gravitational force on the object is the same whether the object is moving or stationary.

C is incorrect because balanced forces do not cause an object at rest to move.

D is incorrect because the ground already provides an upward force balancing the gravitational force, and balanced forces would not cause the rock to move.

Lesson 4 Quiz

1. D   4. A
2. B   5. A
3. A

1. D

A is incorrect because electrical forces can act at a distance.

B is incorrect because the gravitational force can act at a distance.

C is incorrect because magnetic forces can act at a distance.

D is correct because friction acts between two objects that are touching each other.

2. B

A is incorrect because gravity does not pull objects toward your feet unless your feet are directly below the objects.

B is correct because all objects are pulled toward the center of Earth's mass.

C is incorrect because only a magnetic object is affected by forces associated with Earth's poles.

D is incorrect because only a magnetic object is attracted by Earth's poles.

3. A

A is correct because an applied force is a force in which one object directly pushes or pulls on another object.

B is incorrect because the use of a magnet involves a non-contact force, not an applied force.

C is incorrect because electrical forces such as static electricity are non-contact forces.

D is incorrect because air resistance does not involve an object pushing or pulling on another object.

4. A

A is correct because the bowling ball has the most mass, and the more massive an object, the greater the gravitational force acting on it.

B is incorrect because the golf ball and the tennis ball have the least mass, and mass determines gravitational force.

C is incorrect because the soccer ball has a similar volume to that of the bowling ball, but it does not have more mass than the bowling ball, and mass determines gravitational force.

D is incorrect because the golf ball and the tennis ball have the least mass, and mass determines gravitational force.

5. A

A is incorrect because $F = mg$, not $m - g$.

B is incorrect because $F = mg$, not g.

C is incorrect because $F = mg$, not m.

D is correct because $F = mg$, and $g = 9.8$ m/s^2, and so $F = (10.0 \text{ kg}) \cdot (9.8 \text{ m/s}^2) = 98.0$ kg·m/s^2.

Lesson 1 Alternative Assessment

Tic-Tac-Toe: A Need for Speed

Location: Descriptions explain student's location from the reference point of the doorway and from the reference point of the moon.

Average Speed: Calculations show the average speed of a plane that travels 1,000 miles in 2.5 hours. (Speed = 1000/2.5 = 400 miles/hour)

Velocity: Diagrams show two objects going in the same direction with different velocities, two objects traveling at the same speed with different velocities, and two objects with identical velocities. Each speed and velocity is described.

Modeling Speed: Investigations demonstrate what happens when two toy cars are released at the same time from two different ramps of different length. Student describes which car was faster and why.

Map It: Map should accurately represent the classroom and describe how to get from student desk to the door and from the desk to a window.

Graph It: Graph shows a car traveling at different rates for 10 hours. Average speed and distance traveled in 10 hours are indicated.

A-Mazing: Distance shown on graph paper traveling through the maze is longer than the distance as the crow flies.

Changing Speeds: Graphs show the runner running at different speeds and stopping.

Speed But No Velocity?: Diagram or sketch shows an object that returns to the starting point.

Lesson 2 Alternative Assessment

Climb the Ladder: Types of Acceleration

Racing!: Average acceleration = (final velocity – starting velocity)/time = (10 km – 0 km)/18 min = 0.55 km/min^2

More Racing!: Average acceleration = (final velocity – starting velocity)/time = (5 km – 0 km)/16 min = 0.312 km/min^2

Speed: Diagram or words explain what happens to a runner's speed when velocity and acceleration are in the same direction.

Show Speed: Diagram or illustration shows runner's speed when velocity and acceleration are in opposite directions.

Acceleration: Writing should explain what happens to acceleration and speed when a runner changes direction.

Centripetal Acceleration: Drawing shows centripetal acceleration, and labels acceleration, direction, and speed.

Lesson 3 Alternative Assessment

Mix and Match: Forces, Motion, and Newton's Laws

Friction: The effects of friction on the system are described, including any friction-reducing agents. The direction in which friction is acting is noted. Presentation identifies by description or labels areas in which friction is acting.

Gravity: The effects of gravity on the system are described, including the direction in which gravity is acting. Forces that are counteracting gravity are included. Presentation identifies by description or labels direction in which gravity is acting.

Balanced Forces: The forces acting on the system are described, including the direction in which forces are acting. Forces are depicted in such a way that two forces are balancing each other, consistent with the effect on the system. Presentation identifies by description or labels how the balanced forces are acting.

Unbalanced Forces: The forces acting on the system are described, including the direction in which forces are acting. Forces are depicted in such a way that at least two forces are unbalanced, consistent with the effect on the system. Presentation identifies by description or labels how the unbalanced forces are acting.

Newton's Third Law: The forces acting on the system are described, including the direction in which forces are acting and the bodies on which the forces are acting. Forces are depicted in such a way that the two forces are equal, opposite in direction, and are acting on different bodies. Presentation identifies by description or labels that the forces are equal and opposite and are acting on different bodies.

Contact Force: The locations and effects of the contact forces acting on the system are described, including the direction in which forces are acting. The effects on the system are consistent with the direction and location of the forces. Presentation identifies by description or labels locations and directions of the contact forces.

Inertia: The effects of inertia on the system are described, including the direction in which objects are moving as a result. Forces counteracting inertia are included. Presentation identifies by description or labels how inertia is affecting the system.

Lesson 4 Alternative Assessment

Tic-Tac-Toe: How Forces Work

Poetry Slam: Poem includes a details about different types of forces and how they act on objects.

Celestial Objects: Diagrams show how gravity affects the shape of objects and their movement.

Charged Object Skit Skit describes how electrical and magnetic forces push and pull objects.

Be the Teacher: Quiz assesses the main ideas from the lesson and includes an answer key.

Planetary Brochure: Brochures describe the benefits of living with lower surface gravity.

News Report: Webcasts report on a topic related to contact forces, and explain what contact force have to do with the story; for example, what part contact force plays in an event or a product, or why a certain types of contact force has been outlawed.

Comic Strip: Comic includes three examples of everyday actions that help the character figure out how contact forces works.

Puzzle Time: Puzzle includes ten key terms and ideas from the lesson, including *magnetic*, *electrical*, *friction*, and *gravity*.

www.force.net: Web page includes definitions of key terms, images, and examples.

Indiana ISTEP+ Review

Key Concepts

1. B	5. D	9. B
2. B	6. C	10. D
3. A	7. D	
4. D	8. A	

1. B See Unit 2, Lesson 4

A is incorrect because an electrical force is a non-contact force, which acts at a distance.

B is correct because an applied force is a contact force in which one object directly pushes or pulls on another object.

C is incorrect because a gravitational force is a non-contact force, which acts at a distance.

D is incorrect because a magnetic force is a non-contact force, which acts at a distance.

2. B See Unit 2, Lesson 2

A is incorrect because trial 1 is at rest, so its speed did not decrease.

B is correct because trial 2 shows acceleration and velocity in opposite directions, indicating that the cart is slowed; decreasing speed means acceleration in the opposite direction.

C is incorrect because trial 3 shows acceleration and velocity in the same direction, indicating that the speed increased.

D is incorrect because trial 4 shows velocity only, indicating that there was no acceleration, so the cart traveled at a constant speed.

3. A See Unit 2, Lesson 1

A is correct because the average speed is determined by dividing the total distance, 96 km, by the total time, 4 h.

B is incorrect because the average speed is not determined by the average speed of the last hour.

C is incorrect because the average speed must be calculated using the total time, 4 h. It cannot exclude the second hour that the boat was moving at 68 km/h.

D is incorrect because the average speed is the average speed of the entire time sailing, not the average speed of the first 2 h of the boat trip.

4. D See Unit 2, Lesson 2

A is incorrect because multiplying distance by time does yields no useful quantity.

B is incorrect because dividing distance by time yields speed, not acceleration.

C is incorrect because multiplying the change velocity by time yields no useful quantity.

D is correct because acceleration is the change in an object's velocity divided by how long it took for the change to happen.

5. D See Unit 2, Lesson 3

A is incorrect because the net force is the difference in the forces exerted by the two teams, which is not zero, since the total force exerted by each team is not the same (total for Team A = 230 to the left; total for Team B = 235 to the right).

B is incorrect because the net force is the difference in the forces exerted by the two teams, not the total for Team B.

C is incorrect because the net force is 235 N to the right -230 N to the left, or 5 N to the right, so Team B is the winner.

D is correct because the net force is 235 N to the right – 230 N to the left, or 5 N to the right, so team B is the winner.

6. C See Unit 2, Lesson 3

A is incorrect because mass is not measured in Newtons.

B is incorrect because the motion of the box changed, so the forces must be unbalanced.

C is correct because the box accelerated upward, so the upward force of 60 N must have been greater than the downward gravitational force.

D is incorrect because the upward force was an applied force, not a frictional force.

7. D See Unit 2, Lesson 3

A is incorrect because there is also a downward force that must be combined with the upward force for a net force of 50 N upward.

B is incorrect because the downward force of 50 N that must be combined with the upward force of 100 N for a net force of 50 N upward.

C is incorrect because the downward force of 50 N that must be combined with the upward force of 100 N for a net force of 50 N upward.

D is correct because the net force is determined by calculating the difference between the upward and downward forces, 100 N upward – 50 N downward = 50 N upward.

8. A See Unit 2, Lesson 4

A is correct because the gravitational force between two objects is determined by their masses and the distance between them.

B is incorrect because gravitational force depends on mass, not volume alone.

C is incorrect because gravitational force depends on mass, not size alone.

D is incorrect because gravitational force depends on mass, not density alone.

9. B See Unit 2, Lesson 4

A is incorrect because the moon exerts a smaller, not greater gravitational force.

B is correct because having less mass means that the moon exerts less force due to gravity.

C is incorrect because the sun is too far away from both the moon and Earth for its mass to affect the weight of objects on the moon and Earth.

D is incorrect because being closer to the moon's center (shorter distance) would increase, not decrease, the gravitational force.

10. D See Unit 2, Lesson 4

A is incorrect because only an unbalanced force can cause a change in motion.

B is incorrect because an unbalanced force is always needed to change an object's motion.

C is incorrect because only an unbalanced force can cause a change in motion.

D is correct because nothing touched the ball, yet it changed its motion, so a non-contact unbalanced force must have acted on the ball.

Constructed Response

11. See Unit 2, Lesson 3
Key Elements
- The forces on an object are balanced when the object remains at rest or in constant motion (points b and d).
- The evidence of unbalanced forces is the fact that the bus slows down (a), speeds up (c), slows down again (e), and changes direction (f).

Rubric:
2 points Two key elements
1 point One key elements
0 points Other

Extended Response

12. See Unit 2, Lesson 3
Key Elements:
- average speed equals total distance divided by total time

AND

- contact (such as air resistance) and non-contact (such as gravity)

AND

- balanced, because the skydiver travels at a constant speed.

AND (one of the following)
- air resistance from chute opening slows the fall and counteracts gravity
- as forces become balanced, speed becomes constant

Rubric:
4 points Four key elements
3 points Three key elements
2 points Two key elements
1 point One key element
0 points Other

Unit Test A

Key Concepts

1. B	5. D	9. C
2. C	6. D	10. A
3. C	7. A	11. C
4. B	8. A	12. B

1. B

A is incorrect because an object at rest undergoes no change in motion, so it is not accelerating.

B is correct because centripetal acceleration is movement in a circular direction at a constant speed.

C is incorrect because the motion described is not circular.

D is incorrect because motion in a straight line at constant speed in a direction is not centripetal acceleration.

2. C

A is incorrect because the inertia of the box is greater than, not less than, Matthew's force. The box would move if Matthew's force were greater than the inertia of the box.

B is incorrect because a vertical force would not oppose Matthew's push; it would instead be perpendicular to Matthew's push.

C is correct because a force equal and opposite to the force that Matthew exerts prevents the box from moving.

D is incorrect because a force in any direction can cause motion if not opposed by a force in the opposite direction.

3. C

A is incorrect because the speed is constant to the right, as shown by the equal distance between adjacent balls, so there is no acceleration.

B is incorrect because the speed is constant to the left, as shown by the equal distance between adjacent balls, so there is no acceleration.

C is correct because the distance between each ball increases, indicating that acceleration is taking place.

D is incorrect because this sketch shows centripetal acceleration, which happens when there is a change in direction.

4. B

A is incorrect because a person in orbit would still be close enough to Earth for gravity to have an effect on his or her weight.

B is correct because the farther a person moves away from Earth, the smaller is the gravitational force between that person and Earth. Weight is a measure of gravitational force.

C is incorrect because a person's mass would remain constant regardless of his or her distance from Earth.

D is incorrect because the satellites that orbit Earth would not have enough mass to affect the gravitational attraction between a person's mass and Earth's gravity.

5. D

A is incorrect because on a distance-time graph, time is on the horizontal axis.

B is incorrect because although a distance-time graph can be used to determine speed, speed is not on either axis.

C is incorrect because velocity is a measure of speed and direction, and neither speed nor direction is on an axis of a distance-time graph.

D is correct because on a distance-time graph, distance is on the vertical axis.

6. D

A is incorrect because inertia kept the cup in place when the car accelerated.

B is incorrect because the cup did not accelerate forward when the car did.

C is incorrect because the upward force on the cup would increase only if the downward force on the cup increased.

D is correct because inertia kept the cup from moving forward with the car, and gravity caused it to fall.

7. A

A is correct because speed is a measure of how fast something is moving.

B is incorrect because speed is a measure of how fast something is moving, not the direction of movement.

C is incorrect because speed measures how fast something is moving; distance refers to how far something has moved.

D is incorrect because speed is a measure of how fast something is moving; it does not measure time.

8. A

A is correct because speed is a measure of how fast something is moving.

B is incorrect because speed is a measure of how fast something is moving, not the direction of movement.

C is incorrect because speed measures how fast something is moving; distance refers to how far something has moved.

D is incorrect because speed is a measure of how fast something is moving; it does not measure time.

9. C

A is incorrect because rate and time are attributes of speed, and speed is not a force.

B is incorrect because although size (magnitude) is an attribute of force, rate is not; rate is a characteristic of speed.

C is correct because a force can be described as having the attributes of size (magnitude) and direction.

D is incorrect because although direction is an attribute of force, motion is not.

10. A

A is correct because the line for object *A* is the steepest, so object *A* had the greatest average speed.

B is incorrect because while object *B* traveled the greatest distance, the line for object *B* is not the steepest.

C is incorrect because while object *C* traveled for the longest time, the line for object *C* is not the steepest.

D is incorrect because the line for object *D* has the least greatest slope, so object *D* had the lowest average speed.

11. C

A is incorrect because to determine net force, forces that are applied in the same direction are added, not subtracted.

B is incorrect because forces that are applied in the same direction are added to determine net force, and 50 N is the value of only one force.

C is correct because to determine net force, forces that are applied in the same direction are added.

D is incorrect because forces applied in the same direction are added, not multiplied, to determine net force.

12. B

A is incorrect because the car will be moving 10 m/s faster at the end of 5 s, but its acceleration remains 2 m/s^2.

B is correct because the acceleration is a constant 2 m/s per second, or 2 m/s^2.

C is incorrect because the car's speed increases at a rate of 2 m/s per second, so its average acceleration is 2 m/s^2.

D is incorrect because the car's speed is increasing, so acceleration is greater than zero.

Constructed Response

13. Key Elements:

- The arrows are vectors./The length represents the size of the force, and the direction represents the direction of the force. (E.g., *The length of the arrow represents the size of the force. The direction of the arrow represents the direction in which the force is acting*; etc.)

AND

- vertical (up and down) forces; equal in size and opposite in direction (e.g., *The upward force and downward force are balanced because the arrows are the same length, but in opposite direction*; etc.)

AND

- horizontal (right and left) forces; not equal in size and opposite in direction (e.g., *The force pushing to the left and the force pushing to the right are unbalanced because the left arrow is longer than the right arrow*, etc.)

AND

- The box will move to the right (e.g., *The box will move to the right because the net force is 50 N toward the right*; etc.).

Rubric:

2 points Four key elements
1 point Two or three key elements
0 points Other

Extended Response

14. Key Elements:

- Applied force, gravitational force, and magnetic force are acting on the magnets (e.g., *Chandra's hands exert an applied force on the magnets; the magnets exert a magnetic force of repulsion on one another; gravity exerts a downward force on the magnets*; etc.).

See example of completed graphic in the Visual Answers section at the end of this Answer Key.

AND

- Arrows on drawing should show forces.

AND

- Forces are balanced because the objects are not moving (e.g., *The net force shown by the up and down arrows is zero, so the force is balanced. There is an inward force exerted by both hands that balances the repulsion between the magnets. The forces are balanced because the objects are not moving or changing their motion*; etc.).

AND

- Magnetic force would make the magnets move apart, and gravitational force would cause them to fall (e.g., *The gravitational force would cause both magnets to fall. At the same time, a magnetic force of repulsion would cause the magnets to repel one another so that they would likely hit the ground farther apart than they are in the picture*; etc.).

Rubric:
4 points Four key elements
3 points Three key elements
2 points Two key elements
1 point one key element
0 points Other

Unit Test B

Key Concepts

1.	D	5.	B	9.	A
2.	C	6.	C	10.	C
3.	D	7.	A	11.	B
4.	D	8.	C	12.	B

1. D
A is incorrect because these pairs of forces operate at right angles to each other and therefore do not balance each other.

B is incorrect because forces that act at right angles to each other do not balance each other.

C is incorrect because friction (F_f) opposes motion, so if the sneaker were motionless, friction would be less than or equal to—not greater than—the applied force of the spring (F).

D is correct because the force of the spring (F) and the force of friction (F_f) are opposed to each other, so if the sneaker remains motionless, these two forces are balanced.

2. C
A is incorrect because mass is not a force, and a magnetic force is not acting on the book.

B is incorrect because a magnetic force is not acting on the book.

C is correct because gravitational force pushes the book down, and the applied force from the table pushes the book up.

D is incorrect because velocity is not a force, and static electricity (electricity produced by friction) is not acting on the book.

3. D
A is incorrect because the car's speed is equal to the slope of the line, and the slope of the line is not zero. Only a horizontal line has a slope of zero.

B is incorrect because the car's speed is equal to the slope of the line, and the slope is determined by dividing the distance traveled by the total time, yielding 28 m/s, not 14 m/s.

C is correct because the car's speed is equal to the slope of the line, and the slope is determined by dividing the distance traveled (140 m) by the total time (5 s), yielding 28 m/s.

D is incorrect because the car's speed is equal to the slope of the line, and the slope of the line is 28 m/s, not 30 m/s.

4. D
A is incorrect because there is no acceleration and no change in direction.

B is incorrect because there is no acceleration and no change in direction.

C is incorrect because there is a change in linear speed but no change in direction.

D is correct because there is a change in direction, and centripetal acceleration involves a change in direction.

5. B
A is incorrect because the forces exerted by the two objects are equal in magnitude though opposite in direction. Equal force acting on less mass (the ball) causes the ball to accelerate more than the bat.

B is correct because the ball has less mass than the bat, so there is a greater acceleration of the ball.

C is incorrect because the bat and ball exert equal force, regardless of velocity.

D is incorrect because the bat and ball exert equal force; action and reaction still happen because each object has mass.

6. C
A is incorrect because 5 m/s represents speed.

B is incorrect because although 5 m/s^2 has the right units for acceleration, an acceleration vector must also include direction.

C is correct because 5 m/s^2 south has the correct units of acceleration (m/s^2) and a direction (south).

D is incorrect because 5 m/s south represents a velocity vector.

7. A
A is correct because gravitational force pulls all objects down toward Earth's center.

B is incorrect because there was no electrical force acting on the baseball.

C is incorrect because air resistance opposed the horizontal motion of the baseball.

D is incorrect because the applied force was the forward-pushing force provided by the pitcher.

8. C
A is incorrect because the units do not determine that a quantity is a vector.

B is incorrect because a vector must have direction as well as speed.

C is correct because a vector has both speed and direction.

D is incorrect because a vector must have both speed and direction.

9. A
A is correct because the up force is greater than the down force, and the left and right forces are balanced.

B is incorrect because the up and down forces are balanced and the left and right forces are balanced, so there is no acceleration.

C is incorrect because neither the up and down forces nor the left and right forces are balanced, and the object is accelerating up and to the right.

D is incorrect because the up and down forces are balanced, but the left force is greater than the right force, so the object is accelerating to the right.

10. C
A is incorrect because acceleration is inversely proportional to mass ($F = ma$, so $a = F/m$).

B is incorrect because acceleration is inversely proportional to mass.

C is correct because acceleration is inversely proportional to mass, so doubling the mass halves the acceleration.

D is incorrect because acceleration is inversely proportional to mass.

11. B
A is incorrect because m/s is a unit of speed, not acceleration.

B is correct because 200 m/s^2 is the largest value for acceleration among the choices given.

C is incorrect because 0.020 km/s^2, or 20 m/s^2, is smaller than 200 m/s^2.

D is incorrect because 0.002 km/s^2, or 2 m/s^2, is smaller than 200 m/s^2.

12. B

A is incorrect because Blair's maximum speed could have been less than Aaron's, but his average speed had to be greater.

B is correct because Blair ran the same race in less time than Aaron did, so his average speed must have been greater than Aaron's average speed.

C is incorrect because either runner could have run faster during the last 100 m of the race.

D is incorrect because either runner could have run faster during the first 100 m of the race.

Constructed Response

13. Key Elements:

- The arrows are vectors./The length represents the size of the force, and the direction represents the direction of the force. (E.g., *The length of the arrow represents the size of the force. The direction of the arrow represents the direction in which the force is acting*; etc.)

AND

- horizontal (right and left) forces; equal in size and opposite in direction (e.g., *The forces pushing to the right and left are balanced. Forces that are equal in size and opposite in direction are balanced*; etc.)

AND

- vertical (up and down) forces; equal in size and opposite in direction (e.g., *The forces pushing upward and downward are unbalanced because the up arrow is longer than the down arrow. Forces that are not equal in size and opposite in direction are unbalanced*; etc.)

AND

- The box will move up. (E.g., *Force vectors can be combined to indicate net force. When forces are unbalanced, an object will move in the direction of the net force. The box will move upward because the net force is 25 N in an upward direction*; etc.)

Rubric:
2 points Four key elements
1 point Two or three key elements
0 points Zero or one key elements

Extended Response

14. Key Elements:

- forces acting on the riders and their bicycles: gravity, applied force, friction, and air resistance

AND

- forces exerted by the riders on other objects: applied forces (optional: gravitational)

AND

- Gravity would cause the bicycles to continue to accelerate downward./Air resistance and friction would oppose the forward motions.

AND

- There is a net force causing Ayana's bicycle to continue to accelerate down the hill because the downward force of gravity is greater than the opposing forces of friction and air resistance./There is a balanced force between Ayana's hands and the bicycle handles and between Ayana and the bicycle seat.

Rubric:
4 points Four key elements
3 points Three key elements
2 points Two key elements
1 point One key element
0 points Other

Unit 3 Energy, Motion, and Forces

Unit Pretest

1.	A	5. D	9. C
2.	A	6. C	10. B
3.	B	7. D	
4.	A	8. A	

1. A

A is correct because a period is measured in time.

B is incorrect because frequency is measured in hertz.

C is incorrect because amplitude is a distance measurement.

D is incorrect because wavelength is a distance measurement.

2. A

A is correct because the bicycle is moving and therefore has kinetic energy, and energy is the ability to do work.

B is incorrect because it is the bicycle's kinetic energy that gives the bicycle the ability to do work.

C is incorrect because it is the bicycle's kinetic energy that gives the bicycle the ability to do work.

D is incorrect because it is the bicycle's kinetic energy that gives the bicycle the ability to do work.

3. B

A is incorrect some pollution is caused by the trucks and trains that transport fossil fuels.

B is correct because the burning of fossil fuels does not produce radioactive waste products.

C is incorrect because air pollution is produced when fossil fuels are burned.

D is incorrect because habitats can be destroyed during processes used to obtain fossil fuels.

4. A

A is correct because the longest wavelengths of light refract the least. Of the colors listed, red has the longest wavelength.

B is incorrect because the shortest wavelengths of light refract the most. Color 1 refracts the least, so it cannot be blue light.

C is incorrect because the longest wavelengths of light refract the least. Color 1 could not be green light because the wavelength of green light is shorter than the wavelength of red light.

D is incorrect because the longest wavelengths of light refract the least. Color 1 could not be yellow light because the wavelength of yellow light is shorter than the wavelength of red light.

5. D

A is incorrect because the wind energy does work as it pushes on the blades and causes the windmill to turn.

B is incorrect because the kinetic energy of the moving golf club does work by moving the ball over a distance.

C is incorrect because the kinetic energy of the moving water does work as it causes the turbine to move.

D is correct because work involves a force moving an object over a distance, and the barbell did not move.

6. C

A is incorrect because the ball loses energy as it transfers energy to the air and the ground with which it interacts.

B is incorrect because energy can change into mass only during a nuclear reaction.

C is correct because the ball's energy is transferred to the air and the ground.

D is incorrect because energy cannot be destroyed.

7. D

A is incorrect because speed = wavelength × frequency, not amplitude × time.

B is incorrect because speed = wavelength × frequency, not period × amplitude.

C is incorrect because speed = wavelength × frequency, not amplitude × wavelength.

D is correct because speed = wavelength × frequency.

8. A

A is correct because the prop absorbs all colors except green. It will absorb the red light and appear black.

B is incorrect because the prop absorbs all colors except green. It will absorb the red light and appear black, not brown.

C is incorrect because the prop absorbs all colors except green. It will absorb the red light, not reflect it.

D is incorrect because the prop absorbs all colors except green. It would have to reflect all colors to appear white.

9. C

A is incorrect because energy is transferred from the metal to the water, so the metal becomes cooler and the water becomes warmer.

B is incorrect because energy is transferred from the metal to the water, so the metal becomes cooler and the water becomes warmer.

C is correct because heat is the transfer of energy from an object with higher temperature to an object with lower temperature. When the objects reach the same temperature, the final temperature of the water is between the two original temperatures.

D is incorrect because most of the energy transfer is between the two substances. This causes the metal to lose energy and the water to gain energy.

10. B

A is incorrect because power equals energy divided by time, which is 20 W.

B is correct because power is 60 J ÷ 3 s = 20 J/s, or 20 W.

A is incorrect because power equals energy divided by time, which is 20 W.

A is incorrect because power equals energy divided by time, which is 20 W.

Lesson 1 Quiz

1. B	4. C
2. D	5. B
3. A	

1. B

A is incorrect because the ball gained, not lost, energy when it was struck.

B is correct because the ball player's energy was transferred to the ball, which means that work was done on the ball.

C is incorrect because the force was applied in the same direction as the motion.

D is incorrect because it is possible to measure the time and calculate the rate at which work was done on the ball.

2. D

A is incorrect because work is force times distance, and since they all went the same distance, the one who used the most force did the most work. 155 N is less than 160 N.

B is incorrect because work is force times distance, and since they all went the same distance, the one who used the most force did the most work. 120 N is less than 160 N.

C is incorrect because work is force times distance, and since they all went the same distance, the one who used the most force did the most work. 90 N is less than 160 N.

D is correct because work is force times distance, and since they all went the same distance, the one who used the most force did the most work. 160 N is the most force.

3. A

A is correct because power = 2,000 J ÷ 80 s = 25 W.

B is incorrect because power = 2,000 J ÷ 80 s = 25 W, not 50 W.

C is incorrect because power = 2,000 J ÷ 80 s = 25 W, not 60 W.

D is incorrect because power = 2,000 J ÷ 80 s = 25 W, not 100 W.

4. C

A is incorrect because 21,600 J/h is the same as 6 W(J/s), so there is not enough power for all three devices.

B is incorrect because 21,600 J/h is the same as 6 W (J/s), so there is not enough power for the AA/AAA charger.

C is correct because 21,600 J/h is the same as 6 W (J/s), so there is enough power for either the cell phone charger or the PDA charger.

D is incorrect because 21,600 J/h is the same as 6 W (J/s), so there is not enough power for both cell phone charger and PDA charger.

5. B

A is incorrect because Ayanna did 24 N × 1.5 m = 36 J of work, which is more than the amount of work done by Cassie and Michael, but less than the amount of work done by Rafael.

B is correct because Rafael did 18 N × 2.5 m = 45 J of work, which is more than any of the other employees.

C is incorrect because Cassie did 25 N × 1.0 m = 25 J of work, which is less than the amount of work done by Ayanna, Michael, and Rafael.

D is incorrect because Michael did 16 N × 2.0 m = 32 J of work, which is more than the amount of work done by Ayanna and Cassie, but less than the amount of work done by Rafael.

Lesson 2 Quiz

1. D   4. A
2. A   5. B
3. C

1. D

A is incorrect because this is not the law of conservation of energy.

B is incorrect because it is not a true statement.

C is incorrect because this is the law of conservation of matter, not energy.

D is correct because this is the law of conservation of energy.

2. A

A is correct because although the amount of energy in the system does not change, the toy loses energy to the steps as it moves.

B is incorrect because the toy loses energy to the steps as it moves.

C is incorrect because the toy loses energy to the steps as it moves.

D is incorrect because the toy loses energy to the steps as it moves.

3. C

A is incorrect because hair dryers are not solar-powered and do not use chemical energy.

B is incorrect because thermal energy and sound energy, not electromagnetic energy, come from the hair dryer.

C is correct because these are the energy transformations that take place when a hair dryer is used.

D is incorrect because the energy from the circuit is not electromagnetic.

4. A

A is correct because some energy in an energy conversion is transformed to heat, sound, or other unmeasured energy forms.

B is incorrect because most apparent energy loss is due to the transfer of some energy to other forms, such as heat or sound.

C is incorrect because most apparent energy loss is due to the transfer of some energy to other forms, such as heat or sound.

D is incorrect because most apparent energy loss is due to the transfer of some energy to other forms, such as heat or sound.

5. B

A is incorrect because Richard's efficiency is $(270 \text{ J} \div 340 \text{ J}) \times 100\% = 79\%$, which is not the highest of the four workers.

B is correct because Molly's efficiency is $(280 \text{ J} \div 310 \text{ J}) \times 100\% = 90\%$, which is the highest of the four workers.

C is incorrect because Denzel's efficiency is $(230 \text{ J} \div 280 \text{ J}) \times 100\% = 82\%$, which is not the highest of the four workers.

D is incorrect because Janice's efficiency is $(290 \text{ J} \div 350 \text{ J}) \times 100\% = 83\%$, which is not the highest of the four workers.

Lesson 3 Quiz

1. B   4. B
2. D   5. C
3. A

1. B

A is incorrect because although the two liquids have the same temperature, the one with more particles has a higher total kinetic energy. Therefore, the beaker with 1,000 mL has more, not less, thermal energy than the beaker with 100 mL.

B is correct because although the two liquids have the same temperature, the one with more particles has a higher total kinetic energy. Therefore, the beaker with 1,000 mL has more thermal energy than the beaker with 100 mL.

C is incorrect because although the two liquids have the same temperature, the one with more particles has a higher total kinetic energy. Therefore, the beaker with 1,000 mL has more thermal energy than the beaker with 100 mL.

D is incorrect because the relative amounts of thermal energy can be determined with the information provided. Although the two liquids have the same temperature, the one with more particles has a higher total kinetic energy. Therefore, the beaker with 1,000 mL has more thermal energy than the beaker with 100 mL.

2. D

A is in correct because in conduction, energy is transferred from one particle to another without the movement of matter.

B is incorrect because convection is the transfer of energy by the movement of currents within a fluid, and while some convection occurs, most of the energy that reaches you from a campfire is from radiation.

C is incorrect because insulation is a process that inhibits the transfer of energy between objects.

D is correct because radiation is the process in which energy is transferred by electromagnetic waves.

3. A

A is correct because in conduction, energy is transferred from one particle to another without the movement of matter.

B is incorrect because convection is the transfer of energy by the movement of currents within a fluid.

C is incorrect because insulation is a process that inhibits the transfer of energy between objects.

D is incorrect because radiation is the process of transferring energy by electromagnetic waves.

4. B

A is incorrect because in conduction, energy is transferred from one particle to another without the movement of matter.

B is correct because convection is the transfer of energy by the movement of currents within a fluid, and air is a fluid.

C is incorrect because insulation is a process that inhibits the transfer of energy between objects.

D is incorrect because radiation is the process of transferring energy by electromagnetic waves.

5. C

A is incorrect because convection is the transfer of energy by the movement of currents within a fluid, and insulation inhibits energy transfer, and neither convection nor insulation cooks a pizza in a microwave oven.

B is incorrect because although conduction does occur, convection is the transfer of energy by the movement of currents within a fluid, and convection does not cook a pizza in a microwave oven.

C is correct because microwaves transform electromagnetic energy to thermal energy by radiation, and thermal energy is transferred by conduction from one particle to another in the pizza.

D is incorrect because although radiation does occur, convection is the transfer of energy by the movement of currents within a fluid, and convection does not cook a pizza in a microwave oven.

Lesson 4 Quiz

1. A   4. C
2. D   5. D
3. A

1. A

A is correct because B is at the top, or crest, of the wave.

B is incorrect because a trough is the lowest part of a wave and is represented by A and C.

C is incorrect because amplitude is wave height measured from the rest position to the crest or the trough.

D is incorrect because the rest position is halfway between the crest and the trough.

2. D

A is incorrect because sound waves travel most quickly in a solid.

B is incorrect because sound waves travel most quickly in a solid.

C is incorrect because sound waves travel more quickly in a liquid (water) than they do in a gas (air).

D is correct because sound waves travel most slowly in a gas.

3. A

A is correct because waves transfer energy.

B is incorrect because waves transfer energy, not the matter in the medium.

C is incorrect because waves transfer energy, not the medium through which they move.

D is incorrect because waves transfer energy; amplitude is a measure of wave height.

4. C

A is incorrect because different types of electromagnetic waves carry different energies.

B is incorrect because different types of electromagnetic waves have different frequencies.

C is correct because all electromagnetic waves travel at the same speed through empty space.

D is incorrect because different types of electromagnetic waves have different wavelengths.

5. D

A is incorrect because the medium affects the speed of all types of waves.

B is incorrect because mechanical waves require a medium to move.

C is incorrect because the reverse is true; mechanical waves cannot travel through a vacuum, but electromagnetic waves can.

D is correct because electromagnetic waves can travel through a vacuum, but mechanical waves cannot.

Lesson 5 Quiz

1. B   4. D
2. C   5. B
3. A

1. B

A is incorrect because blue paper would absorb, not reflect, red light.

B is correct because blue paper would reflect blue light and absorb red light.

C is incorrect because blue paper would absorb, not reflect, red light.

D is incorrect because blue paper would reflect blue light.

2. C

A is incorrect because the light refracts each time it enters a new medium: first to the 1st pane, second to the air, third to the 2nd pane, and fourth to the air.

B is incorrect because the light refracts each time it enters a new medium: first to the 1st pane 2, second to the air, third to the 2nd pane, and fourth to the air.

C is correct because the light refracts each time it enters a new medium: first to the 1st pane, second to the air, third to the 2nd pane, and fourth to the air.

D is incorrect because the light refracts each time it enters a new medium: first to the 1st pane, second to the air, third to the 2nd pane, and fourth to the air.

3. A

A is correct because soft materials are more likely to absorb sound than hard materials are.

B is incorrect because the metal pan is hard, and soft materials are more likely to absorb sound.

C is incorrect because the wood floor is hard, and soft materials are more likely to absorb sound.

D is incorrect because the glass pitcher is hard, and soft materials are more likely to absorb sound.

4. D

A is incorrect because the glass does not produce its own light.

B is incorrect because a transparent material such as glass is the color that it transmits, not absorbs.

C is incorrect because a transparent material such as glass is the color that it transmits, not reflects.

D is correct because a transparent material such as glass is the color that it transmits.

5. B

A is incorrect because a white, opaque material reflects, not absorbs, light that strikes it.

B is correct because a white, opaque material reflects most of the light that strikes it.

C is incorrect because an opaque material does not transmit light, which means the light cannot be refracted.

D is incorrect because an opaque material does not transmit light that strikes it.

Lesson 6 Quiz

1. A   4. A
2. D   5. B
3. C

1. A

A is correct because water is a renewable energy source, but flooding caused by building dams can destroy habitats.

B is incorrect because a nuclear power plant, not a hydroelectric plant, produces waste that is difficult to store.

C is incorrect because a geothermal plant, not a hydroelectric plant, can only be built near hot springs or volcanoes.

D is incorrect because a plant that burns biomass, not a hydroelectric plant, releases carbon dioxide.

2. D

A is incorrect because nuclear energy produces more, not less, harmful waste.

B is incorrect because nuclear energy generally destroys less, not more, habitats.

C is incorrect because nuclear energy generally creates less, not more, land erosion.

D is correct because nuclear energy generally produces less air pollution than fossil fuels do.

3. C

A is incorrect because biomass energy production contributes more to air pollution than it does to the destruction of habitats.

B is incorrect because biomass energy production contributes more to air pollution than it does to erosion.

C is correct because contributing to air pollution is the biggest environmental drawback of using biomass as an energy source.

D is incorrect because biomass energy production does not generate hazardous waste.

4. A

A is correct because obtaining fossil fuels requires mining or drilling, which can destroy habitats.

B is incorrect because the release of pollutants comes from the burning of fossil fuels, not from obtaining fossil fuels.

C is incorrect because the disruption of migration patterns is more a drawback for hydroelectric power production than it is for obtaining fossil fuels.

D is incorrect because wastes from mining or drilling fossil fuels do not have to be stored; the storage of wastes is necessary for nuclear power production.

5. B

A is incorrect because geothermal power plants do not necessarily disrupt animal migration patterns.

B is correct because hydroelectric power plants can disrupt the migration patterns of fish in the rivers and streams blocked by dams.

C is incorrect because nuclear power plants do not necessarily disrupt animal migration patterns.

D is incorrect because solar power plants do not necessarily disrupt animal migration patterns.

Lesson 1 Alternative Assessment

Climb the Pyramid: *Using Energy*

Scenario: Student concept maps should clearly show how work, energy, and power are related to each other, and should include details on units used and how energy is transferred.

Figure It Out! Student should accurately figure out the power exerted by each of the three students. Student should correctly identify that student 1 was the most powerful.

Quiz: Student quiz should assess the key ideas from the lesson including a definition and description of work, energy, and power including the formulas and units used for each.

History in Science: Student should present brief biographies that include the scientific contributions of two scientists that studied work, energy, or power.

Concentration Cards: Student's cards should include a varied representation of concepts, ideas, and details related to the three key topics, including formulas and units.

Chart: Chart entries should provide detailed information about work and power data. Students should use force, distance, and time to calculate work and power. Data should steadily show the student becoming more powerful.

Lesson 2 Alternative Assessment

Take Your Pick: Energy

Making a Transformation: Skits correctly identify an instance when one form of energy transforms to another form.

Energy Observations: Diagrams accurately identify, label, and describe at least three examples of energy in the room.

Match the Pairs: Five cards each show one type of energy, and five other cards each pair with one of the first five cards.

Where Did the Energy Go? Sketches show energy transformations and account for all of the initial energy. The forms of energy are labeled in each sketch.

Puzzling Terms: Puzzles include at least four terms dealing with energy conservation and energy conversion. They also include answer keys.

Be Efficient! Memos explain what efficiency is, what qualities should be considered when buying new buses, and how energy-efficient school buses can save the school district money.

Experimenting with Energy: Designs describe the law of conservation of energy, list a hypothesis, and detail a method that will test the hypothesis.

What's the Difference? Descriptions compare the efficiency of CFLs with incandescent lights, and explain how much of the input energy ends up as visible light in each case.

Lesson 3 Alternative Assessment

Points of View: Thermal Energy and Its Transfer

Vocabulary: Definition of *radiation* is correct. Journal entry compares and contrasts the meanings of words that are related to *radiation*.

Examples: Posters identifies three examples of conductors and three examples of insulators, and describes the qualities that make them good conductors or insulators.

Illustrations: Cartoons show several methods of thermal energy transfer. Captions identify the methods of transfer and explain how the methods are related.

Analysis: Explanations describe why the beverage got cooler and how the thermal energy was transferred.

Details: Presentations describe convection in ocean water, where the water is moving during convection, why it is moving, how water temperature is measured, and how to measure to show thermal energy transfer.

Lesson 4 Alternative Assessment
Take Your Pick: Waves and Energy

Everyday Waves: Posters show a situation in which a wave is involved, and the wave is indicated and labeled. Poster also explains whether the wave is mechanical or electromagnetic.

Making Waves: Models show transverse and longitudinal waves, and the waves are labeled.

You Ask the Questions: Papers contain at least five questions and answers about amplitude, wavelength, wave speed, and frequency.

Helping a Friend: Dialogues include the definition of a wave and describe how a wave is different from its medium.

The Wave Game: Students create eight game cards (one for each wave listed) and put each type of wave in the correct category (electromagnetic or mechanical).

Paragraph Paraphrase: Students paraphrase information about amplitude, wavelength, wave speed, and frequency, including the most important information from the lesson.

Which Wave Are You? Skits show the differences and similarities between transverse and longitudinal waves. Actors talk about the characteristics of the waves, and they act out the motions of the waves.

Compare and Contrast Waves: Presentations compare and contrast mechanical and electromagnetic waves. Presentations also give examples of both types of waves.

Lesson 5 Alternative Assessment
Points of View: Light and Sound

Vocabulary: Story tells what happens to a group of light beams that leave the sun, enter Earth's atmosphere, and interact with different media, such as water and grass.

Examples: Lists include three examples of objects that reflect light, three objects that scatter light, and three objects that do not transmit light. Characteristics common to each group are listed.

Analysis: Explanation describes why a white shirt glows a brilliant purple when lit with ultraviolet light.

Observations: Observations note discuss the way the pencil looks bent in the water and explain why the pencil looks this way.

Details: Work explains why sound waves spread out and correctly notes what occurs when the sound waves encounter each obstacle.

Lesson 6 Alternative Assessment
Tic-Tac-Toe: *Our Energy Use*

Be the Teacher: The quiz should cover the important facts from the lesson about renewable and nonrenewable resources, fossil fuels, and alternative energy sources.

Collage: Student collage should include at least six energy resources and should identify whether the resources are renewable or nonrenewable.

Pro/Con Grid: Grid should provide relevant information about the advantages and disadvantages of the energy resources featured in the lesson.

Skit: Student skit should include discussion of the key ideas from the lesson, including advantages and disadvantages of various energy sources.

Commercial: Commercials should explain how the product uses an alternative energy source and how it compares to products that use other types of energy resources.

Poem: Poem should include an analysis of how at least one aspect of human energy use affects the environment.

Invention: Design should focus on how the machine using one or more alternative energy sources. An explanation of how the machine would affect the environment should be included.

Puzzle Time: Puzzle should include key terms from the lesson. Clues should show that student understand key ideas.

Web Site: Site should include at least three pages and should include a glossary of terms, examples of various energy sources, and images.

Indiana ISTEP+ Review
Key Concepts

1. C	6. D	11. C
2. D	7. B	12. D
3. A	8. B	13. D
4. A	9. C	14. A
5. C	10. A	

1. C See Unit 3, Lesson 5

A is incorrect because the light ray is reflecting, not refracting.

B is incorrect because the light ray is scattering in all directions, not refracting.

C is correct because the light refracts, or changes direction, as it moves into and out of the material.

D is incorrect because the light ray is absorbed as it passes through the material.

2. D See Unit 3, Lesson 2

A is incorrect because the total amount of energy will not change.

B is incorrect because energy will move from the warmer object to the cooler, and the total amount of energy will not change.

C is incorrect because energy will move from the warmer metal to the cooler water, but mass will not be affected.

D is correct because energy will move from the warmer metal to the cooler water, and the total amount of energy will not change.

3. A See Unit 3, Lesson 6

A is correct because a dam for a hydroelectric plant can block the normal path of migrating fish.

B is incorrect because hydroelectric plants do not release gaseous pollutants.

C is incorrect because only nuclear plants produce radioactive waste.

D is incorrect because hydroelectric plants do not overheat the water.

4. A See Unit 3, Lesson 1

A is correct because power is work divided by time.

B is incorrect because power is work divided by time, not work multiplied by time.

C is incorrect because power is work divided by time, not work divided by time, multiplied by 10.

D is incorrect because power is work divided by time, not work minus time.

5. C See Unit 3, Lesson 4

A is incorrect because the ability to record sounds is not evidence of energy from waves.

B is incorrect because the visible spectrum is not evidence of energy from waves.

C is correct because the vibrations you feel are evidence of the energy carried by the sound waves .

D is incorrect because shadows are not evidence of energy from waves.

6. D See Unit 3, Lesson 3

A is incorrect because energy as heat moves by conduction, not radiation, from the warmer potatoes to the spoon.

B is incorrect because energy as heat moves by conduction, not radiation.

C is incorrect because energy as heat moves from a warmer material, the potatoes, to a cooler material, the spoon.

D is correct because energy as heat moves by direct contact from the warmer potatoes to the cooler spoon.

7. B See Unit 3, Lesson 1

A is incorrect because wind turbines do work generating electricity by harnessing wind energy.

B is correct because energy is the ability to do work, and wind turbines use wind energy to produce electrical energy.

C is incorrect because the wind turbines do not produce the movement of air, but use the movement of air (wind) to do work.

D is incorrect because wind turbines do not use electrical energy, they generate it by using wind energy to do work.

8. B See Unit 3, Lesson 2

A is incorrect because energy transfers from warmer materials to cooler materials.

B is correct because energy transfers from warmer materials to cooler materials.

C is incorrect because the melting of the ice cube is not a chemical change, and so chemical potential energy is not transferred.

D is incorrect because the melting of the ice cube is not a chemical change, and so chemical potential energy is not transferred.

9. C See Unit 3, Lesson 4

A is incorrect because some transverse waves—that is, electromagnetic waves—can travel through empty space.

B is incorrect because only electromagnetic waves can travel through empty space.

C is correct because all waves transfer energy.

D is incorrect because waves do not transfer particles.

10. A See Unit 3, Lesson 1

A is correct because the power is 300 J ÷ 1.5 s = 200 W, which is the most power used for any of the tasks.

B is incorrect because the power is 320 J ÷ 2.0 s = 160 W, which is less than Gina's 200 W.

C is incorrect because the power is 180 J ÷ 4.0 s = 45 W, which is less than Gina's 200 W.

D is incorrect because the power is 540 J ÷ 3.0 s = 180 W, which is less than Gina's 200 W.

11. C See Unit 3, Lesson 1

A is incorrect because wheels are not a power system.

B is incorrect because an axle is not a power system.

C is correct because an engine is a power system.

D is incorrect because a battery is not a power system for a gasoline-burning car (although it could be for a battery-powered car).

12. D See Unit 3, Lesson 5

A is incorrect because wave II travels much slower than the other waves, but electromagnetic waves travel in air and water close to the speed of light, which is the fastest speed possible.

B is incorrect because electromagnetic waves all travel close to the speed of light in air and water, but wave II is traveling much slower than the speed of light.

C is incorrect because wave II travels much slower than the speed of light, but electromagnetic waves travel close to the speed of light in air and water.

D is correct because waves I and III both travel close to the speed of light in air and water.

13. D See Unit 3, Lesson 2

A is incorrect because energy cannot be created or destroyed.

B is incorrect because the experiments would not have been completed if there was not enough energy.

C is incorrect because energy cannot be created or destroyed.

D is correct because the total quantity of energy does not change, so the rest of the energy must have been transferred into some undetected form.

14. A See Unit 3, Lesson 3

A is correct because energy travels from the sun to Earth by radiation. Radiation is the transfer of energy through electromagnetic waves.

B is incorrect. Current from a blower is an example of convection because warmth is carried by moving air.

C is incorrect because feeling warmth by direct contact with a warmer object is conduction.

D is incorrect because feeling warmth by direct contact with a warmer object is conduction.

Constructed Response

15. See Unit 3, Lesson 5

Key Elements:

• from air to water the light ray will slow down, but its direction will not change

AND

- from water to air the light ray will speed up, but its direction will not change

Rubric:
2 points Two key elements
1 point One key element
0 points Other

Extended Response

16. See Unit 3, Lesson 6
Key Elements:
One out of each set: (one key element each)

- nuclear beneficial – does not release carbon dioxide

- nuclear harmful – produces radioactive waste that must be stored

AND

- biomass beneficial – renewable resource

- biomass beneficial – recycles organic waste

- biomass harmful – burning it releases carbon dioxide

AND

- solar beneficial – renewable

- solar beneficial – does not contribute to air pollution

- solar harmful – solar plants require large amounts of land

AND

- hydroelectric beneficial – renewable

- hydroelectric harmful – flooding of land can destroy habitats

- hydroelectric harmful – can disrupt fish migration

- hydroelectric harmful – can cause erosion problems

Rubric:
4 points Four key elements
3 points Three key elements
2 points Two key elements
1 point One key element
0 points Other

Unit Test A
Key Concepts

1.	A	6.	D	11.	C
2.	D	7.	A	12.	A
3.	B	8.	B	13.	B
4.	A	9.	D	14.	C
5.	B	10.	B	15.	C

1. A
A is correct because thermal energy is the total kinetic energy of all particles in a substance.

B is incorrect because this statement describes the temperature of a substance, not its thermal energy.

C is incorrect because thermal energy is the total kinetic energy of all particles in a substance. It does not include potential energy.

D is incorrect because thermal energy is the total kinetic energy of all particles in a substance. It does not include potential energy.

2. D
A is incorrect because a period is a measure of time, not distance.

B is incorrect because frequency is a measure of the number of waves in a given time.

C is incorrect because amplitude is a measure of the height, not the length, of a wave.

D is correct because wavelength is the distance between corresponding parts of consecutive waves.

3. B
A is incorrect because conduction involves the transfer of energy through direct contact of particles, not through motion of particles.

B is correct because convection is the transfer of energy through the motion of particles in a fluid.

C is incorrect because insulation does not take place as the result of the motion of particles.

D is incorrect because radiation is a form of energy transfer that does not require matter.

4. A
A is correct because energy is the ability to do work.

B is incorrect because the ability to do work is due to energy, not the type of material used to make an object.

C is incorrect because an object's shape is not generally related to its ability to do work.

D is incorrect because an object's size is not generally related to its ability to do work.

5. B
A is incorrect because power equals energy divided by time, not energy divided by the square of time.

B is correct because power equals energy divided by time, so the correct answer is 1,350 J ÷ 5 s = 270 W.

C is incorrect because power equals energy divided by time, not energy multiplied by time.

D is incorrect because power equals energy divided by time, not energy multiplied by the square of time.

6. D
A is incorrect because no light waves reflect off the glass surface.

B is incorrect because yellow light travels through the glass.

C is incorrect because the glass cannot be translucent for red light if no red light passes through the glass.

D is correct because the yellow light travels through the glass, which means the glass is transparent for yellow light.

7. A
A is correct because energy is defined as the ability to do work.

B is incorrect because energy is the ability to do work, not the resistance to motion.

C is incorrect because energy is the ability to do work, not the speed of an object.

D is incorrect because energy is the ability to do work, not the amount of force in a given time.

8. B
A is incorrect because hydroelectric plants use water, which is a renewable resource.

B is correct because nuclear plants use the element uranium, which is a nonrenewable resource.

C is incorrect because solar plants use solar energy, which is a renewable resource.

D is incorrect because wind plants use wind energy, which is a renewable resource.

9. B

A is incorrect because a mechanical wave slows down when it moves from a solid into a gas.

B is correct because a mechanical wave speeds up when it moves from a liquid into a solid.

C is incorrect because a mechanical wave cannot travel in a vacuum.

D is incorrect because a mechanical wave cannot travel in a vacuum.

10. B

A is incorrect because gears do not provide propulsion.

B is correct because the power source for a windmill is the wind.

C is incorrect because there is no chemical energy in this system.

D is incorrect because no fossil fuel is used in powering a windmill.

11. C

A is incorrect because all colors of light reflect off white paper.

B is incorrect because all colors of light reflect off white paper.

C is correct because all colors of light, including red and blue, reflect off white paper.

D is incorrect because all colors of light reflect off white paper.

12. A

A is correct because energy can be transferred from one system to another.

B is incorrect because, according to the law of conservation of energy, energy cannot be created or destroyed.

C is incorrect because the energy of the battery is not dependent on a force moving over a distance.

D is incorrect because, according to the law of conservation of energy, energy cannot be created or destroyed.

13. B

A is incorrect because conduction is the transfer of energy from one particle to another without the movement of matter.

B is correct because convection is the transfer of energy by the movement of currents within a fluid.

C is incorrect because insulation is a process that inhibits the transfer of energy between objects.

D is incorrect because radiation is the process of transferring energy through electromagnetic waves.

14. C

A is incorrect because, according to the law of conservation of energy, the total energy cannot change.

B is incorrect because, according to the law of conservation of energy, the total energy cannot change.

C is correct because, according to the law of conservation of energy, the total energy cannot change.

D is incorrect because, according to the law of conservation of energy, the total energy cannot change.

15. C

A is incorrect because geothermal power plants release very few contaminants into the air that can cause acid rain.

B is incorrect because hydroelectric power plants do not release contaminants into the air that can cause acid rain.

C is correct because the burning of fossil fuels releases contaminants into the air that can cause acid rain.

D is incorrect because nuclear power plants do not release contaminants into the air that can cause acid rain.

Constructed Response

16. Key Elements:

- has potential energy because it is above the ground; energy is the ability to do work

AND

- any valid description of how you could give the ball more energy and thereby increase its ability to do work (e.g., *give it more energy by pushing it, give it more energy by putting it on a high shelf*, etc.)

Rubric:
2 points Two key elements
1 point One key element
0 points Other

Extended Response
17. Key Elements
- Light refracts each time it enters a different medium.

AND

- White light is made up of different wavelengths, which refract at different angles when they enter and exit a medium.

AND

- Color 1: red; Color 2: yellow; Color 3: green; Color 4: blue

AND

- Only yellow light would exit, not different colors, because it is a single wavelength (a single color) of light.

Rubric:
4 points Four key elements
3 points Three key elements
2 points Two key elements
1 point One key element
0 points Other

Unit Test B
Key Concepts

1.	B	6.	A	11.	D
2.	A	7.	B	12.	C
3.	D	8.	C	13.	D
4.	C	9.	B	14.	D
5.	A	10.	A	15.	D

1. B
A is incorrect because thermal energy depends on the energy of particles in the water, not the size of the container.

B is correct because increasing the temperature increases the kinetic energy of the molecules of the water.

C is incorrect because decreasing the temperature decreases the kinetic energy of molecules, which causes the thermal energy to decrease.

D is incorrect because the amount of water and its total kinetic energy would not change if Lisa divided the water into two parts.

2. A
A is correct because ray 1 travels through the material without reflecting or without being absorbed or scattered.

B is incorrect because ray 2 is absorbed; it does not travel through the material.

C is incorrect because ray 3 is scattered; it does not travel through the material.

D is incorrect because ray 4 is reflected; it does not travel through the material.

3. D

A is incorrect because although an electromagnetic wave does not require a medium to travel, it is affected by changes in media (e.g., light through a prism).

B is incorrect because an electromagnetic wave travels faster, not slower, in a vacuum.

C is incorrect because in a vacuum, an electromagnetic wave moves at the speed of light, not at half the speed of light.

D is correct because in a vacuum, an electromagnetic wave travels at the speed of light. When the wave enters a medium, it slows down.

4. C

A is incorrect because wind energy, not electricity, keeps the turbine moving.

B is incorrect because the turbine's height above the ground does not give it energy; energy from the wind gives the turbine the ability to do work.

C is correct because energy from the wind gives the turbine the ability to do work.

D is incorrect because the changing direction of the turbine's blades does not give the turbine energy; energy from the wind gives the turbine the ability to do work.

5. A

A is correct because the burning of biomass releases carbon dioxide into the atmosphere, which contributes to air pollution.

B is incorrect because geothermal power plants do not significantly contribute to air pollution.

C is incorrect because nuclear power plants do not significantly contribute to air pollution.

D is incorrect because the solar generation of electricity does not significantly contribute to air pollution.

6. A

A is correct because the mug heats her hands by conduction.

B is incorrect because the mug is in direct contact with her hands, so it heats them through conduction.

C is incorrect because the cocoa is not an insulator.

D is incorrect because the convection does not work well in solids.

7. B

A is incorrect because the battery does not prevent heat buildup; the battery provides energy, which gives the circuit the ability to do work.

B is correct because the battery provides chemical energy, and the energy gives the circuit the ability to do work.

C is incorrect because the battery provides energy, not electrical resistance, and the energy gives the circuit the ability to do work.

D is incorrect because the battery does not inhibit electron flow; the battery provides energy, which gives the circuit the ability to do work.

8. C

A is incorrect because power equals energy divided by time, not energy divided by the cube of time.

B is incorrect because power equals energy divided by time, not energy divided by the square of time.

C is correct because power equals energy divided by time, so 72 J ÷ 2 s = 36 W.

D is incorrect because power equals energy divided by time, not energy multiplied by time.

9. B

A is incorrect because the remaining 90% of electrical energy is transformed into thermal energy.

B is correct because the remaining 90% of electrical energy is transformed into heat.

C is incorrect because energy cannot be destroyed; the remaining 90% of electrical energy is instead transformed into thermal energy.

D is incorrect because the energy is not saved but is transformed into thermal energy.

10. A

A is correct because a wave is a disturbance that transfers energy through matter or space.

B is incorrect because a wave does not transfer matter.

C is incorrect because a wave is not a type of energy, even though it transfers energy.

D is incorrect because a wave is not a type of matter.

11. D

A is incorrect because wheels are not a power source.

B is incorrect because gears are not a power source.

C is incorrect because the chain is not a power source.

D is correct because the rider is the source of the energy that powers the bicycle.

12. C

A is incorrect because the distance is calculated by dividing the work (energy) by the force used.

B is incorrect because the units for distance should be measured in meters.

C is correct because the distance is calculated by dividing the work (energy) by the force used, so 240 J ÷ 120 N = 2 m.

D is incorrect because the distance is calculated by dividing the work (energy) by the force used.

13. D

A is incorrect because only green light reflects off green paper. Red light would be absorbed.

B is incorrect because only green light reflects off green paper. Blue light would be absorbed.

C is incorrect because both red and blue light would be absorbed by green paper.

D is correct because only green light reflects off green paper. Both red and blue light would be absorbed.

14. D

A is incorrect because energy cannot be created, and the total energy of the person and the box does not change.

B is incorrect because the energy of the box cannot increase without energy being transferred to it.

C is incorrect because energy cannot be created, and the total energy of the person and the box does not change.

D is correct because total energy does not change; energy is transferred from the person to the box.

15. D

A is incorrect because a laboratory burner transfers energy to a container of water mostly by radiation, not through work.

B is incorrect because work is force times the distance over which the force is applied, but the force the student uses to keep the backpack up is not in the same direction as her movement, so no work is done.

C is incorrect because the piece of furniture does not move, so no work is done.

D is correct because work is force times the distance over which the force is applied; the woman applies a force to the luggage in the same direction the luggage moves, so work is done.

Constructed Response

16. Key Elements

- Habitats can be destroyed by flooding land when reservoirs are created.

OR

- Dams can disrupt migration of fish and can cause erosion problems.

AND

- Nuclear power plants use uranium, a nonrenewable resource.

OR

- Nuclear power plants make radioactive waste that must be stored.

Rubric:
2 points Two key elements
1 point One key element
0 points Other

Extended Response

17. Key Elements

- The water transfers heat by direct contact, which is conduction.

AND

- The silver and stainless steel spoons will feel hot, the plastic spoon will feel warm, and the wood spoon temperature will not have changed.

AND

- insulators: plastic and wood; conductors: stainless steel and silver

AND

- Radiation could come in the form of a heat source at some distance away, such as a fire under the bowl or sunlight falling on the spoons and bowl.

Rubric:
4 points Four key elements
3 points Three key elements
2 points Two key elements
1 point One key element
0 points Other

Unit 4 Earth Structures
Unit Pretest

1. A	5. A	9. B
2. A	6. C	10. D
3. B	7. D	
4. D	8. C	

1. A

A is correct because tsunamis are generally caused by undersea earthquakes.

B is incorrect because tsunamis caused by meteorites are rare, and no meteorite strike took place then.

C is incorrect because wind cannot generate a tsunami.

D is incorrect because earthquakes, not typhoons, cause tsunamis.

2. A

A is correct because a compass has a needle that points to Earth's magnetic North Pole.

B is incorrect because a microscope is used to see very small things, not detect Earth's magnetic field.

C is incorrect because a telescope is used to see objects that are very far in the distance, not detect Earth's magnetic field.

D is incorrect because a calculator is used to make mathematical calculations, not detect Earth's magnetic field.

3. B

A is incorrect because the retreat of a continental glacier does not form valleys.

B is correct because alpine glaciers can turn V-shaped valleys into U-shaped valleys like the one shown by causing erosion and breaking up rock.

C is incorrect because the kettle lakes are not part of the valley shown in the illustration.

D is incorrect because the deposition of glacial drift would not form a valley.

4. D

A is incorrect because microorganisms do not add water to soil.

B is incorrect because microorganisms are too small to dig burrows.

C is incorrect because microorganisms cannot move rock fragments.

D is correct because microorganisms decompose dead organisms and return nutrients to the soil.

5. A

A is correct because the plates separate from each other at a divergent boundary.

B is incorrect because the plates slide past each other at a transform boundary.

C is incorrect the plates collide at a convergent boundary.

D is incorrect because at a divergent boundary, the plates move apart. A plate is sometimes sub ducted under another plate at convergent boundaries.

6. C

A is incorrect because the thin and solid outermost layer describes Earth's crust.

B is incorrect because the innermost layer of iron and nickel describes the inner core.

C is correct because the hot, slow-flowing layer of rock between the crust and the core describes the mantle.

D is incorrect because the liquid layer that encloses a solid ball of iron and nickel describes the outer core.

7. D

A is incorrect because the footwall moves up when a normal fault occurs.

B is incorrect because the hanging wall drops down when a normal fault occurs.

C is incorrect because, when a normal fault occurs, most of the movement is up and down, not side to side.

D is correct because the hanging wall drops down when a normal fault occurs.

8. C

A is incorrect because these materials contain nonmetallic elements.

B is incorrect because none of these materials are made up of only one type of atom.

C is correct because all of these materials contain a combination of silicon and oxygen atoms.

D is incorrect because all of these materials contain a combination of silicon and oxygen atoms. Therefore, they are silicate minerals.

9. B

A is incorrect because shield volcanoes have gentle slopes and quiet eruptions.

B is correct because cinder cone volcanoes have steep sides and violent eruptions.

C is incorrect because composite volcanoes have alternating quiet and violent eruptions.

D is incorrect because composite volcanoes have steep sides and have alternating quiet and violent eruptions.

10. D

A is incorrect because valleys generally form because of erosion by surface water, not groundwater.

B is incorrect because canyons generally form because of erosion by surface water, not groundwater.

C is incorrect because human-made channels do not form because of erosion.

D is correct because caverns form when groundwater dissolves and erodes rock underground.

Lesson 1 Quiz

1. C   4. A
2. C   5. A
3. B

1. C

A is incorrect because all other minerals are softer than diamond.

B is incorrect because many minerals, such as calcite and gypsum, are common and inexpensive.

C is correct because all minerals have an orderly internal, crystal structure.

D is incorrect because many minerals, such as quartz, do not contain carbon atoms.

2. C

A is incorrect because many silicate minerals contain silicon dioxide.

B is incorrect because minerals do not come from living things.

C is correct because minerals are crystalline, which means they have an orderly internal structure.

D is incorrect because many minerals, such as quartz, can form when melted rock cools to form crystals.

3. B

A is incorrect because silicate minerals cannot be pure elements if they contain atoms of at least two different elements (silicon and oxygen).

B is correct because a compound is composed of atoms of two or more elements joined by chemical bonds.

C is incorrect because silicate minerals are not metallic minerals.

D is incorrect because silicate minerals contain at least two different kinds of atoms (silicon and oxygen).

4. A

A is correct because silicate minerals contain a combination of silicon and oxygen and may also include one or more metals.

B is incorrect because silicate minerals contain atoms of silicon and oxygen.

C is incorrect because pure carbon minerals, such as graphite and diamond, are not silicate minerals.

D is incorrect because compounds that contain carbon and hydrogen are generally organic in origin.

5. A

A is correct because carbonates consist of carbon and oxygen.

B is incorrect because minerals containing a combination of carbon and oxygen do not contain a halide ion, such as chloride, fluoride, bromide, or iodide.

C is incorrect because silicate minerals consist of silicon and oxygen.

D is incorrect because oxides contain a single oxygen ion.

Lesson 2 Quiz

1. B   4. C
2. A   5. C
3. D

1. B

A is incorrect because Earth's crust does not rise in subsidence.

B is correct because *subsidence* is areas of crust sinking to a lower elevation. Sediments can collect in these basins.

C is incorrect because earthquakes are not necessarily common in areas of subsidence. Uplift is the opposite of subsidence.

D is incorrect because volcanoes have nothing to do with subsidence.

2. A

A is correct because the igneous rock must first change into sediment before sedimentary rock can form.

B is incorrect because if the rock melted and became magma, it would form igneous rock when it solidified.

C is incorrect because the rock's minerals do not have to dissolve for sedimentary rock to form.

D is incorrect because high pressure and temperature would have changed the igneous rock into metamorphic rock.

3. D

A is incorrect because rift zones form at a divergent boundary, not at a convergent boundary where two plates move toward each other.

B is incorrect because the deep cracks in a rift zone form when two plates move away from each other at a divergent boundary, not at a convergent boundary.

C is incorrect because rift zones do not form at convergent boundaries.

D is correct because deep cracks form between two plates that are moving away from each other.

4. C

A is incorrect because intrusive igneous rock is a result of underground-cooled magma.

B is incorrect because an extrusive igneous rock forms when lava cooled above the ground surface.

C is correct because coal is an organic sedimentary rock, which forms from the remains of plants or animals.

D is incorrect because coal is an organic sedimentary since it forms from the remains of plants or animals. Clastic sedimentary rock forms from fragments of preexisting rock.

5. C

A is incorrect because sedimentary limestone does not contain iron minerals that have cooled and aligned with Earth's magnetic field.

B is incorrect because metamorphic rocks, such as marble, do not melt during their formation, so there are no iron minerals to align with Earth's magnetic field.

C is correct because iron minerals in igneous basalts line up with Earth's magnetic field as they cool.

D is incorrect because sedimentary sandstones do not contain iron minerals that have cooled and aligned with Earth's magnetic field.

Lesson 3 Quiz

1. C   4. A
2. D   5. B
3. B

1. C

A is incorrect because an arête is a sharp ridge separating two cirques, which are glacial landforms.

B is incorrect because a valley is a landform sometimes formed by glacial movement.

C is correct because groundwater can hollow out pockets in limestone rock and can eventually form a cave.

D is incorrect because a cirque is a landform made by a glacier.

2. D

A is incorrect because an alluvial fan forms because of a change in slope and speed, not from an increase in water volume.

B is incorrect because sediment falls out because the land is flatter, not because the land is steeper.

C is incorrect because an alluvial fan forms as a stream spreads out and becomes wider.

D is correct because as the stream entered an area with a lower slope, it spread out and moved slower, and the slower speed caused sediment to drop out.

3. B

A is incorrect because a stalactite is a deposition formation that hangs from the ceiling.

B is correct because a stalagmite forms by deposition on a cave floor.

C is incorrect because cirques are landforms made by retreating glaciers above ground.

D is incorrect because stalagmites are formed by deposition, not by erosion.

4. A

A is correct because a glacier retreating will cause glacial drift to be deposited at the front end and sides of the glacier.

B is incorrect because a glacier growing in size will cause more erosion, not deposition of glacial drift.

C is incorrect because a glacier getting thicker will cause more erosion, not deposition of glacial drift.

D is incorrect because a glacier increasing in speed will cause erosion, not deposition of glacial drift.

5. B

A is incorrect because the snow is turned into ice by the weight of snow above it that compresses it, not by cold wind blowing across it.

B is correct because the snow is turned into ice by the weight of snow above it that compresses it.

C is incorrect because the snow is turned into ice by the weight of snow above it that compresses it. The snow does not melt as it falls and then freezes once it hits the ground.

D is incorrect because the snow is turned into ice by the weight of snow above it that compresses it, not by the temperature of the ground.

Lesson 4 Quiz

1. A   4. A
2. A   5. C
3. D

1. A

A is correct because weathering is the process by which rocks are broken down into smaller pieces by physical and chemical means.

B is incorrect because erosion is the process that moves rocks by wind, air, or water.

C is incorrect because weathering breaks down rocks, it does not build up material.

D is incorrect because weathering breaks down rocks, but does not change them into a different type of rock.

2. A

A is correct because rain causes chemical weathering, and wind causes physical weathering.

B is incorrect because the deposition of soil on top of the granite would help protect the granite from weathering agents.

C is incorrect because weathering does not happen to rocks deep within the ground, where heat from magma exists.

D is incorrect because underground pressure helps form rocks, not weather them.

3. D

A is incorrect because the water that seeps into the soil will cause chemical weathering.

B is incorrect because exfoliation is not the process by which the tortoise breaks up rocks.

C is incorrect because erosion does not aid in soil formation.

D is correct because the mixing action of larger burrowing animals helps the function of decomposers and the aeration of the soil.

4. A

A is correct because the organic and chemical nutrients that plants need to grow are most abundant in horizon A

B is incorrect because rock fragments have little to do with soil fertility.

C is incorrect because soil fertility is the soil's ability to hold and supply nutrients to plants, not the ability to hold or supply water.

D is incorrect because the solid rock in horizon D contains little organic material, so does not contribute to soil fertility.

5. C

A is incorrect because of 100 g, 25 percent is air and silt is 18 percent for only 43 percent of the 100 g sample.

B is incorrect because silt is 18% and sand is 18% for only 36% of the 100 g sample.

C is correct because air is 25% and water is 25% for only 50% of the 100 g sample.

D is incorrect because clay is 9% and organic matter is 5% for only 14% of the 100 g sample.

Lesson 5 Quiz

1.	C	4.	D
2.	C	5.	B
3.	B		

1. C

A is incorrect because the crust is much thinner than the inner core is, and the inner core is a physical layer.

B is incorrect because the crust is much thinner than the outer core is, and the outer core is a physical layer..

C is correct because the crust is the thinnest layer of Earth.

D is incorrect because the crust is much thinner than the mantle is.

2. C

A is incorrect because there are five physical layers and only three compositional layers.

B is incorrect because all of the compositional layers are included in the physical layers.

C is correct because the physical layers of the inner core and outer core are both included in the compositional layer of the core.

D is incorrect because the lithosphere, not the asthenosphere, includes the compositional layer of the crust.

3. B

A is incorrect because the rigid upper part, not the fluid part, of the mantle is also part of the lithosphere.

B is correct because the rigid upper part of the mantle is also part of the lithosphere.

C is incorrect because the rigid upper part, not the soft moving part, of the mantle is also part of the lithosphere.

D is incorrect because the rigid upper part of the mantle is part of the lithosphere, and the lower part of the mantle is slow flowing, not stationary.

4. D

A is incorrect because the tectonic plates move on top of the asthenosphere, not the outer core.

B is incorrect because the tectonic plates move on top of the asthenosphere, not the lithosphere.

C is incorrect because the tectonic plates move on top of the asthenosphere, not the mesosphere.

D is correct because the tectonic plates move on top of the asthenosphere.

5. B

A is incorrect because the inner and outer cores are made mostly of iron and nickel, not lead and iron.

B is correct because the inner and outer cores are made mostly of iron and nickel.

C is incorrect because the inner and outer cores are made mostly of iron and nickel, not lead and mercury.

D is incorrect because the inner and outer cores are made mostly of iron and nickel, not nickel and mercury.

Lesson 6 Quiz

1.	D	4.	B
2.	B	5.	A
3.	C		

1. D

A is incorrect because convection currents are movements in matter due to differences in density.

B is incorrect because sea-floor spreading is found where some, but not all, tectonic plates meet.

C is incorrect because convergent boundaries are found where some, but not all, tectonic plates meet.

D is correct because the place where two plates of lithosphere meet is called a tectonic plate boundary.

2. B

A is incorrect because at a transform boundary two plates slide past each other, not move apart.

B is correct because two plates move apart at a divergent boundary and can form a rift that fills with water.

C is incorrect because the two plates moved and were not stationary.

D is incorrect because two plates collide, not move apart, at a convergent boundary.

3. C

A is incorrect because sea-floor spreading describes the movement of tectonic plates away from mid-ocean ridges, but does not describe the mechanism of the movement.

B is incorrect because continental drift is the hypothesis that Earth's continents once formed a single landmass, but it does not explain how tectonic plates move..

C is correct because mantle convection, ridge push and slab pull are the three mechanisms that have been proposed to explain the movement of tectonic plates.

D is incorrect because sea-floor spreading describes the movement of tectonic plates away from mid-ocean ridges, and continental drift is the hypothesis that Earth's continents once formed a single landmass, but neither explains how tectonic plates move.

4. B

A is incorrect because a continental rise is a gently sloping section of the continental margin.

B is correct because continental drift is the hypothesis that all the continents were once part of one supercontinent that broke apart.

C is incorrect because a continental shelf is a gently sloping section of the continental margin.

D is incorrect because a continental slope is a steeply inclined section of the continental margin.

5. A

A is correct because there is a convergent boundary between the Cocos Plate and the Caribbean Plate.

B is incorrect because there is no indication on this map that the Philippine Plate and the Pacific plate are converging.

C is incorrect because there is no indication on this map that the South American Plate and the African plate are converging.

D is incorrect because the Indo-Australian Plate and the Scotia plate do not share a boundary.

Lesson 7 Quiz

1. B   4. C
2. D   5. B
3. D

1. B

A is incorrect because the stress that slides a body in different directions is called shear stress.

B is correct because compression is defined as stress that squeezes and shortens a body.

C is incorrect because the stress that stretches a body is called tension.

D is incorrect because the stress that pulls a body apart is called tension.

2. D

A is incorrect because a syncline is characteristic of a folded mountain, which is formed by compression, not tension.

B is incorrect because an anticline is characteristic of a folded mountain, which is formed by compression, not tension.

C is incorrect because a folded mountain is formed by compression, not tension.

D is correct because tension is stress that stretches and pulls a body apart. This process can create fault-block mountains.

3. D

A is incorrect because when the footwall moves up a normal fault occurs.

B is incorrect because when the hanging wall moves up a reverse fault occurs.

C is incorrect because when the hanging wall drops down a normal fault occurs.

D is correct because the walls slide past each other when a strike-slip fault occurs.

4. C

A is incorrect because tension stretches rocks apart and makes them break, not fold.

B is incorrect because, although some shear stress is involved as mountains fold, the primary cause of the folding is compression.

C is correct because folded mountains form when compression at convergent tectonic plate boundaries folds and uplifts rock layers.

D is incorrect because volcanic activity, although it can build mountains, does not build folded mountains.

5. B

A is incorrect because tension is stress that stretches and pulls rocks apart, but the eruption of magma, or melted rock, creates volcanic mountains.

B is correct because volcanic mountains form when melted rock erupts onto Earth's surface.

C is incorrect because shear stress slides rock by pushing parts of the rock in different directions, but the eruption of melted rock creates volcanic mountains.

D is incorrect because compression is stress that squeezes and shortens rock, but the eruption of melted rock creates volcanic mountains.

Lesson 8 Quiz

1. C   4. B
2. D   5. B
3. D

1. C

A is incorrect because tsunamis are one result of earthquakes.

B is incorrect because earthquakes happen when the potential energy from rock movement, not in a fault, is suddenly released.

C is correct because earthquakes are caused by movement of tectonic plates along a fault. Tectonic plates can move past each other, collide, or overrun each other.

D is incorrect because shaking of the lithosphere is a result of an earthquake.

2. D

A is incorrect because tension takes place when plates diverge, not when they converge.

B is incorrect because stretching takes place when plates diverge or move past one another, not when they converge.

C is incorrect because shear stress takes place at transform plate boundaries.

D is correct because compression takes place when two plates push together.

3. D

A is incorrect because taking shelter indoors under a desk or table prevents human injuries.

B is incorrect because large cracks in the ground do not usually form.

C is incorrect because violent winds are not an effect of an earthquake.

D is correct because injuries and damage most often happen when buildings and other structures collapse.

4. B

A is incorrect because the rock in the interior of a plate is not stronger than the rock at the boundary.

B is correct because the source of energy for earthquakes comes from deformation of rocks by tectonic plate motion, which generally happens at plate boundaries.

C is incorrect because earthquakes are caused by the energy of moving plates, not the energy transferred from magma.

D is incorrect because earthquakes happen at all types of plate boundaries, not just boundaries where one plate moves over another.

5. B

A is incorrect because elastic rebound does not involve the collapse of rocks due to pressure.

B is correct because elastic rebound is the release of energy from stretched or compressed rocks returning to previous shape.

C is incorrect because elastic deformation is not caused by gravity.

D is incorrect because earthquakes are caused by stress, not heat.

Lesson 9 Quiz

1. D 4. C
2. A 5. B
3. C

1. D

A is incorrect because volcanoes often occur at plate boundaries, but they do not form plate boundaries.

B is incorrect because a caldera, or deep depression, forms following a volcanic eruption.

C is incorrect because a magma chamber forms beneath Earth's surface.

D is correct because a volcanic mountain forms when lava builds up, on Earth's surface, over time.

2. A

A is correct because a crater is the relatively small steep-walled depression around a volcano's vent caused by eruptions.

B is incorrect because a fissure is an opening in Earth's surface.

C is incorrect because a caldera is a large depression that can form after a volcanic eruption when the magma chamber empties. The vent no longer exists.

D is incorrect because although a lava plateau is a steep-walled feature, it does not form around a vent.

3. C

A is incorrect because both lava and pyroclastic materials erupt onto Earth's surface.

B is incorrect because shield volcanoes have quiet eruptions with lava flows.

C is correct because pyroclastic materials are ejected from violent eruptions.

D is incorrect because lava is associated with nonviolent eruptions.

4. C

A is incorrect because hot spots are not found along convergent boundaries.

B is incorrect because hot spots are not found along divergent boundaries.

C is correct because hot spots form over mantle plumes.

D is incorrect because hot spots are not found along rift zones.

5. B

A is incorrect because both magma and lava are molten rock.

B is correct because magma chambers can be deep underground. Lava is magma that has reached Earth's surface.

C is incorrect because lava is magma, or molten rock, that has reached Earth's surface.

D is incorrect because a volcano is any place where gas, ash, or melted rock come out of the ground.

Lesson 1 Alternative Assessment

Tic-Tac-Toe: Matter and Minerals

You Ask the Questions: Quizzes contain at least six questions (of different types) about the ways minerals can form.

Trading Definitions: Cards identify, picture, and define elements, atoms, and compounds, and include a few examples.

Distinguished Work: Collages distinguishes between minerals and nonminerals, and describes the characteristics of each.

Presenting Properties: Presentations compare and contrast properties of common minerals, and include illustrations or diagrams.

You Decide: Cards tell what student know about minerals before reviewing the lesson, and what student learned about minerals.

Picturing Minerals: Posters show common minerals and describe the characteristics of minerals.

Pair Match Up: Cards describe physical properties of minerals. Matching cards include information that pairs only with one mineral.

What Am I?: Skits portray two different minerals and their properties.

Guess the Mineral: Game show ways to identify minerals. Cards name minerals and describe how to identify them.

Lesson 2 Alternative Assessment

Mix and Match: Changes to Rock Types

Igneous rock: Igneous rock and the way it is formed are correctly identified.

Sedimentary rock: Sedimentary rock and the way it is formed are correctly identified.

Metamorphic rock: Metamorphic rock and the way it is formed are correctly identified.

Weathering: Weathering and at least two of its possible causes are identified.

Erosion: Erosion is correctly identified and its causes are discussed.

Deposition: Deposition is correctly identified and its causes are discussed.

Lesson 3 Alternative Assessment

Mix and Match: Pathways of Erosion and Deposition

Photograph of a landform: Each erosion and deposition process is correctly identified and described.

Observations of a stream or river: Each example of surface stream processes is explained correctly (role of gravity, gradient, discharge, particle load, particle size and how each relate to the rate of erosion and deposition).

An aerial photograph of an alluvial fan: Description of alluvial fan, its characteristics, and actions that caused its formation are correctly explained.

Observations of a local farm: Each erosion and deposition process is correctly identified and described.

Website describing national parks: Each erosion and deposition process is correctly identified and described.

Descriptions or photographs of a flood: The flood, its characteristics, and the erosion and deposition it causes are described correctly.

Topographical map: The land, its characteristics, and the action that caused its formation are described correctly.

Descriptions or photographs of glaciers: Description of how glaciers move and how they erode or affect land is correct.

Geological map: Description of the land, its characteristics, and what action caused its formation is correct.

Lesson 4 Alternative Assessment

Mix and Match: *All About Soil*
A.   Student should use the same type of information source from Column A to gather information about the soil topics he or she chooses.
B.   Student should choose two soil topics from Column B.
C.   Use the following guidelines to evaluate student's presentation of analysis.
Realistic illustration: Student's illustration should show the important features their soil topic.

Schematic diagram, with a key: Students should create a scientific diagram that uses symbols to provide data about soil in a certain area.

Lesson 5 Alternative Assessment

Take Your Pick: Earth's Physical and Compositional Layers
Picturing Earth's Layers: Posters show Earth's solid compositional layers. The layers are labeled and briefly described.

What Are Your Thoughts?: Cards describe what student knew about Earth's compositional layers before completing the lesson and the most interesting thing student learned about Earth's compositional layers during the lesson.

Down to the Core: Venn diagrams correctly identify the similarities and differences between Earth's inner and outer cores.

The Layer Quiz: Cards show the names of Earth's layers and some of the properties of the layers.

Seeing Inside: Presentations describe how seismic waves and their speed help scientists learn about the inside of Earth.

Your Turn to Teach: Lesson accurately describes the layers of the solid Earth.

Blast from the Past: Timelines show past theories about Earth's internal structure in the correct sequence.

What's in a Layer?: Presentations compare and contrast the two ways of looking at Earth's internal structure.

Lesson 6 Alternative Assessment

Climb the Pyramid: Exploring Tectonic Plates
A Puzzling Picture: Puzzle pieces fit together to form one large landmass. Student demonstrations and explanations accurately portray plate tectonics.

Plate Interview: Interview presents ten questions and answers. The answers are ones that could have come from Alfred Wegener in 1912.

Sea-floor Spreading: Writing describes the process of sea-floor spreading and uses the Mid-Atlantic Ridge as an example. Description tells how material reaches the surface and why the ridge is higher than the surrounding oceanic plates.

Density Differences: Poem or song explains how density differences below Earth's plates cause the plates to move and change shape.

Flipbook: Flipbook shows what happens at a convergent boundary, a divergent boundary, and a transform boundary.

Collision Diorama: Diorama includes labels, and shows convergent boundaries formed between two continental plates, a continental plate and an oceanic plate, or two oceanic plates.

Lesson 7 Alternative Assessment

Climb the Ladder: Faults, Folds, and Mountains
Quiz Cards: Three cards include the terms *compression*, *tension*, and *shear stress*. Three other cards include the definitions for these terms.

To a Fault: Poster describes and illustrates the three types of faults.

Flipping Forward: Flipbook shows how a folded mountain forms.

On the Range: Description describes a famous mountain range, what type of range it is, and the way it formed.

Plate Talk: Skit describes what might happen to a tectonic plate that is pushing against another plate, what might happen to the other tectonic plate, and why.

You're the Expert!: Report notes where the oldest rock is located in the fold, describes the shape of the fold, and how the syncline occurred.

Lesson 8 Alternative Assessment

Climb the Ladder: Earthquake Exercises
Earthquake Poster: Poster shows how an earthquake occurs and how elastic deformation can take place. Labels show the focus, epicenter, and fault.

Word Swap: Puzzles use one vocabulary word from the lesson, and include a paragraph that tells about the word.

Earthquake Events: Flipchart shows the sequence of events that cause an earthquake and how the ground moves during an earthquake.

Earthquake Article: Article describes being in an earthquake, what caused the quake, when it hit, what the aftermath was like, and how people's lives were affected.

Shaky Story: Story tells what happens during an earthquake, what the characters do, and how they react.

Boundary Action: Models show a divergent boundary, a convergent boundary, and a transform plate boundary. The direction of movement is labeled.

Lesson 9 Alternative Assessment

Points of View: Volcanoes and Volcanic Activity
Vocabulary: The root of volcano is listed, along with other words in the lesson that contain the root. Each word is defined.

Illustrations: Trading cards show and label the three types of volcanoes, and describe how each type is similar to and different from the other types.

Analysis: Presentations describe how Earth's surface might be different if volcanoes did not exist and which landforms and landmasses might not exist if it weren't for volcanoes.

Details: Letters explain that volcanoes can also form in other areas, describe the other areas, and explain how these volcanoes occur.

Models: Models accurately depict a shield volcano. They also label the volcano's vent, lava flow, and magma chamber. Models describe how a shield volcano is different from and similar to other types of volcanoes.

Indiana ISTEP+ Review
Key Concepts

1. B	6. D	11. A
2. D	7. C	12. B
3. A	8. B	13. D
4. B	9. A	14. A
5. C	10. B	15. A

1. B See Unit 4, Lesson 2

A is incorrect because sub duction happens where one tectonic plate slides under another.

B is correct because magma flows upward at the center of a rift zone as the two plates move apart.

C is incorrect because the diagram shows magma moving upward, not lava solidifying.

D is incorrect because the rift zone forms as two oceanic plates diverge.

2. D See Unit 4, Lesson 8

A is incorrect because earthquakes happen at plate boundaries, and the energy of an earthquake moves out in all directions from the focus .

B is incorrect because stress takes places at plate boundaries regardless of the direction of motion.

C is incorrect because earthquakes happen at plate boundaries, and energy travels from them whether there are mountains or not.

D is correct because the Florida coast is not located at a plate boundary.

3. A See Unit 4, Lesson 3

A is correct because acids in ground water dissolve limestone and may create caves over time.

B is incorrect because metamorphic rock forms when rock is exposed to high temperatures or high pressures or both, but not when rock is exposed to acidic groundwater.

C is incorrect because sand would not result from the dissolution of limestone by acidic water.

D is incorrect because molten rock is formed from very hot temperatures deep within Earth.

4. B See Unit 4, Lesson 4

A is incorrect because bedrock is solid rock that lies below layers of soil.

B is correct because soil formation begins with rock breaking up into small pieces.

C is incorrect because ice wedging involves water freezing and thawing in cracks of rock.

D is incorrect because rock is an inorganic material. Organic material is made of once-living material.

5. C See Unit 4, Lesson 3

A is incorrect because although alpine glaciers create U-shaped valleys from V-shaped valleys, continental glaciers create flattened landscapes, not V-shaped valleys.

B is incorrect because alpine glaciers create rugged landscapes, and continental glaciers create flattened landscapes.

C is correct because alpine glaciers produce rugged landscapes, and continental glaciers produce flat landscapes.

D is incorrect because alpine glaciers create rugged landscapes, and continental glaciers create flattened landscapes.

6. D See Unit 4, Lesson 7

A is incorrect because the blocks in a strike-slip fault move primarily horizontally.

B is incorrect because the blocks in a strike-slip fault move primarily horizontally.

C is incorrect because the blocks in a strike-slip fault move in different directions.

D is correct because the blocks in a strike-slip fault move horizontally in opposite directions.

7. C See Unit 4, Lesson 2

A is incorrect because gravity would not cause crystals to be aligned with each other.

B is incorrect because crystals in igneous rock could not change position after the rock has formed, and gravity would not cause crystals to be aligned with each other.

C is correct because magnetite crystals would align with Earth's magnetic field as the magnetite crystals cooled from magma or lava.

D is incorrect because crystals in igneous rock could not change position after the rock has formed,

8. B See Unit 4, Lesson 8

A is incorrect because A represents the focus not the epicenter.

B is correct because the epicenter is located on the surface directly above the focus.

C is incorrect because this line is part of the fault not the epicenter.

D is incorrect because this line indicates the path by which seismic waves first reach Earth's surface.

9. A See Unit 4, Lesson 7

A is correct because fault-block mountains form when tension causes faults along which some blocks of rock drop down relative to other blocks.

B is incorrect because shear stress pushes rocks in different directions but does not form fault-block mountains. Some shear stress may be involved as faults occur, but the primary cause of fault-block mountains is tension.

C is incorrect because compression may form folded mountains, but not fault-block mountains.

D is incorrect because volcanic activity, although it can build mountains, does not form fault-block mountains.

10. B See Unit 4, Lesson 3

A is incorrect because the sediment does not play a role in whether the lake will dry up; the sediment is necessary to form a shoreline to contain the water.

B is correct because without the sediment, the water would not stay contained.

C is incorrect because although vegetation needs sediment in order to grow, vegetation is not necessary for the formation of the lake.

D is incorrect because sediment does not play a role in ice melting.

11. A See Unit 4, Lesson 5

A is correct because the core is the central part of Earth.

B is incorrect because the crust is the outermost layer of Earth.

C is incorrect because the lithosphere is the solid outer physical layer of Earth that is made up of the crust and the upper part of the mantle.

D is incorrect because the mesosphere is the slow-flowing physical layer of Earth in the mantle.

12. B See Unit 4, Lesson 9

A is incorrect because a quiet eruption results in a gentle flow of lava.

B is correct because a violent eruption releases pyroclastic materials.

C is incorrect because most moderate eruptions pour out lava.

D is incorrect because gentle and moderate eruptions are associated with the flow of lava, not the release of pyroclastic materials.

13. D See Unit 4, Lesson 5

A is incorrect because plate tectonics is a theory that describes the movement of the plates on the asthenosphere, which is the soft layer of the mantle.

B is incorrect because chemical composition, not structural features, is used to identify these layers of Earth.

C is incorrect because Earth is divided into five layers based on physical properties.

D is correct because the three layers of core, mantle, and crust are identified based on the chemical substances they contain.

14. A See Unit 4, Lesson 2

A is correct because the ash falling to Earth's surface is an example of deposition.

B is incorrect because erosion transports soil and sediments to new locations.

C is incorrect because subsidence is the sinking of regions of the Earth's crust.

D is incorrect because weathering is the disintegration and decomposition of rocks.

15. A See Unit 4, Lesson 9

A is correct because plates move toward each other at a convergent plate boundary.

B is incorrect because plates move away from each other at a divergent plate boundary.

C is incorrect because plates slide past each other at a transform boundary.

D is incorrect because plates usually do not move in the same direction at the same time.

Constructed Response

16. See Unit 4, Lesson 4
Key Elements:
• The uppermost soil horizon is dark in color because it contains humus.

AND

(One of the following)

• Living things break down the remains of plants and animals. This decayed organic matter becomes part of the soil.

• Living things can loosen and mix soil as they travel through it.

Rubric:
2 points: Two Key Elements
1 point: One Key Element
0 points: Other

Extended Response

17. See Unit 4, Lesson 7
Key Elements:
• These are folded mountains.

• The anticline and syncline folds in the mountains are clearly visible. or: Folds are visible, but there is no evidence of faults or volcanic activity, so these cannot be fault-block mountains or volcanic mountains.

AND

• Compression was the type of stress that formed these mountains.

• Arrows should be drawn to show that the rock was being squeezed together from the lower left to the upper right. There should be two arrows, one in the upper right and one in the lower left. The arrows should both be pointing in toward the rock.

Rubric:
4 Points Four Key Elements
3 Points Three Key Elements
2 Points Two Key Elements
1 Point One Key Element
0 Points Other

Unit Test A
Key Concepts

1.	D	6.	D	11.	A
2.	D	7.	A	12.	A
3.	B	8.	C	13.	D
4.	D	9.	A	14.	C
5.	D	10.	C	15.	B

1. D

A is incorrect because deposition describes eroded material that is being laid down.

B is incorrect because erosion describes weathered material that is being transported from one place to another.

C is incorrect because subsidence describes the sinking of Earth's crust to a lower elevation.

D is correct because weathering causes rocks to break into fragments.

2. D

A is incorrect because weathering does not change a sedimentary rock into a metamorphic rock.

B is incorrect because erosion and deposition do not change a sedimentary rock into a metamorphic rock.

C is incorrect because melting and solidification do not change a sedimentary rock into a metamorphic rock.

D is correct because the sedimentary rock, shale, changes into the metamorphic rock, slate, after exposure to heat and pressure.

3. B

A is incorrect because the innermost layer of Earth's interior is the core.

B is correct because the thin and solid outermost layer of Earth is the crust.

C is incorrect because the hot, slow-flowing layer of Earth's interior above the core is the mantle.

D is incorrect because the layer of Earth on which the tectonic plates move is the asthenosphere, which is part of the mantle.

4. D

A is incorrect because canyons form by erosion, but the landform shown is a sinkhole.

B is incorrect because a cavern is a large cave, and a collapsed cave forms a sinkhole.

C is incorrect because channels form by erosion, but the landform shown is a sinkhole.

D is correct because a sinkhole forms when the roof of a cave collapses, as the picture shows.

5. D

A is incorrect because cleavage is the tendency of a mineral to break along specific planes of weakness to form smooth, flat surfaces.

B is incorrect because color is determined visually and not by scratching it against a plate to determine streak.

C is incorrect because luster describes how the surface of a mineral reflects light.

D is correct because streak is the color of a mineral in a powdered form. Streak is observed by rubbing the mineral across a porcelain plate.

6. D

A is incorrect because humus is found mostly in horizon A, not in bedrock.

B is incorrect because horizon B contains little organic matter.

C is incorrect because parent rock is another name for bedrock.

D is correct because humus is organic matter made of decayed plants and animals.

7. A

A is correct because the focus is the point beneath the surface at which an earthquake originates.

B is incorrect because B indicates the earthquake epicenter, not the focus.

C is incorrect because the line labeled C is the fault along which the earthquake occurred, not the focus.

D is incorrect because the series of circles labeled D represent waves of energy travelling away from the focus, but not the focus itself.

8. C

A is incorrect because a fault is a break in the rock, along which movement has occurred.

B is incorrect because the focus is the point beneath Earth's surface where an earthquake originates.

C is correct because the epicenter is the point on Earth's surface directly above the focus.

D is incorrect because an earthquake originates at a particular point on a tectonic plate boundary.

9. A

A is correct because a shield volcano has gently sloping sides and is formed by nonexplosive eruptions.

B is incorrect because a composite volcano has alternating nonexplosive and explosive eruptions.

C is incorrect because pyroclastic describes a type of material ejected from volcanoes, not a type of volcano.

D is incorrect because a cinder cone volcano has steep sides formed by explosive eruptions.

10. C

A is incorrect because tectonic plates are not part of Earth's core, but blocks of Earth's crust and the uppermost part of the mantle.

B is incorrect because tectonic plates are blocks of the Earth's crust and only the uppermost part of the mantle. The lithosphere is the uppermost part of the mantle and the crust.

C is correct because tectonic plates are blocks of Earth's lithosphere that consist of Earth's crust and the rigid, uppermost part of Earth's mantle.

D is incorrect because Earth's asthenosphere is the soft layer of the mantle upon which the lithosphere moves.

11. A

A is correct because the landform shown in the illustration is a glacier flowing between mountains.

B is incorrect because the landform shown in the illustration is a glacier, which can leave material behind called *glacial drift*.

C is incorrect because the landform shown in the picture is a glacier, not an erosional feature of a mountainside like a cirque. .

D is incorrect because the landform shown in the picture is an alpine glacier, not a continental glacier.

12. A

A is correct because *J* points to the hanging wall that is downthrown in a normal fault.

B is incorrect because *K* points to a footwall in the diagram of a reverse fault.

C is incorrect because *L* points to one side of a strike-slip fault, which has moved horizontally, not vertically..

D is incorrect because *M* points to one side of a strike-slip fault, which has moved horizontally, not vertically..

13. D

A is incorrect because at a divergent boundary, the plates move away from each other, not toward each other.

B is incorrect because at a transform boundary, two plates slide past each other; they do not move away from each other.

C is incorrect because plates move away from each other at a divergent boundary; they do not slide past each other.

D is correct because plates slide past each other at a transform boundary.

14. C

A is incorrect because ice blocks are large pieces of ice, not molten rock.

B is incorrect because magma is not solid rock; it is molten rock.

C is correct because magma is molten rock.

D is incorrect because volcanic ash is made up of very tiny particles of solid rock.

15. B

A is incorrect because Earth has a north and south pole, not two north poles.

B is correct because Earth's magnetic field has lines of force that behave like a bar magnet, with a north and south pole.

C is incorrect because convection currents in Earth's mantle flow in circular patterns due to unequal heating.

D is incorrect because waves traveling outward from an earthquake's focus describe seismic waves, not Earth's magnetic field.

Constructed Response
16. Key Elements:
- The outermost layer is the crust.

- The crust is the layer of solid rock that makes up Earth's surface.

AND

- The middle layer is the mantle.

- The mantle is the layer of hot, slow-flowing material between Earth's crust and core.

AND

Any two of the following: (one key element each)

- The innermost layer is the core.

- It is made of mostly of molten metal.

- The outer core is molten liquid metal.

- There is so much pressure on the inner core that it is a dense solid.

Rubric:
2 points Six key elements
1 point Three, four, or five key elements
0 points other

Extended Response
17. Key Elements
- A mineral's color is the color it appears in white light. The color of a mineral is the result of how that mineral absorbs certain colors of light.

AND

- Luster is how a mineral reflects light. It is a measure of its reflectivity.

AND

- From the table, diamond can be inferred to be the most reflective or most lustrous. It is described as having a brilliant luster.

AND

- Gold is yellow in color and metallic in luster.

Rubric:
4 points Four key elements
3 points Three key elements
2 points Two key elements
1 point One key element
0 points other

Unit Test B
Key Concepts

1.	A	6.	D	11.	B
2.	C	7.	B	12.	C
3.	A	8.	B	13.	A
4.	B	9.	D	14.	B
5.	C	10.	D	15.	C

1. A
A is correct because flowing water can break down rock, cause rock fragments to scrape against each other and against the sand on the stream bottom, and result in pebbles that are worn smooth.

B is incorrect because the force of gravity would not cause the rounding of pebbles in a stream.

C is incorrect because the movement of ice would imply that the pebbles were rounded by a glacier.

D is incorrect because freezing and thawing would not cause the rounding of pebbles in a stream.

2. C
A is incorrect because a compass needle points to Earth's magnetic north pole, not to the south.

B is incorrect because a compass needle points to Earth's magnetic north pole, not to the east.

C is correct because a compass needle points to Earth's magnetic north pole.

D is incorrect because a compass needle points to Earth's magnetic north pole, not to the west.

3. A
A is correct because the core is the innermost part of Earth below the mantle.

B is incorrect because the solid outer layer of Earth is the crust.

C is incorrect because the hot, slow-flowing layer of rock beneath the crust is the mantle.

D is incorrect because the layer of Earth on which the tectonic plates move is the asthenosphere, which is one of the physical layers of Earth.

4. B
A is incorrect because these five layers are divided based on physical properties, not composition.

B is correct because these five layers are divided based on physical properties.

C is incorrect because these five layers are divided based on physical properties, not chemical properties.

D is incorrect because these five layers are divided based on physical properties, not on elemental properties.

5. C
A is incorrect because acid in decaying leaves cannot displace soil to expose rock.

B is incorrect because acids increase chemical weathering of rock.

C is correct because acids are agents of chemical weathering, and decaying leaves add organic matter to soil.

D is incorrect because chemical weathering and soil formation occur more rapidly when soil is more acidic.

6. D
A is incorrect because a sinkhole forms when the roof of a cave collapses; sinkholes do not form from canyons.

B is incorrect because a sinkhole forms when the roof of a cave collapses; sinkholes do not form from ponds.

C is incorrect because a sinkhole forms when the roof of a cave collapses; sinkholes do not form from valleys.

D is correct because a sinkhole forms when the roof of a cave collapses.

7. B
A is incorrect because the feldspar sample has a mass of 16 g divided by a volume of 6.2 mL to equal a density of 2.6 g/mL.

B is correct because the galena sample has a mass of 9 g divided by a volume of 1.2 mL to equal a density of 7.5 g/mL.

C is incorrect because the garnet sample has a mass of 12 g divided by a volume of 3.0 mL to equal a density of 4.0 g/mL.

D is incorrect because the quartz sample has a mass of 10 g divided by a volume of 3.7 mL to equal a density of 2.7 g/mL.

8. B

A is incorrect because a scratch test determines hardness and not acidity.

B is correct because carbonates, and some other minerals, will react with hydrochloric acid to produce bubbles of carbon dioxide gas.

C is incorrect because the density of hydrochloric acid cannot be used to identify other minerals.

D is incorrect because acids tend to react with bases and not with other acids.

9. D

A is incorrect because the epicenter is the point on Earth's surface directly above the focus.

B is incorrect because rocks move along the fault.

C is incorrect because the line labeled C represents the fault on which the earthquake is taking place.

D is correct because energy travels as waves outward from the focus in every direction.

10. D

A is incorrect because Africa is a single tectonic plate, so there are no plate boundaries within the continent.

B is incorrect because the fact that there were no earthquakes has to do with the locations of tectonic plate boundaries, not with landmass.

C is incorrect because faults exist in rocks throughout the world.

D is correct because the continent of Africa is located on a single continental tectonic plate; so, there are no plate boundaries along which earthquakes would take place.

11. B

A is incorrect because a cone-shaped piece of paper would represent a volcano, not a lava plateau.

B is correct because a lava plateau has steep sides and a relatively flat surface.

C is incorrect because a depression in modeling clay could represent a crater or other landform.

D is incorrect because a deep cut in modeling clay would represent a volcanic fissure.

12. C

A is incorrect because condensation occurs when a gas changes into a liquid.

B is incorrect because conduction is the transfer of energy from one object to another by direct contact.

C is correct because convection is the transfer of energy by the movement of matter.

D is incorrect because radiation is the transfer of energy by electromagnetic waves.

13. A

A is correct because the hanging wall moves up along a reverse fault due to compressional tension.

B is incorrect because the footwall does not move up along a reverse fault.

C is incorrect because the walls mainly move up or down, not from side to side, along a reverse fault.

D is incorrect because the hanging wall moves up along a reverse fault.

14. B

A is incorrect because although it must be below freezing for a glacier to form, there must also be lots of snow, so it will not usually be dry.

B is correct because for a glacier to form it must be cold and more snow must fall than melts, so the snow can be compacted into a glacier.

C is incorrect because although there must be a fair amount of precipitation, it must be cold, not mild, for a glacier to form.

D is incorrect because although it must be below freezing for a glacier to form, more snow must fall than melts.

15. C

A is incorrect because some continental plates (for example, the Indian Plate) are smaller than oceanic plates (for example, Pacific Plate).

B is incorrect because oceanic crust is thinner than continental crust.

C is correct because continental crust is thicker than oceanic crust.

D is incorrect because some continental plates (for example, North American Plate) are larger than oceanic plates (for example, the Juan de Fuca Plate).

Constructed Response

16. Key Elements:

Any one of the following:

- No; because the mountain with the lowest elevation in the table was also formed by faults.

- No; because the next four highest mountains listed in the table were formed in other ways besides by faults.

AND

- Mt. Greylock and Mt. McKinley were both formed by faults. The elevation of Mt. McKinley is nearly 17,000 feet greater than the elevation of Mt. Greylock.

AND

Any one of the following:

- No; Long's Peak was formed by a glacier and not by movement of tectonic plates so it is not on the boundary of a tectonic plate.

- No; Mauna Kea in Hawaii is on a different tectonic plate (Pacific Plate) from all the others.

- No; All of the mountains listed are on the North American Plate except Mauna Kea.

Rubric:
2 points Three Key Elements
1 point One or two Key Elements
0 points Other

Extended Response

17. Key Elements:

Any three of the following: (one key element each)

- Water fills small cracks and freezes.

- Ice forces the crack open.

- When the ice thaws the crack remains.

- Eventually the rock breaks down into a soil component.

AND

- Water expands as it freezes.

AND

Any one of the following:

- The frequency of freeze/thaw cycles could increase.

- Each freeze/thaw cycle leaves more small cracks. These cracks fill with water that freezes, which widens the cracks and breaks the rock into smaller fragments.

Rubric:
4 Points Five Key Elements
3 Points Four Key Elements
2 Points Three Key Elements
1 Point Two Key Elements
0 Points Other

Unit 5 The Changing Earth
Unit Pretest

1. C   5. A   9. B
2. D   6. C   10. C
3. A   7. D
4. B   8. D

1. C
A is incorrect because radiometric dating shows that Earth is about 4.6 billion years old, not 40 billion years old.

B is incorrect. Based on radiometric dating of rock from our solar system, Earth is about 4.6 billion years old.

C is correct because radiometric dating of rock from our solar system indicates that Earth is about 4.6 billion years.

D is incorrect because Earth is about 4.6 billion, not 4.6 million, years old.

2. D
A is incorrect because a sinkhole is a depression in the ground.

B is incorrect because although a sedimentary rock can contain fossils, sedimentary rock itself is not a fossil.

C is incorrect because crystals were never alive; they are solids whose particles are arranged in a particular pattern.

D is correct because a fossil is the physical evidence of an organism that once lived.

3. A
A is correct because the geologic time scale divides Earth's immense history into distinct time units.

B is incorrect because relative dating is a way to determine the relative ages of rocks.

C is incorrect because absolute dating is a way to determine the absolute ages of rocks.

D is incorrect because the principle of superposition refers to the position of rock layers relative to each other.

4. B
A is incorrect because the chart indicates that modern humans have existed only for about 200,000 years.

B is correct because eras are used as time units in the chart. In the geologic time scale, an era is shorter than an eon but longer than a period.

C is incorrect because the chart indicates that Earth is 4.6 billion years old.

D is incorrect because according to the chart, fish evolved before birds did.

5. A
A is correct because the igneous intrusion cut through all of the sedimentary layers (by the law of crosscutting relationships).

B is incorrect because it was deposited before the igneous intrusion cut through it.

C is incorrect because it was deposited before the igneous intrusion cut through it, and it is likely older than the top layer.

D is incorrect because it was deposited before the igneous intrusion cut through it, and it is likely the oldest of the sedimentary layers.

6. C
A is incorrect because the fossil does not provide any evidence to indicate that your area was once farther from the ocean than it is now.

B is incorrect because the fossil does not provide any evidence to indicate that your area was once more mountainous than it is now.

C is correct because the animal would have died and been buried by sediment in a seashore environment.

D is incorrect because the climate in your area could be the same even though the area may have been closer to the ocean.

7. D
A is incorrect because the rock layer would be younger than a rock layer that contains fossil A.

B is incorrect because the rock layer would be older than a rock layer containing fossil D.

C is incorrect because the rock layer would be older than a rock layer that contains fossil D, but it could not be determined whether the rock layer

containing B is older or younger than a layer containing C since their ranges overlap.

D is correct because the rock layer would be older than a rock layer that contains fossil D.

8. D
A is incorrect because Precambrian time accounts for 90 percent of Earth's time, not 10 percent.

B is incorrect because Precambrian time accounts for 90 percent of Earth's history, not 30 percent.

C is incorrect because Precambrian time accounts for 90 percent of Earth's history, not 60 percent.

D is correct because 90 percent of Earth's history occurred during Precambrian time.

9. B
A is incorrect because coprolites are fossilized dung, and the image shows the fossil of the body of a fish.

B is correct because the diagram shows a fossil of a fish.

C is incorrect because an ice core is a long cylinder of ice obtained from a glacier or ice cap, and the image shows a fossil.

D is incorrect because tree rings are structures in the cross-sections of tree trunks that indicate growth, and the image shows a fossil.

10. C
A is incorrect because stable isotopes do not decay.

B is incorrect because stable isotopes do not decay.

C is correct because radioactive decay takes place when an unstable isotope breaks down into a stable isotope.

D is incorrect because this interaction does not describe radioactive decay.

Lesson 1 Quiz

1. B   4. A
2. D   5. B
3. C

1. B
A is incorrect because a bone is a structure that may be fossilized as a result of having been preserved in rock, ice, amber, or hardened asphalt.

B is correct because a trace fossil is a structure, such as tracks or dung, that form as a result of an organism's activity on soft sediment.

C is incorrect because a frozen fossil is a structure, such as skin, bones, and fur that are found in ice.

D is incorrect because a petrified fossil is a structure, such as bone, that forms as the result of minerals replacing soft body tissues.

2. D

A is incorrect because the fish species could still exist.

B is incorrect because there is not enough information provided about the relative age of the fossil.

C is incorrect because fossils are usually found in sedimentary rock.

D is correct because the fish fossil indicates that the rocks were once under water.

3. C

A is incorrect because the Rocky Mountains do not have a tropical climate.

B is incorrect because the Rocky Mountains are no longer under an ocean.

C is correct because grizzly bears live in this mountain biome.

D is incorrect because the Rocky Mountains are not an arctic biome.

4. A

A is correct because fossils provide evidence of how geologic processes have changed Earth's surface; the presence of similar fossils in the two areas would suggest that the landmasses were once connected.

B is incorrect because living things provide little evidence of the movement of landmasses over millions of years.

C is incorrect because trees are not old enough to provide evidence of processes that occur over millions of years.

D is incorrect because it is the similarities in the fossils that are important, not the number of different fossils.

5. B

A is incorrect because tropical ferns are not associated with cold climates.

B is correct because tropical ferns grow in warm, humid climates.

C is incorrect because the question relates to environment and climate change, not geologic change.

D is incorrect because tropical ferns do not grow in cool, dry climates.

Lesson 2 Quiz

1. B 4. A
2. C 5. A
3. D

1. B

A is incorrect because determining mineral composition is not part of relative dating, which is used to compare the ages of rocks.

B is correct because relative dating is used to determine the order in which rock layers formed and the relative age of each rock layer.

C is incorrect because classifying rocks by their type is not a way to determine which rock is older than another rock.

D is incorrect because radioactive isotopes are used to determine the absolute age, not the relative age, of rocks.

2. C

A is incorrect because this property alone does not allow fossils to be used for relative dating.

B is incorrect because this property does not allow scientists to determine the relative ages of the sedimentary layers.

C is correct because rock that contains fossils of organisms similar to those that live today is most likely younger than rock that contains fossils of earlier organisms.

D is incorrect because it is rarely possible to determine a fossil's exact age; even if exact ages of fossils could be measured, this information is not needed to determine relative ages of rock layers.

3. D

A is incorrect because animals that lived in the past may or may not be more complex than those living today.

B is incorrect because many animals that exist today have not existed throughout Earth's history.

C is incorrect because animals today have descended from animals that once existed, so fossil and modern animals share many characteristics.

D is correct because characteristics of animals evolve. Those on Earth today have descended from animals that existed in the past.

4. A

A is correct because by dating the layers above and below the layer containing the ammonites, the age of the layer containing the ammonites can be determined. The ammonites are in a sedimentary rock layer, which cannot be dated using radiometric dating techniques.

B is incorrect because fossils can almost never be accurately dated using radiometric methods.

C is incorrect because sedimentary rocks cannot be accurately dated using radiometric methods.

D is incorrect because fossils do not have a half life, only radioactive isotopes have half lives.

5. A

A is correct because absolute dating includes different methods that scientists use to measure the age of rock.

B is incorrect because scientists study composition using methods of chemical analysis, not absolute dating.

C is incorrect because scientists study physical structure using methods such as microscopic analysis, not absolute dating.

D is incorrect because scientists study geographic distribution using field surveys and other methods, not absolute dating.

Lesson 3 Quiz

1. C 4. C
2. B 5. D
3. C

1. C

A is incorrect because the organisms could not have crossed a body as large as the Atlantic Ocean.

B is incorrect because the observation does not suggest that the Atlantic Ocean was ever a large body of freshwater.

C is correct because continents move. The fossils are the same because they represent organisms that lived on a single landmass at one time.

D is incorrect because organisms evolve; most organisms alive today are different from those that lived millions of years ago.

2. B

A is incorrect because it lists time divisions from smallest to largest.

B is correct because eons are divided into eras, eras are divided into periods, and periods are divided into epochs.

C is incorrect because an eon is larger than an era, a period, and an epoch.

D is incorrect because a period is shorter than an eon and an era.

3. C

A is incorrect because the rock's age would reveal how old the rock is but not how it was formed.

B is incorrect because although color might help identify an igneous rock (formed in a volcanic eruption), the color of a sedimentary rock does not generally provide clues about how the rock was formed.

C is correct because the texture of a sedimentary rock can provide clues about how and where the rock was formed.

D is incorrect because the fossils in a sedimentary rock would likely reveal little about how the rock was formed.

4. C

A is incorrect because this trace fossil provides evidence for environmental changes over time. A fish fossil indicates that the area was once an aquatic environment.

B is incorrect because a bone embedded in rock is not necessarily a fossil, and does not provide evidence for climate change over time.

C is correct because the width of a tree ring can determine the climatic conditions that existed during the life of the tree. A thick tree ring means there were good growing conditions during the life of the tree.

D is incorrect because a mammoth frozen in ice can provide evidence for how life forms have changed over time.

5. D

A is incorrect because Precambrian time ended more than 543 million years ago.

B is incorrect because the Paleozoic era ended about 248 million years ago.

C is incorrect because the Mesozoic era ended about 65 million years ago.

D is correct because the Cenozoic era began about 65 million years ago and continues today.

Lesson 1 Alternative Assessment

Climb the Ladder: *Fossil Hunters*

Fossil Club: Web pages summarize the five ways fossils form, and include one picture of each type of fossil.

Club Pamphlet: Pamphlets describe the five ways fossils are formed. Pamphlets include a picture of each type.

Climate Quiz: Quizzes contain at least five questions that deal with Earth's climates and the changes they have undergone.

Climate Clues: News reports describe the fossil findings and tell what the plant evidence indicates about the climate in the past.

Not a Trace: Lectures define trace fossils, provide examples, and explain how to distinguish them from other fossils.

Fossil Television: Scripts and performances describe how scientists use trace fossils to learn about animals.

Lesson 2 Alternative Assessment

Tic-Tac-Toe: *Create a Museum Exhibit*

Half-Life Breakdown: Posters or displays explain what a half-life is, and discuss how scientists use half-life in radiometric dating.

You Ask the Questions: Quizzes contain at least four questions that deal with index fossils and the ways scientists use them.

Relative Brochure: Brochures compare disturbed and undisturbed sedimentary rock layers. They also explain how the laws of superposition and crosscutting are used to order disturbed and undisturbed rock layers. Brochures should include diagrams.

Dating Description: Presentations list and describe the different methods of relative dating. They include information about dating rock layers that are disturbed and undisturbed.

Decay Drama: Skits explain how radioactive decay makes it possible for scientists to date objects.

Fossil Persuasion: Speeches explain what index fossils are and why they are needed in the museum exhibit.

Meeting the Requirements: Web pages explain the requirements fossils must meet to be considered index fossils.

Come on Down!: Press releases explain what relative dating is and why people should visit the exhibit.

Old Rock and Roll?: Songs describe how scientists use absolute dating to determine the ages of rocks.

Lesson 3 Alternative Assessment

Choose Your Meal: *Geologic Dinner Time*

Sedimentary CSI: Video or Web clips describe how the composition of sedimentary rock provides evidence of the environment in which the rock formed. Clips also include explanations and visuals of composition and texture.

Functional Fossils: Models show a plant or animal fossil and describe how the fossil provides clues about changing climates and how organisms have changed over time.

Continental Breakfast: Poems or songs describe the theory of continental drift. They should also summarize the evidence that supports the changing positions of the landmasses.

A Scientist's Story: Stories include a scientist who is researching how landforms have changed over time in a particular area. Stories also explain how Earth's features indicate slow changes over time.

This Just In! News reports describe continental drift. Reports also include the evidence that supports the changing positions of the landmasses.

Climatic Conference Speeches explain the evidence that supports the theory that Earth's climates have changed over time. Speeches include information about tree rings, sea-floor sediments, and ice cores.

Post the Evidence Posters display evidence that suggests Earth's climates have changed over time. Posters include information pertaining to tree rings, sea-floor sediments, and ice cores.

Tipping the Scale Plans or models demonstrate the organization of Earth's geologic history. Plans or models include the geologic time scale's eons, eras, periods, and epochs.

Indiana ISTEP+ Review
Key Concepts
1. D   5. A
2. A   6. B
3. D   7. D
4. C   8. A

1. D See Unit 5, Lesson 3

A is incorrect because Earth is approximately 4.6 billion years old.

B is incorrect because life first appeared on Earth about 3.5 billion years ago, based on analyses of these fossils.

C is incorrect because Earth was about 1.1 billion years old when life first appeared.

D is correct because about 1.1 billion years passed between Earth's formation—about 4.6 billion years ago—and the appearance of the first life forms, about 3.5 billion years ago.

2. A See Unit 5, Lesson 1

A is correct because the fossil record documents how organisms have changed over time.

B is incorrect because continental drift is a geologic change.

C is incorrect because climatic changes represent an environmental change and do not provide evidence for biological change.

D is incorrect because ice core analysis provides information about past environmental conditions.

3. D See Unit 5, Lesson 3

A is incorrect because eons are the largest units of geologic time.

B is incorrect because eras are the next largest units of geologic time.

C is incorrect because periods are the third largest units of geologic time.

D is correct because epochs are the smallest of these four units geologic time.

4. C See Unit 5, Lesson 2

A is incorrect because it is not a key characteristic of index fossils.

B is incorrect because abundance is a key characteristic of index fossils.

C is correct because a short span of existence is a key characteristic of index fossils.

D is incorrect because distinctiveness is a key characteristic of index fossils.

5. A See Unit 5, Lesson 3

A is correct because the Mesozoic era ended about 65 million years ago, with the start of the Cenozoic era.

B is incorrect because the chart does not indicate when reptiles evolved.

C is incorrect because the Paleozoic era lasted approximately 295 million years.

D is incorrect Earth's geologic history begun when the planet formed about 4.6 billion years ago.

6. B See Unit 5, Lesson 2

A is incorrect because the rock layers must be older than 2.5 million years to contain Fossils A and B.

B is correct because the range of the ages of the fossils can be used to estimate the age of the rock layer.

C is incorrect because the scientist cannot determine the exact age of the rock layers based on the data given in the table.

D is incorrect because the scientist cannot determine the exact age of the rock layers based on the data given in the table.

7. D See Unit 5, Lesson 3

A is incorrect because the geologic time scale does not help scientists to arrange rock layers.

B is incorrect because the geologic time scale itself cannot be used to determine the absolute ages of rocks.

C is incorrect because the fossils are used to help determine the arrangement of the geologic time scale.

D is correct because Earth's history is immense and more easily studied when divided into distinct time periods.

8. A See Unit 5, Lesson 1

A is correct because index fossils existed for short periods of time; their presence in the two rock layers indicates a similar relative age for the rocks.

B is incorrect because the rock layers would not contain similar index fossils if they formed at different times.

C is incorrect because there is not enough information to determine if the rock layers were undisturbed.

D is incorrect because there is not enough information to determine if the rock layers have unconformities.

Constructed Response
9. See Unit 5, Lesson 3
Key Elements:
• The climate was once warmer (when the layer with the plant fossil formed), and then it got colder (after the layer that was covered with an ice sheet formed).

AND

• Relative dating is a method of dating in which a fossil is compared to other objects to find out if it is older of younger than those objects. Absolute dating is a method of dating in which the age of an object is measured in years, not relative to other objects.

Extended Response
10. See Unit 5, Lesson 2
Key Elements:
• An index fossil is a fossil that is used to determine the age range of a rock layer.

AND

- An index fossil is very distinctive, so it is easy to identify. An index fossil is abundant.

AND

- An index fossil is widely distributed. An index fossil represents an organism that was on Earth for only a short time.

AND

- When an index fossil is found in a rock, it means that the rock must have formed at the same time as the index fossil. So, when scientists find that fossil, they know how old the rock is.

Rubric:
4 points Four key elements
3 points Three key elements
2 points Two key elements
1 point One key element
0 points Other

Unit Test A

Key Concepts

1.	C	5.	B	9.	B
2.	A	6.	A	10.	C
3.	D	7.	B	11.	D
4.	C	8.	D	12.	B

1. C

A is incorrect because it shows the time units from largest to smallest.

B is incorrect because epoch and period are reversed, and so are era and eon.

C is correct because it shows the time units from smallest to largest.

D is incorrect because era and eon follow epoch and precede period.

2. A

A is correct because comparing fern fossil to the cactus plants in the same geographic area can provide information about changes in climate over time.

B is incorrect because ice cores are used to show climate change over time, but would not be used in an area with no ice.

C is incorrect because a comparison of a fossil and a living organism would not provide information about changes in the atmosphere.

D is incorrect because a comparison of a fossil and a living organism would not provide information about the absolute age of the rock in which the fossil was found.

3. D

A is incorrect because the fault cuts through all of the layers and rocks, so it is the youngest feature.

B is incorrect because rock 1 cuts through rock 2, so rock 1 is younger.

C is incorrect because rock 2 cuts through layer 1, so rock 2 is younger.

D is correct because the fault, rock 1, and rock 2 cut through layer 1, so they formed after layer 1 formed.

4. C

A is incorrect; Earth is 4.6 billion years old.

B is incorrect because Earth is 4.6 billion years old.

C is correct because radiometric dating of rocks indicates that Earth is 4.6 billion years old.

D is incorrect because Earth is 4.6 billion years old.

5. B

A is incorrect because mammals did not evolve until after the Paleozoic era, and they became dominant only during the Cenozoic era.

B is correct because mammals became dominant during the Cenozoic era.

C is incorrect because mammals did not exist during Precambrian time.

D is incorrect because although mammals evolved in the Mesozoic era, they did not become dominant until the Cenozoic era.

6. A

A is correct because the more similar a fossil is to a living organism, the more likely the fossil and the living organism are separated by a shorter span of time.

B is incorrect because the fossil in Rock *B* would most likely be older than the fossil in Rock *A*. The greater the differences between a fossil and a living organism, the more likely they are separated by long spans of time.

C is incorrect because the fossils represent organisms that lived at different times in Earth's history; they indicate that the rock layers are not the same age.

D is incorrect because index fossils can be used to determine relative ages of rocks in which they are found.

7. B

A is correct because Ricardo is modeling what happens when a shell or bone makes an impression in sedimentary rock, which is an example of fossil formation.

B is incorrect because Ricardo is not modeling how to take a long cylinder of ice from an ice cap.

C is incorrect because Ricardo is not modeling how a gap in the rock record forms when rock layers are eroded or when sediment is not deposited over a long time.

D is incorrect because Ricardo is not modeling an ordered arrangement of rock layers.

8. D

A is incorrect because bone fossils are not necessarily helpful in estimating rock ages unless they have certain properties, such as widespread distribution and short geologic lifespan.

B is incorrect because fossils are not classified as trapped.

C is incorrect because trace fossils are not necessarily helpful in estimating rock ages unless they have certain properties, such as widespread distribution and short geologic lifespan.

D is correct because index fossils have the properties necessarily to estimate the ages of rock layers, such as widespread distribution and short geologic life span.

9. B

A is incorrect because *absolute decay* is not a correct term. Determining the absolute age of an event or object is absolute dating.

B is correct because the diagram shows the radioactive decay of carbon-14.

C is incorrect because *relative dating* does not involve using radioactive isotopes.

D is incorrect because *unconformity* is a gap in the geologic rock record. Unconformities are used to determine the relative age of a rock layer.

10. C

A is incorrect because the Cenozoic era is the most recent era and has the most information about life forms.

B is incorrect because life forms with hard parts evolved during the Paleozoic era and many of these hard parts were preserved as fossils.

C is correct because life forms during Precambrian time had soft bodies and very few were preserved as fossils.

D is incorrect because fossils from the Mesozoic era are relatively plentiful.

11. D

A is incorrect because human ancestors are associated with a later era.

B is incorrect because human ancestors are associated with a later era.

C is incorrect because humans evolved much later in geologic time.

D is correct because humans evolved during the Cenozoic era.

12. B

A is incorrect because eons are the largest geologic time units.

B is correct because eras are divided into periods.

C is incorrect because eons are divided into eras.

D is incorrect because ages are the smallest geologic time units.

Constructed Response

13. Key Elements:
• tree rings

AND

• Tree rings provide scientists with information about Earth's climatic conditions that existed during the life of a tree.

Rubric:
2 points Two key elements
1 point One key element
0 points Other

Extended Response

14. Key Elements:
• The geologic time scale is the standard method used to divide Earth's history into smaller, more manageable parts.

AND

• Major events such as mass extinctions and the break-up of continents are used to define the boundary between one time unit and the next.

AND

• Timelines should show that Precambrian time lasted from 4.6 bya to 544 mya. The Paleozoic era lasted from 544 mya to 248 mya. The Mesozoic era lasted from 248 mya to 65 mya. The Cenozoic era began 65 mya and continues today.

AND

• Sample details might include the following: Precambrian time makes up 90 percent of Earth's history. Organisms with hard parts formed during the Paleozoic era. The Mesozoic era is known as the "Age of Dinosaurs." The Cenozoic era is known as the "Age of Mammals." Accept all accurate details.

Unit Test B

Key Concepts

1. B	5. A	9. D
2. C	6. A	10. C
3. C	7. A	11. B
4. B	8. D	12. A

1. B

A is incorrect because high latitudes are cold parts of Earth, and tropical ferns cannot survive in cold areas.

B is correct because tropical ferns are found in equatorial regions.

C is incorrect because mid-altitudes are temperate parts of Earth, and tropical ferns are not found in temperate climates.

D is incorrect because the poles are some of the coldest parts of Earth, and tropical ferns cannot survive in cold areas.

2. C

A is incorrect because index fossils, though common, are not geographically limited.

B is incorrect because index fossils are representative of organisms that lived for a short period, not a long period, of geologic time.

C is correct because index fossils represent species that were widespread and common.

D is incorrect because these characteristics are not associated with index fossils.

3. C

A is incorrect because information provided by ocean sediments goes back further in time than information provided by ice cores.

B is incorrect because ice cores can provide information that goes back more than 100,000 years.

C is correct because the line representing ice cores extends past the point marked 100,000 years on the timeline.

D is incorrect because the figure lists other sources of information, including tree rings and ocean sediments.

4. B

A is incorrect because climate is an environmental, not a biological, factor.

B is correct because organisms provide biological information.

C is incorrect because rocks are geologic, not biological, factors.

D is incorrect because rocks are geologic, not biological, factors.

5. A

A is correct because petrified objects are fossils that form when minerals slowly replace a dead organism's tissues.

B is incorrect because fossils are unlikely to be found in urban areas that have been paved.

C is incorrect because the Bronx Zoo is home to living animals and plants.

D is incorrect because trenches are the deepest parts of oceans and are difficult to reach.

6. A

A is correct because pine trees would not have lived in an aquatic environment.

B is incorrect because fossils of fish would likely be found in rocks once covered by seawater.

C is incorrect because fossils of seashells would likely be found in rocks once covered by seawater.

D is incorrect because fossils of sharks would likely be found in rocks once covered by seawater.

7. A

A is correct because an epoch is a subdivision of a period, which in turn is a subdivision of an era.

B is incorrect because eras also cover recent geologic time.

C is incorrect because eras can also be characterized by mass extinctions.

D is incorrect because eras are also shorter than eons.

8. D

A is incorrect because climate is usually considered to be an environmental factor.

B is incorrect because DNA relationships provide little information about geologic processes.

C is incorrect because comparing frozen fossils from two different places would likely give biological information and not information about geologic processes.

D is correct because fossils can be used to determine when a rock likely formed.

9. D

A is incorrect because feathers for warmth would not be an adaptation in a desert.

B is incorrect because a tropical rain forest is always warm, so an adaptation for warmth is not necessary.

C is incorrect. The equator and the regions near it are the hottest on Earth, so an adaptation such as feathers to keep warm is not necessary.

D is correct because the feathers could be an adaptation to help keep the dinosaurs warm in cold weather.

10. C

A is incorrect because catastrophic events rather than slow processes distinguish geologic eras from one another.

B is incorrect because the location of the poles is not used to distinguish geologic eras.

C is correct because mass extinctions and other catastrophic events often serve as the boundaries between geologic eras.

D is incorrect because earthquakes are too common to be used to divide geologic time into different eras.

11. B

A is incorrect because organisms first appear in the fossil record during Precambrian time.

B is correct because organisms with hard body parts did not evolve until the Paleozoic era.

C is incorrect because Precambrian time makes up 90 percent of Earth's geologic history.

D is incorrect because rock layers do exist from Precambrian time.

12. A

A is correct because dinosaurs were dominant during the Mesozoic era.

B is incorrect because dinosaurs were extinct by the beginning of the Cenozoic era.

C is incorrect because only simple organisms are associated with Precambrian time.

D is incorrect because dinosaurs had not yet evolved by the end of the Paleozoic era.

Constructed Response

13. Key Elements:
- The intrusion is younger than the bottom layer.

AND

- The law of crosscutting relationships states that a feature such as an intrusion or fault is younger than any other body of rock that it cuts through.

Rubric:
2 points Two key elements
1 point One key element
0 points Other

Extended Response

14. Key Elements:
- The drawing represents the radioactive decay of an isotope.

AND

- The parent isotope is thorium-232. The daughter isotope is lead-208.

AND

- During radioactive decay, the unstable isotope thorium-232 emits particles and energy as it decays. When thorium decays, it produces lead-208. Over time, there will be less thorium and more lead.

AND

- Lead-208 is a stable isotope, so when all the thorium has decayed to lead, the decay process ends.

Rubric:
4 points Four key elements
3 points Three key elements
2 points Two key elements
1 point One key element
0 points Other

Unit 6 The Cell
Unit Pretest

1.	D	5.	B	9.	D
2.	A	6.	C	10.	D
3.	A	7.	C		
4.	B	8.	D		

1. D

A is incorrect because DNA is one of the structures in an organism and, by itself, cannot carry out all the functions of life.

B is incorrect because a nucleus is an organelle in eukaryotes, and, by itself, cannot carry out all the functions of life.

C is incorrect because cytoplasm is part of the structure of an organism and, by itself, cannot carry out all the functions of life.

D is correct because a prokaryote is a single-celled organism with structures that can carry out all the functions of life.

2. A

A is correct because water makes up about two-thirds of each cell in the human body, and is used in most cell processes.

B is incorrect because salt makes up less than 1% of the human body.

C is incorrect because carbon dioxide is a waste product that is toxic to humans in large quantities.

D is incorrect because sodium bicarbonate is baking soda and is not naturally found in the human body.

3. A

A is correct because the presence of a nucleus is a characteristic of eukaryotic cells and is not found in prokaryotic cells.

B is incorrect because cytoplasm is found in both prokaryotic and eukaryotic cells.

C is incorrect because a cell membrane is found in both prokaryotic and eukaryotic cells.

D is incorrect because genetic material is found in both prokaryotic and eukaryotic cells.

4. B

A is incorrect because although plants have cell walls, the cell wall does not carry out photosynthesis.

B is correct because chloroplasts, which are not found in animal cells, use energy from the sun to make sugar.

C is incorrect because lysosomes are found in animal cells, not plant cells.

D is incorrect because both plant and animal cells have nuclei.

5. B

A is incorrect because connective tissue is a type of animal tissue.

B is correct because the fruit of a plant is ground tissue, which stores nutrients in a plant.

C is incorrect because protective tissue covers and protects parts of a plant.

D is incorrect because transport tissue carries water and nutrients throughout a plant.

6. C

A is incorrect because endocytosis is a process in which materials are taken in by a cell, and the diagram shows the cell cycle.

B is incorrect because exocytosis is a process in which materials are eliminated by a cell, and the diagram shows the cell cycle.

C is correct because the diagram shows the cell cycle, in which a cell divides to make two new cells.

D is incorrect because cellular respiration is the process in which cells make ATP, and the diagram shows the cell cycle.

7. C

A is incorrect because the sun is not a living organism.

B is incorrect because a plant is made up of cells, and the cell is the basic unit of life.

C is correct because it shows a cell, which is the basic unit of life.

D is incorrect because an insect is made up of cells, and the cell is the basic unit of life.

8. D

A is incorrect because replacing damaged and dying cells is the main reason for cell division, not material exchange.

B is incorrect because although the cell membrane facilitates material exchange, cells don't exchange materials to keep the cell membrane functioning.

C is incorrect because cells do not exchange materials to release energy into their environments. Cells store energy for their own use.

D is correct because cells exchange materials with the environments around them so they can get rid of wastes and take in nutrients.

9. D

A is incorrect because both prokaryotic cells and eukaryotic cells have cytoplasm.

B is incorrect because both prokaryotic and eukaryotic cells have cell membranes.

C is incorrect because genetic material is present in both types of cells.

D is correct because eukaryotic cells have membrane-bound organelles, and prokaryotic cells do not.

10. D

A is incorrect because organs are made of tissues.

B is incorrect because some organisms are made of different types of organ systems, and each organ system is made up of different organs.

C is incorrect because organ systems are made up of different organs. Each organ is made up of different types of tissue, and each type of tissue is made up of different types of cells.

D is correct because organ systems are made up of different organs.

Lesson 1 Quiz

1.	A	4.	B
2.	A	5.	C
3.	B		

1. A

A is correct because all organisms reproduce.

B is incorrect because some unicellular organisms are eukaryotes, which have nuclei.

C is incorrect because unicellular organisms can be prokaryotes or eukaryotes.

D is incorrect because unicellular organisms can be prokaryotes or eukaryotes.

2. A

A is correct because cell division results in the production of new cells.

B is incorrect because not all cells have nuclei, and cells without nuclei also reproduce.

C is incorrect because although cells can move around, movement alone does not result in cell division.

D is incorrect because although all cells have membranes, the presence of a cell membrane alone does not result in cell division.

3. B

A is incorrect because DNA is contained within most cells and is necessary for cell division, one of the many necessary life processes.

B is correct because an organism is made up of one or more cells and carries out all of its own activities for life.

C is incorrect because organelles are structures contained within most cells that help the cell to perform life processes.

D is incorrect because cytoplasm is the region inside the cell membrane that includes the fluid and all of the organelles except the nucleus.

4. B

A is incorrect because prokaryotes do not have nuclei.

B is correct because the DNA in prokaryotes is contained in part of the cytoplasm.

C is incorrect because flagella are hairlike structures that help some prokaryotes to move around.

D is incorrect because membrane-bound organelles are a characteristic of eukaryotic cells.

5. C

A is incorrect because the excretion of waste does not lead to the production of more cells.

B is incorrect because the presence of cytoplasm does not lead to the production of more cells.

C is correct because cell division is the process by which cells reproduce to make more cells.

D is incorrect because taking in nutrients from the environment does not lead to the production of more cells.

Lesson 2 Quiz

1. B   4. B
2. A   5. D
3. C

1. B

A is incorrect because gold is an element not found in the body.

B is correct because water is an essential compound made of one oxygen and two hydrogen atoms.

C is incorrect because nitrogen is an element, not a compound.

D is incorrect because hydrogen peroxide is a compound not found in the body.

2. A

A is correct because carbohydrates provide cells with energy.

B is incorrect because proteins are made up of amino acids.

C is incorrect because phospholipids, not carbohydrates, form cell membranes.

D is incorrect because enzymes, not carbohydrates, help chemical processes happen.

3. C

A is incorrect because proteins are made up of amino acids.

B is incorrect because calcium, not lipids, is used to repair broken bones.

C is correct because phospholipids are lipids that contain phosphorus and make up the cell membrane.

D is incorrect because nucleic acids, not lipids, carry information in the cell. DNA is a type of nucleic acid.

4. B

A is incorrect because lipids are fats and oils, not enzymes.

B is correct because enzymes are proteins that help chemical processes happen in cells.

C is incorrect because nucleic acids are made of nucleotides, not enzymes.

D is incorrect because carbohydrates are sugars, starches, and fiber, not enzymes.

5. D

A is incorrect because taking in salt would further reduce the concentration of water molecules inside the cell.

B is incorrect because water concentration does not initiate cell division.

C is incorrect because water moves out of the cell when the environment around a cell has low concentrations of water.

D is correct because water moves into the cell when the concentration of water outside the cell is lower than the concentration of water inside the cell. Too much water could cause the cell to burst.

Lesson 3 Quiz

1. A   4. B
2. C   5. C
3. B

1. A

A is correct because the cytoskeleton is a web of proteins that supports a cell and can help to move materials inside the cell. Some organisms use it to move the entire organism.

B is incorrect because the nucleus is the membrane-bound organelle that contains the genetic material.

C is incorrect because cell membranes enclose cells and separate their cytoplasm from the environment.

D is incorrect because DNA contains the information needed for cell processes, such as making proteins.

2. C

A is incorrect because the cytoskeleton supports the cell's shape.

B is incorrect because DNA is found inside the nucleus in eukaryotes. It is located in part of the cytoplasm in prokaryotes.

C is correct because the cell membrane separates the cell from its environment.

D is incorrect because DNA consists of the genetic information needed by the cell.

3. B

A is incorrect because the size of the nuclei does not influence protein production.

B is correct because ribosomes are the organelles that make proteins.

C is incorrect because mitochondria are not directly involved with protein production.

D is incorrect because cell membranes are not directly involved with protein production.

4. B

A is incorrect because the Golgi complex packages and distributes materials in both plant and animal cells.

B is correct because lysosomes are responsible for breaking down waste materials inside animal cells. Plant cells do not contain lysosomes.

C is incorrect because ribosomes are organelles where proteins are made in both plant and animal cells.

D is incorrect because the rough endoplasmic reticulum is involved in the production and processing of proteins in both plant and animal cells.

5. C

A is incorrect because chloroplasts are the site for photosynthesis, the plant process that uses carbon dioxide, water, and sunlight to produce sugar and oxygen.

B is incorrect because lysosomes are the organelles that break down waste materials in animal cells.

C is correct because mitochondria are the site for cellular respiration, which breaks down sugar to produce ATP in plant and animal cells.

D is incorrect because the nucleus contains the genetic material in plant and animal cells.

Lesson 4 Quiz

1. C   4. B
2. A   5. D
3. B

1. C

A is incorrect because the organs described are not part of the reproductive systems of either plants or animals.

B is incorrect because nervous tissues, not cardiovascular tissues, send messages throughout the body, and they are present only in animals.

C is correct because the tissues and organs of the cardiovascular system and the xylem and phloem in plants function in the transport of materials.

D is incorrect because bone, connective tissue, and other parts of the skeletal system provide structure and support in some animals, not the cardiovascular system.

2. A

A is correct because growth is a main reason why cells divide.

B is incorrect because cells can remove waste without dividing.

C is incorrect because cells can take in and use oxygen without dividing.

D is incorrect because only photosynthetic organisms make their own food, and cell division is not related to making more food.

3. B

A is incorrect because cells obtain energy using cellular respiration to break down food, not from mitosis.

B is correct because skin cells divide to replace dead or damaged skin cells.

C is incorrect because mitosis does not prevent bruises.

D is incorrect because skin cells divide to form new skin cells, not muscle cells.

4. B

A is incorrect because passive transport does not require the cell to use energy and active transport does.

B is correct because active transport requires energy to move substances against a concentration gradient. Passive transport does not require the cell to use energy.

C is incorrect because diffusion is passive transport, which does not require the cell to use energy.

D is incorrect because exocytosis is active transport, which requires the cell to use energy.

5. D

A is incorrect because hibernation is a behavioral, not a physical, response.

B is incorrect because migration is a behavioral, not a physical, response.

C is incorrect because performing tricks for food is a behavioral, not a physical, response.

D is correct because a plant turning toward the light is a physical response to the direction of the light source.

Lesson 5 Quiz

1. A   4. D
2. B   5. B
3. C

1. A

A is correct because after fertilization, cells divide to form the embryo, which develops into all the specialized tissues and organs of a multicellular organism.

B is incorrect because cell division does not take place before fertilization.

C is incorrect because the development of an embryo and specialized tissues cannot take place before cell division.

D is incorrect because the embryo cannot develop before fertilization.

2. B

A is incorrect because photosynthesis does not occur in fruit.

B is correct because a leaf is an organ that contains chloroplasts, which trap light energy for photosynthesis.

C is incorrect because photosynthesis does not happen in petals.

D is incorrect because photosynthesis does not happen in roots.

3. C

A is incorrect because ground tissue is a plant tissue that stores nutrients.

B is incorrect because muscle tissue moves bones or organs in the body.

C is correct because nerve tissue is made of nerve cells (neurons) that carry signals to and from different parts of the body.

D is incorrect because protective tissue surrounds and protects structures.

4. D

A is incorrect because only multicellular organisms have more than one cell.

B is incorrect because multicellular organisms generally live longer than unicellular organisms.

C. is incorrect because both unicellular and multicellular organisms perform functions necessary for life..

D is correct because multicellular organisms have cells that develop from an embryo into specialized tissues and organs, and unicellular organisms do not have specialized tissue and organs.

5. B

A is incorrect because skin cells are part of epithelial tissue and do not transport materials.

B is correct because red blood cells transport oxygen and carbon dioxide throughout the body.

C is incorrect because nerve cells carry electrical signals from stimuli; they do not carry oxygen or carbon dioxide.

D is incorrect because muscle cells are part of tissue that enables motion; they do not carry oxygen and carbon dioxide throughout the body.

Lesson 1 Alternative Assessment

Tic-Tac-Toe: The Basic Form of Life

Historical Cell Fiction: Writing describes a conversation that could have happened between three scientists who developed the cell theory. May include information about how the discoveries of Schwann, Schlieden, and Virchow contributed to the development of the cell theory.

Something in Common: Drawing includes a eukaryotic and a prokaryotic cell. The major parts of each cell are labeled. Yarn or string connects the common parts, such as the cell membrane and cytoplasm.

A Great Adventure: Guidebook relates the functions of cell organelles to rides at an amusement park. Guidebook describes each ride and what it does. It includes a color-coded map.

A Simple Cell: Poem describes a prokaryotic cell, and includes facts about a bacteria or archaea.

How It Works: Essay explains why it is good to be small, and includes information about why a cell must be small, and why it cannot survive if it is too large.

Time Capsule: Journal entries are written from the point of view of Theodor Schwann, and describe how three things he concluded about cells.

A Model of a Cell: Model shows each organelle in a different color and labels each organelle. The model also includes a key.

Public Service Announcement: Announcement includes information about the importance of the cell theory and includes a drawing.

A New Report: Report includes information about a one-celled organism that lives inside of the human body. Report includes the name of the bacterium, what it does, and where it can be found.

Lesson 2 Alternative Assessment

Points of View: Exploring Atoms and Molecules

Vocabulary: Each vocabulary word is defined using students own words, and then each word is defined using a dictionary or textbook definition. Last, each term is used in a sentence.

Details: Descriptions explain how sugars and starches are related to carbohydrates, how amino acids are related to proteins, and how DNA and nucleotides are related to nucleic acids.

Illustrations: Pictures show an atom, a molecule, and a compound such as a water molecule. An illustration shows how atoms, molecules, and compounds are related to cells.

Analysis: Diagram explains how molecules, atoms, elements, and compounds relate to one another.

Models: Models show cell membranes and how the phospholipid molecules form this membrane.

Lesson 3 Alternative Assessment

Mix and Match: Structure and Function of Cell Organelles

The difference between prokaryotes and eukaryotes: The differences between prokaryotes and eukaryotes are correctly described. (Prokaryotic cells have a cell membrane, cytoplasm, and genetic material, but the genetic material in a prokaryote is not contained in a nucleus. All eukaryotic cells have cell membranes, cytoplasm, organelles, and genetic material contained in the nucleus.)

The general characteristics of the eukaryotic cell: The general characteristics of the eukaryotic cell are described. (All eukaryotic cells have cell membranes, cytoplasm (which includes membrane-bound organelles), and genetic material contained in the nucleus of each cell. Eukaryotes also have common organelles that include mitochondria, ribosomes, endoplasmic reticulum, Golgi complex.)

How mitochondria function: The way mitochrondria function is correctly explained.

(Mitochondria are double-membrane organelles. Many folds in the inner membrane increase the surface area inside the mitochondria available to perform cellular respiration. Cellular respiration is the process cells use to break down sugars to release energy stored in the sugar, Mitochondria transfer the energy released from sugar to a molecule called ATP. Cells use ATP to do work.)

How the ribosomes, ER and Golgi complex work together: How ribosomes, ER, and Golgi complex work together is correctly described.

(Ribosomes are organelles that make proteins. The ER is a system of folded membranes in which proteins, lipids, and other materials are made. The ER transports substances throughout the cell. Rough ER is found near the nucleus. Ribosomes on the rough ER make proteins. Rough ER delivers the proteins throughout the cell. Smooth ER does not have ribosomes and it makes lipids. Lipids and proteins are delivered to the Golgi complex from the ER to be modified and transported in a vesicle for use in or out of the cell.)

The cell wall and large central vacuoles of plants: The differences and similarities between cell walls and the large central vacuoles of plants are correctly described. (Cell walls are found outside the cell membrane and provide structure and protection to the cell. The large central vacuole in a plant cell is a membrane-bound cavity that stores water. Central vacuoles also help support the cell.)

Chloroplasts and lysosomes: The differences between chloroplasts found in plant cells and the lysosomes found in animal cells are correctly described. (Chloroplasts trap the energy of sunlight and use it to make sugar in plants. Lysosomes are responsible for digestion in animals.)

Lesson 4 Alternative Assessment

Climb the Ladder: Maintaining Homeostasis

Illustrate a Poster: Poster shows the process of photosynthesis and cellular respiration. Explanations tell how these two processes are essential for cell survival and how the two processes relate.

Build a Model: 3-D model shows the processes of photosynthesis and cellular respiration. Model is labeled. Explanation describes both processes and why they are essential to cell survival.

Write a Picture Book: Picture book shows the different stages of the cell cycle. The nucleus, chromosomes, and chromatids are labeled. One sentence on each page explains what happens at each stage of the cell cycle.

Be a Broadcaster: News report describes what happens as a cell divides.

Write a Skit: Skit describes passive and active transport and explains how these methods of transport help cells maintain balance.

Create an Animation: Animation demonstrates passive and active transport. Description explains both types of transport and how these help the cell maintain balance.

Lesson 5 Alternative Assessment

Tic-Tac-Toe: Design Artificial Organs

Structure and Function: Descriptions highlight two organs and how the structure of each helps it to function. Then one organ is analyzed to describe the type of structure that would be ideal for its function and why.

Diagram: Diagram includes at least two organ systems, and describes how they work together.

Organ Journal: Journal entries describe two organ systems for artificial life, and include a diagram of the organs.

Human Cell Types: Descriptions explain the function of 10 human cell types. Students pick one cell type and tell why they would want to design artificial life with this cell type, or why this cell type could never be made artificially.

Building a System: Skits describe the four levels of organization in a multicellular organism (cell, tissue, organ, organ system).

Instruction Booklet: Instruction booklet names the organs in an organ system and describes how the system is used.

Designer Cell: Design includes both structure and function of an imaginary specialized cell.

Life in a Pond: Poems compares adaptations of a single-celled paramecium with those of a multicellular sunfish in a freshwater pond.

Which Tissue? Speech explains the functions of four types of tissues in humans, and makes an argument about which tissue is the most useful.

Indiana ISTEP+ Review

Key Concepts

1. A	5. B	9. C
2. C	6. A	10. C
3. D	7. B	
4. B	8. B	

1. A See Unit 6, Lesson 1

A is correct. The nucleus contains the cell's DNA.

B is incorrect because a nucleus is an organelle.

C is incorrect because the cytoplasm fills the inside of the cell and surrounds the nucleus.

D is incorrect because the cell membrane covers the cell's surface and is not on the inside of the cell.

2. C See Unit 6, Lesson 5

A is incorrect because cells are the most basic (smallest) level of cellular organization.

B is incorrect because specialized cells are not able to perform all functions necessary for life; they perform specialized functions.

C is correct because specialized tissues and organs have specific functions, and must work together to meet the needs of the organism.

D is incorrect because tissues and organs have specialized functions, not similar functions. Also, if they worked independently of each other, the needs of the organism would not be met.

3. D See Unit 6, Lesson 1

A is incorrect because a eukaryotic cell has its DNA contained in a nucleus, and the DNA in cell B is in its cytoplasm.

B is incorrect because both cells have cytoplasm.

C is incorrect because both cells have cell membranes.

D is correct because a eukaryotic cell has a nucleus, and cell A has a nucleus.

4. B See Unit 6, Lesson 2

A is incorrect because nearly two-thirds of the cell's mass is made up of water.

B is correct because nearly two-thirds of the cell's mass is made up of water.

C is incorrect because nearly two-thirds of the cell's mass is made up of water.

D is incorrect because nearly two-thirds of the cell's mass is made up of water.

5. B See Unit 6, Lesson 5

A is incorrect because the statement is false; multicellular organisms live longer than unicellular organisms.

B is correct because the statement is true; unicellular organisms are smaller than multicellular organisms.

C is incorrect because the statement is false; unicellular organisms are made of just one cell.

D is incorrect because the statement is false; unicellular organisms have just one cell, not multiple cells that work together.

6. A See Unit 6, Lesson 3

A is correct because plant cells have cell walls, and animal cells do not.

B is incorrect because although the cell is a plant cell, both plant and animal cells have nuclei.

C is incorrect because the cell has structures, such as a cell wall, that are found only in plant cells.

D is incorrect because the diagram shows chloroplasts and a cell wall, which means that this is a plant cell.

7. B See Unit 6, Lesson 4

A is incorrect because excretion of wastes is not part of cell division.

B is correct because the cells of an organism divide and make new cells so that an organism can grow.

C is incorrect because cellular respiration, not cell division, is the process that cells use to obtain energy from food.

D is incorrect because the exchange of materials with the environment helps maintain homeostasis and is not a reason for cell division.

8. B See Unit 6, Lesson 5

A is incorrect because an organ system and an organism are larger than an organ.

B is correct because tissue is made of cells, an organ is made of tissues, an organ system is made of organs, and an organism is made of organ systems.

C is incorrect because tissue is larger than a cell, and an organ system is larger than an organ.

D is incorrect because tissue is larger than a cell, and an organism is larger than an organ system.

9. C See Unit 6, Lesson 3

A is incorrect because plant cells have cell walls and do not have lysosomes.

B is incorrect because fungus cells have cell walls.

C is correct because animal cells have ribosomes, mitochondria, and lysosomes but not cell walls.

D is incorrect because prokaryotic cells do not have mitochondria or lysosomes but do have cell walls.

10. C See Unit 6, Lesson 5

A is incorrect because the nervous system is involved with the transfer of signals.

B is incorrect because the skeletal system involves bones.

C is correct because the circulatory system involves the movement of fluids and nutrients throughout the body, similar to the movement of water and nutrients throughout a plant's vascular system.

D is incorrect because the respiratory system is involved with the movement of oxygen and the taking in of oxygen and expelling of carbon dioxide from the body.

Constructed Response
11. See Unit 6, Lesson 5
Key Elements:
- organ: leaf OR stem OR root
- organ system: leaf and stem system (shoot system) OR root system
- organism: plant

AND (any ONE of the following):
- leaf—involved in photosynthesis which provides food for the plant.
- stem—provides support for the plant to hold it upright; contains tissues that transport water, nutrients, and food throughout the plant.
- root— reach into the soil to obtain water and nutrients; contain tissue that helps transport the water and nutrients up to the rest of the plant.

Rubric:
2 points Four key elements
1 point Two or three key elements
0 points Other

Extended Response
12. See Unit 6, Lesson 1
Key Elements:
Data table correctly describes, organizes, and displays all information: (two key elements)
- all columns/rows labeled appropriately
- table organized/labeled so that data relationships can be determined
- all data entered correctly

Exemplary response:

Structure	Prokaryotic cell	Eukaryotic cell
cell membrane	Yes	Yes
cytoplasm	Yes	Yes
nucleus	No	Yes

AND (any ONE of the following):
- cell membrane—surrounds cell, allows certain materials into and out of cell
- cytoplasm—gives cell shape, supports cell organelles
- nucleus—in eukaryotes, contains DNA, directs cell activities

AND (one of the following):
- Prokaryotes—organelles not surrounded by membrane (no membrane-bound organelles); eukaryotes—organelles surrounded by membrane (membrane-bound organelles).
- Prokaryotes – DNA in cytoplasm; eukaryotes – DNA contained in nucleus.

Rubric:
4 points Four key elements
3 points Three key elements
2 points Two key elements
1 point One key element
0 points Other

Unit Test A
Key Concepts
1. D   5. A   9. C
2. C   6. D   10. B
3. C   7. C   11. A
4. B   8. A   12. D

1. D

A is incorrect because an organelle is a structure inside a cell and is not a type of cell.

B is incorrect because a membrane is a structure that surrounds a cell and is not a type of cell.

C is incorrect because a eukaryotic cell has a nucleus, and this cell does not have a nucleus.

D is correct because a prokaryotic cell has no nucleus, but contains its DNA in the cytoplasm.

2. C

A is incorrect because chloroplasts perform photosynthesis; ribosomes produce proteins.

B is incorrect because chloroplasts perform photosynthesis; vacuoles store water and food.

C is correct because the main function of the chloroplasts is to perform photosynthesis.

D is incorrect because the chloroplasts perform photosynthesis; the cell wall surrounds and protects plant cells.

3. C

A is incorrect because in a multicellular organism, each type of cell performs one function according to its location and role in the organism.

B is incorrect because different types of cells in multicellular organisms perform different functions.

C is correct because in a multicellular organism, each type of cell has a specialized function.

D is incorrect because organelles do not perform all functions; each organelle has a particular function.

4. B

A is incorrect because although iron is found in the blood, it is not one of the six most common elements found in humans.

B is correct because oxygen is one of the six most common elements found in humans.

C is incorrect because helium is not found in humans.

D is incorrect because although water is found in humans, it is not an element.

5. A

A is correct because the diagram shows an organ system. A lung is an organ in the body's respiratory system.

B is incorrect because a lung is an organ. It is made of different types of tissue.

C is incorrect because a lung is an organ. There can be many organs in a multicellular organism.

D is incorrect because a lung is an organ. It is part of an organ system.

6. D

A is incorrect because a cytoskeleton is the web of proteins that helps support and give structure to the cell.

B is incorrect because lysosomes are much smaller than nuclei and each cell may contain many lysosomes in the cytoplasm.

C is incorrect because each cell may contain many mitochondria in the cytoplasm.

D is correct because a nucleus is the single, membrane-bound organelle that is usually found near the center of a cell.

7. C

A is incorrect because although plant cells have cell walls, animal cells do not.

B is incorrect because although fungal cells have cell walls, animal cells do not.

C is correct because plant cells have cell walls. Some bacteria, archaea, fungi and protists also have cell walls.

D is incorrect because animal cells do not have a cell wall.

8. A

A is correct because cells divide to make new cells that can replace damaged or dead cells.

B is incorrect because cellular respiration is the process by which certain cells make ATP, not the process by which cells make new cells.

C is incorrect because cells are not replaced through endocytosis.

D is incorrect because cells do not grow larger to make up for lost cells.

9. C

A is incorrect because organism, not organ, is the most specialized level of structural organization. Organ would be on the third level of the diagram.

B is incorrect because organism, not tissue, is the most specialized level of structural organization. Tissue would be on the fourth level of the diagram.

C is correct because in multicellular organisms like animals, organism is more specialized than organ, tissue, or organ system.

D is incorrect because organism, not organ system, is the most specialized level of structural organization. Organ system would be on the second level of the diagram.

10. B

A is incorrect because nuclei are found inside cells.

B is correct because a cell membrane surrounds all cells, and a cell wall surrounds the cell membrane in plant cells, fungal cells, and bacterial cells.

C is incorrect because both the cytoplasm and the cytoskeleton are found within cells.

D is incorrect because the cytoplasm is found within cells.

11. A

A is correct because all cells need energy to perform all cell function.

B is incorrect because some cells, such as anaerobic bacteria, do not require oxygen to survive.

C is incorrect because all cells must be able to eliminate wastes, not absorb wastes, to survive.

D is incorrect because most cells do not grow continuously but stop growing once they have reached a certain size.

12. D

A is incorrect because function is the job that each part does.

B is incorrect because structure is the actual arrangement of the parts.

C is incorrect because organization is the way the parts are arranged.

D is correct because specialization is being fit for one particular purpose; each type of blood cell is specialized for a function. Specialized cells work together to form tissues, organs, and organ systems.

Constructed Response

13. Key Elements (any **three** of the following; one key element each):

- cell—neuron (nerve cell)

- tissue—nerves

- organs—either of the following: brain, spinal cord

- organ system—central nervous system

AND

neuron (nerve cell); send and receive messages from nearby neurons

Rubric:
2 points Four key elements
1 point Two or three key elements
0 points Other

Extended Response

14. Key Elements (any **two** of the following; one key element each):

- cell membrane—surrounds cell, allows certain materials into and out of cell

- cytoplasm—gives cell shape, supports cell organelles

- nucleus—contains DNA, directs cell activities

- mitochondria—where cellular respiration takes place (production of ATP)

- ribosomes—where protein synthesis takes place

- endoplasmic reticulum (ER)—either of the following: movement of materials; where proteins and lipids are made

AND

eukaryote; has nucleus and organelles surrounded by membrane

AND

animal; lacks cell wall, large central vacuole, and chloroplasts found in plant cells

Rubric:
4 points Four key elements
3 points Three key elements
2 points Two key elements
1 point One key element
0 points Other

Unit Test B

Key Concepts

1. A	5. A	9. D
2. C	6. C	10. C
3. B	7. C	11. D
4. B	8. A	12. D

1. A

A is correct because both membrane-bound organelles and nuclei are found only in eukaryotic cells.

B is incorrect because organelles without membranes are found only in prokaryotic cells.

C is incorrect because although a cell membrane is found in both types of cells, organelles without membranes are found only in prokaryotic cells.

D is incorrect because DNA in cytoplasm is a characteristic of prokaryotic cells.

2. C

A is incorrect because organism, not organ, is the most specialized level of structural organization. Organ would be on the third level of the diagram.

B is incorrect because organism, not tissue, is the most specialized level of structural organization. Tissue would be on the fourth level of the diagram.

C is correct because in multicellular organisms like animals, organism is more specialized than organ, tissue, or organ system.

D is incorrect because organism, not organ system, is the most specialized level of structural organization. Organ system would be on the second level of the diagram.

3. B

A is incorrect because in a multicellular organism, different types of cells have different functions.

B is correct because a multicellular organism contains different types of cells, and each type has a specialized function.

C is incorrect because a multicellular organism contains groups of cells that have the same function.

D is incorrect because a multicellular organism contains specialized cells that have different functions.

4. B

A is incorrect because although hydrogen, oxygen, and salts are found in cells, none is a main type of molecule in cells.

B is correct because the four main types of molecules in living things are carbohydrates, lipids, nucleic acids, and proteins.

C is incorrect because nutrients include more than one type of molecule, and carbon dioxide is a waste molecule, not a type of molecule found in living cells.

D is incorrect because atoms make up molecules; they are not a type of molecule. And chemical compounds include more than one type of molecule.

5. A

A is correct because each new cell has the same genetic information as the original cell.

B is incorrect because the two new cells are smaller than the original cell. They will eventually grow to the size of the original cell.

C is incorrect because each new cell receives a complete set of genetic information that was present in the original cell.

D is incorrect because the two cells will continue the cell cycle until they die.

6. C

A is incorrect because the cytoskeleton consists of stringy proteins dispersed throughout a cell.

B is incorrect because DNA is stringy material found inside the nucleus.

C is correct because mitochondria have folded inner membranes.

D is incorrect because ribosomes do not have double membranes.

7. C

A is incorrect because the diagram shows that the tongue is an organ that is part of the digestive system. An organ is made of different types of cells.

B is incorrect because the tongue is an organ. An organ is part of an organ system.

C is correct because the diagram shows that the tongue is an organ that is part of the digestive system. An organ is made up of two or more types of tissue that work together to perform a specific function.

D is incorrect because the diagram shows that the tongue is an organ that is part of the digestive system.

8. A

A is correct because the central vacuole functions in water storage and in supporting the structure of a plant cell.

B is incorrect because ribosomes are sites of protein synthesis, and lysosomes are sites of digestion.

C is incorrect because mitochondria are sites of cellular respiration, and chloroplasts are sites of photosynthesis.

D is incorrect because lysosomes are sites of waste disposal, and the nucleus stores the genetic material.

9. D

A is incorrect because a cell that is not maintaining homeostasis is unlikely to divide.

B is incorrect because cell processes do not continue operating normally if homeostasis is not maintained.

C is incorrect because if a cell is not maintaining homeostasis, it will be less able to eliminate wastes efficiently.

D is correct because internal conditions must remain stable in order for cell processes to continue operating normally.

10. C

A is incorrect because the roots are an organ. An organ is a group of tissues that work together.

B is incorrect because the roots are an organ that is part of an organ system.

C is correct because the roots are an organ. An organ is a group of tissues that work together.

D is incorrect because the roots are an organ that is part of an organ system.

11. D

A is incorrect because the structures are ribosomes, which produce proteins; they do not transport substances.

B is incorrect because the structures are ribosomes, and ribosomes do not contain DNA and do not have folded inner membranes.

C is incorrect because the structures are ribosomes, and ribosomes make proteins; mitochondria produce ATP for the cell.

D is correct because ribosomes are shown in the diagram; ribosomes are the cell's smallest organelles, and they do not have membranes.

12. D

A is incorrect because although plant cells have cell walls, nuclei are in both plant and animal cells.

B is incorrect because although plant cells have chloroplasts, both plant and animal cells contain ribosomes.

C is incorrect because although lysosomes are found only in animal cells, both plant and animal cells contain mitochondria.

D is correct because both cell walls and large, central vacuoles are in plant cells but not in animal cells.

Constructed Response

13. Key Elements (any **three** of the following; one key element each)**:**

- cell—blood cell
- tissue—blood
- organs—either of the following: heart, blood vessels
- organ system—circulatory system

AND

circulatory system; transport of oxygen, nutrients, and wastes throughout body

Rubric:
2 points Four key elements
1 point Two or three key elements
0 points Other

Extended Response

14. Key Elements:

Water content decreases with age.

AND

- On average, individual cells contain about the same amount of water as indicated for body average (50 percent elderly, 70 percent adult, 90 percent infant).

AND

Drink more water.

AND (one key element):

- Cells contain water.
- Reactions take place in water.
- Water keeps cells, tissues, organs, organ systems, and organisms functioning properly.

Rubric:
4 points Four key elements
3 points Three key elements
2 points Two key elements
1 point One key element
0 points Other

ISTEP+ Practice Test 1
Key Concepts

1.	B	8.	D	15.	C
2.	A	9.	B	16.	B
3.	C	10.	C	17.	D
4.	D	11.	A	18.	A
5.	D	12.	A	19.	C
6.	B	13.	C	20.	D
7.	D	14.	A		

1. B See Unit 3, Lesson 1

A is incorrect because in this example, energy is not being used to move an object over a distance, so no work is done.

B is correct because the girl moves herself and the can up the ladder, so work is done.

C is incorrect because in this example, energy is not being used to move an object over a distance, so no work is done.

D is incorrect because in this example, energy is not being used to move an object over a distance, so no work is done.

2. A See Unit 3, Lesson 3

A is correct because radiation is the transfer of energy through electromagnetic waves, and the sun's energy travels from the sun to Earth by radiation.

B is incorrect because air warmed by the blower is transferred by the movement of air currents, which is an example of convection.

C is incorrect because feeling warmth by direct contact with a warmer object is conduction.

D is incorrect because feeling warmth by direct contact with a warmer object is conduction.

3. C See Unit 1, Lesson 3

A is incorrect because both groups were located in Earth's magnetic field.

B is incorrect because both groups were located in Earth's magnetic field.

C is correct because if the needle is magnetized, each of its poles is attracted to the opposite magnetic pole of Earth.

D is incorrect because a magnetized needle would point north no matter where it was on the cork.

4. D See Unit 3, Lesson 4

A is incorrect because wave 1 is closest to the earthquake source, so it has the most energy and has the most, not the least, effect on Earth's surface.

B is incorrect because the energy of a wave decreases with distance, and wave 2 reaches Earth's surface at a point closer to the source than waves 3 and 4 do.

C is incorrect because the energy of a wave decreases with distance, and wave 3 reaches Earth's surface at a point closer to the source than wave 4 does.

D is correct because energy of a wave decreases with distance, and wave 4 reaches Earth at the farthest point from the source, so it has the least effect on Earth's surface.

5. D See Unit 2, Lesson 3

A is incorrect because friction is a force that happens when two objects rub together.

B is incorrect because the normal force is a contact force that opposes the force of gravity.

C is incorrect because a mechanical force is caused by the push or pull of one object or material directly on another.

D is correct because a magnetic force can affect objects that are not in contact with one another.

6. B See Unit 3, Lesson 1

A is incorrect because power is a measure of how quickly energy is converted from one form to another, not how quickly energy is transferred between objects.

B is correct because power is a measure of how quickly energy is converted from one form to another, such as how quickly a car engine converts chemical energy to mechanical energy.

C is incorrect because this definition describes a watt, the unit of power, but not power itself.

D is incorrect because power is determined by dividing energy by time, not by dividing work by time.

7. D See Unit 5, Lesson 3

A is incorrect because an age is the shortest unit of geologic time.

B is incorrect because an epoch is between a period and an age in length.

C is correct because an eon is longer than any of the other units of geologic time.

D is incorrect because an era is longer than three of the other units, but it is shorter than an eon.

8. D See Unit 2, Lesson 3

A is incorrect because the upward force is balanced by an equal and opposite downward force.

B is incorrect because the downward force is balanced by an equal and opposite upward force.

C is incorrect because the shoe is moving to the right, not the left. The direction of motion must be in the direction of the net force.

D is correct because the net force is in the direction of motion, which is to the right.

9. B See Unit 1, Lesson 2

A is incorrect because the up and down forces are not balanced. The net force acting on the box is in the upward direction.

B is correct because the up and down forces are balanced and the left and right forces are balanced. There is no net force acting on the box, and the motion remains unchanged.

C is incorrect because neither the up and down forces nor the left and right forces are balanced. The net force acting on the box is up and to the right.

D is incorrect because the left and right forces are not balanced. The net force acting on the box is to the right.

10. C See Unit 3, Lesson 2

A is incorrect because energy is conserved when it is transferred from one system to another.

B is incorrect because energy is conserved when it is transferred from one system to another.

C is correct because the law of conservation of energy states that energy cannot be created or destroyed but can only change in form when it is transferred from one system to another.

D is incorrect because energy can change into mass only during nuclear reactions, not when it is transferred between systems.

11. A See Unit 4, Lesson 5

A is correct because the core is at the center of Earth.

B is incorrect because the asthenosphere is part of the mantle.

C is incorrect because the lithosphere is the solid, outer layer of Earth that consists of the crust and the rigid upper part of the mantle.

D is incorrect because the mantle is the middle layer of Earth, located between Earth's crust and core.

12. A see Unit 4, Lesson 6

A is correct because tectonic plate movement, which causes earthquakes and volcanoes, occurs as a result of convection currents in the mantle, which form because the mantle is warmer at the bottom than at the top.

B is incorrect because radioactive materials in Earth release heat but are not the result of heat.

C is incorrect because tides are the result of the moon's gravitational pull on Earth.

D is incorrect because erosion and deposition are caused by the movement of wind and water on Earth's surface.

13. C See Unit 4, Lesson 2

A is incorrect because cooling takes place when magma forms igneous rock.

B is incorrect because melting changes rock into magma.

C is correct because sediment is deposited and then hardens under pressure to form sedimentary rock

D is incorrect because weathering can change metamorphic rock into sediment, but it cannot change sediment into sedimentary rock.

14. A See Unit 6, Lesson 1

A is correct because Schwann concluded that cells are the basic unit of all life.

B is incorrect because not all cells have nuclei and, to Schwann, the cell was the basic unit of life.

C is incorrect because organelles are parts of cells and, to Schwann, the cell was the basic unit of life.

D is incorrect because to Schwann, the cell was the basic unit of life; cells make up an organism so an organism cannot be a basic unit of life.

15. C See Unit 6, Lesson 3

A is incorrect because a lysosome more closely resembles a sac than flattened membranes. Lysosomes function in digestion and breakdown, not in protein and lipid modification and distribution.

B is incorrect because ribosomes are tiny, round structures that do not look like flattened membranes. Ribosomes function in protein synthesis.

C is correct because the Golgi complex is a system of flattened membranes that functions in protein and lipid modification and distribution.

D is incorrect because a central vacuole, which aids in storage and support in plant cells, more closely resembles a sac than flattened membranes.

16. B See Unit 6, Lesson 3

A is incorrect because the rough endoplasmic reticulum does not contain DNA.

B is correct because the rough endoplasmic reticulum is covered with ribosomes.

C is incorrect because mitochondria, not the Golgi complex, produce ATP.

D is incorrect because chloroplasts, not the Golgi complex, perform photosynthesis.

17. D See Unit 3, Lesson 3

A is incorrect because although the roots are connected to the stem, this does not describe what roots do in the plant.

B is incorrect because having root hairs helps the roots function, but the presence of root hairs does not describe a function of roots.

C is incorrect because roots can be of various lengths, and the length of roots is not a function of roots.

D is correct because taking in nutrients is one of the functions of roots.

18. A See Unit 1, Lesson 2

A is correct because when animals move in the top layer of soil (humus), they create paths for water to follow, making the humus porous.

B is incorrect because animals live where they can acquire food, water, and oxygen, which is generally nearer the surface of the soil.

C is incorrect because animals are more likely to affect upper layers of soil, such as the soil in the A horizon.

D is incorrect because animals also affect soil by making soil porous and by adding nutrients to soil.

19. C See Unit 6, Lesson 4

A is incorrect because living cells divide to replace dead cells; nearby cells do not grow larger.

B is incorrect because living cells divide to replace dead cells; once dead, cells cannot be revived.

C is correct because cellular division creates new cells to replace those that die.

D is incorrect because, once specialized, cells remain specialized; they do not assume the function of other cells.

20. D See Unit 3, Lesson 6

A is incorrect because drilling and mining processes do not produce carbon dioxide or other forms of air pollution, so this choice best fits in cell 2.

B is incorrect because although the vehicles that transport fossil fuels can produce air pollution, this choice best fits in cell 4, as improper transporting of fossil fuels can lead to spills that cause pollution.

C is incorrect because converting fossil fuels to usable forms can produce harmful byproducts, so this choice best fits in cell 1.

D is correct because burning fossil fuels releases pollutants such as carbon dioxide into the air, which contribute to acid rain and other environmental problems.

Constructed Response

21. See Unit 5, Lesson 2
Key Elements:
• Fossil H will be in rock layers that are younger than layers that contain fossil F.

AND

• Scientists can compare fossils of species that lived in the past to one another and to species living on Earth today. This helps them learn how the species are related and how they evolved (changed over time). For example, they can use fossils to learn that multicellular organisms evolved later than single-celled organisms.

Rubric:
2 points Two key elements
1 point One key element
0 points Other

22. See Unit 3, Lesson 1
Key Elements:
• any example of energy from wind being used to produce electrical energy (e.g., *The blades on a windmill turn from the energy in wind,* etc.)

AND

• The kinetic energy from the wind is transferred to the turning turbine blades, which transform it into electrical energy in a generator.

AND

• any example of energy from moving water being used to produce electrical energy (e.g., *The blades of a turbine in a dam turn from energy from running water,* etc.)

AND

• The potential energy from the water at the top of a dam is transformed to kinetic energy as the water falls; this kinetic energy is transferred to the turning turbine blades, which transform it into electrical energy in a generator.

Rubric:
2 points Two key elements
1 point One key element
0 points Other

23. See Unit 6, Lesson 5
Key Elements:
• During fertilization, a male sex cell joins with (fertilizes) a female sex cell.

AND

• After fertilization, cells of the embryo divide and form specialized tissues, which further develop and form organs that are part of specialized organ systems. (Answers should include at least three of the following levels of organization: cells, tissues, organs, organ systems, organism.)

Rubric:
2 points Two key elements
1 point One key element
0 points Other

Extended Response

24. See Unit 6, Lesson 2
Key Elements:
• Water makes up nearly two-thirds of the mass of living cells.

AND

• Phospholipids are molecules that form much of the cell membrane. The cell membrane is responsible for moving water and other material in and out of a cell.

AND

• If a cell has too much water, the cell can burst and die.

AND

• If a cell has too little water, it can shrivel and die.

Rubric:
4 points Four key elements
3 points Three key elements
2 points Two key elements
1 point One key element
0 points Other

25. See Unit 4, Lesson 3
Key Elements:
• Gravity causes a glacier to move.

AND

- As it moves, a glacier picks up materials, such as rocks, that become embedded in the ice. These materials abrade the lands over which glaciers move, causing dramatic changes in the landscape.

AND

- An alpine glacier forms in a valley between mountains, and a continental glacier forms on flat land.

AND

- Alpine glaciers produce rugged landscape features.

AND

- any two of the following: arêtes, cirques, horns, hanging valleys, and flatter-bottomed U-shaped valleys formed from V-shaped valleys

AND

Continental glaciers can spread over entire continents and smooth and flatten landscapes.

AND

- and any **two** of the following: drumlins, erratics, and kettle lakes

Rubric:
4 points Four key elements
3 points Three key elements
2 points Two key elements
1 point One key element
0 points Other

ISTEP+ Practice Test 2

Key Concepts

1. D	8. D	15. A
2. B	9. A	16. B
3. A	10. D	17. D
4. C	11. A	18. D
5. C	12. B	19. C
6. C	13. D	20. C
7. C	14. D	

1. D See Unit 3, Lesson 3
A is incorrect because letter Z represents radiation; conduction is the transfer of energy from one particle to another without the movement of matter, which is represented by letter Y.

B is incorrect because letter Z represents radiation; convection is the transfer of energy by the movement of currents within a fluid, which is represented by the letter X.

C is incorrect because insulation is a process that inhibits the transfer of energy between objects.

D is correct because radiation is the process in which energy is transferred by electromagnetic waves; fire transfers energy in waves through the air.

2. B See Unit 5, Lesson 3
A is incorrect because the units in this sequence are ordered from longest to shortest.

B is correct because this is the correct sequence; they can be inferred using the clues in the table.

C is incorrect because the only units in correct positions in this sequence are epoch and period.

D is incorrect because era and epoch in this sequence are switched.

3. A See Unit 3, Lesson 4
A is correct because although the energy of the wave might move matter in the medium, the wave does not carry matter.

B is incorrect because a wave moves only energy, not matter, through a medium.

C is incorrect because in a longitudinal wave, energy is transferred in the direction of vibration.

D is incorrect because in a transverse wave, energy is transferred in a direction perpendicular to the direction of vibration.

4. C See Unit 4, Lesson 3
A is incorrect because this choice does not include all of the primary factors that affect soil formation, and it also includes three that do not—rainfall, temperature, and wind.

B is incorrect because this choice does not include all of the primary factors that affect soil formation, and it also includes one that does not—sunshine.

C is correct because these factors work together to form soil.

D is incorrect because this choice is missing some of the primary factors that affect soil formation—parent rock and some types of living things, such as bacteria.

5. C See Unit 2, Lesson 3
A is incorrect because mass is not a force, and magnetic force is not acting on the cup.

B is incorrect because magnetic force is not a force acting on the cup.

C is correct because gravitational force pushes the cup down, and the normal force pushes the cup up.

D is incorrect because velocity is not a force.

6. C See Unit 2, Lesson 3
A is incorrect because the up force is greater than the down force, and the left and right forces are balanced, so the object is accelerating straight upward.

B is incorrect because the up and down forces are balanced and the left and right forces are balanced, so there is no acceleration.

C is correct because neither the up and down forces nor the left and right forces are balanced, and the object is accelerating up and to the right.

D is incorrect because the up and down forces are balanced, but the left force is greater than the right force, so the object is accelerating to the right.

7. C See Unit 1, Lesson 2
A is incorrect because cells must contain water to survive.

B is incorrect because adding more salt decreases water in the cells.

C is correct because higher salt concentration causes water to leave cells, and lower salt concentration causes water to enter cells.

D is incorrect because the salt concentration of the water affects how water enters or leaves the plant cells.

8. D See Unit 3, Lesson 6
A is incorrect because burning fossil fuels can cause air pollution, such as carbon dioxide, a greenhouse gas, so this choice belongs in cell 3.

B is incorrect because transporting fossil fuels might cause spills that can cause pollution that harms the environment, so this choice belongs in cell 4.

C is incorrect because converting fossil fuels to usable forms can produce harmful byproducts, so this choice belongs in cell 1.

D is correct because obtaining fossil fuels by drilling into land or the ocean floor can destroy habitats and pollute water and soil.

9. A See Unit 2, Lesson 3

A is correct because the explosion of the burning fuel exerts an upward force to overcome the downward force of Earth's gravity.

B is incorrect because the exploding gases are what create thrust.

C is incorrect because the friction between the rocket and the ground is not the force that keeps the rocket from going into space; gravity is the force that keeps the rocket on Earth.

D is incorrect because friction is not a force that must be overcome in order to propel the rocket into space. Friction would be a force to consider if the rocket were being moved along the ground.

10. D See Unit 3, Lesson 2

A is incorrect because this does not explain why the kinetic energy is less than the potential energy.

B is incorrect because energy can change forms, but it cannot be destroyed.

C is incorrect because energy can change forms, but it cannot be destroyed.

D is correct because the potential energy of the fuel is converted to kinetic energy as well as to light, thermal energy, and sound energy.

11. A See Unit 4, Lesson 5

A is correct because the diagram shows much more volume in the mantle than in the crust.

B is incorrect because the diagram does not show mass, and the crust has less mass than the other layers.

C is incorrect because the core is at the center of Earth.

D is incorrect because the diagram does not show density, and the crust is not denser than the core or the mantle.

12. B See Unit 3, Lesson 1

A is incorrect because energy is not being used, so no work is done.

B is correct because energy moves the ball across a distance.

C is incorrect because the ball stays in the glove and does not move, so no work is done.

D is incorrect because reading does not move an object through a distance, so no work is done.

13. D See Unit 4, Lesson 6

A is incorrect because if the students were modeling plate boundaries, they would be using two solid objects that touch each other.

B is incorrect because if the students were modeling continental drift, they would likely be using a solid object that represents a single landmass breaking apart or two solid objects that come together.

C is incorrect because if the students were modeling the movement of tectonic plates, they would likely be using two solid objects that move on a fluid surface.

D is correct because as it melts, the ice cube releases food coloring that circulates in the beaker, modeling convection currents in the mantle.

14. D See Unit 5, Lesson 2

A is incorrect because the position of fossils do not help scientists learn relative ages of rock layers; only by comparing different fossils in different rock layers can scientists learn about relative ages of the layers.

B is incorrect because although scientists can learn about the relative age of rock layers by comparing fossils in rock layers around the world, simply locating those areas is not helpful.

C is incorrect because comparing the fossils in a single layer does not help scientists learn when other layers were deposited, which is needed in order to determine the relative ages of the layers.

D is correct because by comparing known fossils in many different rock layers, scientists can learn the approximate time when each layer was deposited.

15. A See Unit 6, Lesson 1

A is correct because a cell has all the structures needed to perform all of the tasks necessary for life.

B is incorrect because a cell nucleus is just part of a cell and does not have all the structures needed to perform all of the tasks necessary for life.

C is incorrect because a cell membrane is just part of a cell and does not have all the structures needed to perform all of the tasks necessary for life.

D is incorrect because although a multicellular organism can perform all of the tasks necessary for life, it is composed of cells, which are a smaller unit than the organism.

16. B See Unit 6, Lesson 3

A is incorrect because mitochondria produce ATP, not sugar.

B is correct because chloroplasts perform photosynthesis, which produces sugar, and mitochondria perform cellular respiration, which uses the energy in sugar to produce ATP.

C is incorrect because enzymes are proteins and are made on the ribosomes.

D is incorrect because ribosomes, not chloroplasts, are the sites of protein production.

17. D See Unit 6, Lesson 3

A is incorrect because ribosomes do not contain DNA.

B is incorrect because ribosomes do not produce ATP.

C is incorrect because prokaryotes do not have a nucleus.

D is correct because ribosomes in eukaryotes are usually attached to the endoplasmic reticulum, and ribosomes in prokaryotes are usually loose in the cytoplasm.

18. D See Unit 6, Lesson 5

A is incorrect because the circulatory system carries cellular wastes to the lungs and the kidneys, but it does not remove them from the body.

B is incorrect because the respiratory system brings oxygen into the body, but it does not carry any nutrients to the cells.

C is incorrect because the circulatory system carries cellular wastes to the lungs and the kidneys, but it does not remove them from the body; the respiratory system brings oxygen into the body, but it does not carry any nutrients to the cells.

D is correct because the circulatory system carries nutrients and water to cells, and the respiratory system removes cellular wastes from the body.

19. C See Unit 6, Lesson 4

A is incorrect because cells in the inner ear are stable and rarely divide in adults.

B is incorrect because muscle cells are stable and rarely divide in adults. Exercise can increase their size, but not their number.

C is correct because cells in skin are replaced often in the body.

D is incorrect because nerve cells are usually stable and rarely divide in the adult.

20. C See Unit 6, Lesson 4

A is incorrect because cells in the inner ear are stable and rarely divide in adults.

B is incorrect because muscle cells are stable and rarely divide in adults. Exercise can increase their size, but not their number.

C is correct because cells in skin are replaced often in the body.

D is incorrect because nerve cells are usually stable and rarely divide in the adult.

Constructed Response

21. See Unit 4, Lesson 2
Key Elements:
- Weathering breaks up igneous rock into sediment, and erosion moves the sediment to a place where it builds up and cements together under pressure to form sedimentary rock.

AND

- Intense heat and high pressure cause metamorphic rock to form.

Rubric:
2 points Two key elements
1 point One key element
0 points Other

22. See Unit 4, Lesson 2
Key Elements:
- They must know that the needle of a compass always points north.

AND

- A compass points north because the needle of the compass is magnetized. One end of a magnetized needle points to Earth's north magnetic pole, and the other end points to Earth's south magnetic pole.

Rubric:
2 points Two key elements
1 point One key element
0 points Other

23. See Unit 4, Lesson 3
Key Elements:
- Karst topography is a type of irregular landscape characterized by caverns, sinkholes, and underground drainage. Karst topography forms in limestone or other soluble rock.

AND

- A sinkhole is a circular depression that forms when rock dissolves, when overlying sediment fills an existing cavity, or when the roof of an underground cavern or mine collapses.

Rubric:
2 points Two key elements
1 point One key element
0 points Other

Extended Response

24. See Unit 6, Lesson 5
Key Elements:
- Multicellular organisms are made up of more than one cell. They tend to be larger in size than unicellular organisms, and they tend to have longer life spans than unicellular organisms.

AND

- Most multicellular organisms reproduce through sexual reproduction. During sexual reproduction, a male sex cell fertilizes a female sex cell. This process is called fertilization.

AND

- After fertilization, a small cluster of cells divides to form the embryo.

AND

- An embryo differentiates into different types of cells, which form specialized types of tissue, which form organs, which are part of organ systems, which make up a multicellular organism. (Answers should include at least three of the following levels of organization: cells, tissues, organs, organ systems, organism.)

Rubric:
4 points Four key elements
3 points Three key elements
2 points Two key elements
1 point One key element
0 points Other

25. See Unit 3, Lesson 1
Key Elements:
- Chemical energy from a battery is transformed to electrical energy to run a CD player.

AND

- Mechanical (kinetic) energy from a windmill changes to electrical energy, which changes to light and thermal energy when a lamp is turned on.

AND

- Differences in temperatures (thermal energy) cause air to move (mechanical or kinetic energy).

AND

- Sound energy changes to mechanical (kinetic) energy when a loud noise makes windows rattle.

Visual Answers

Unit 2 Unit Test A, question 14, page 44

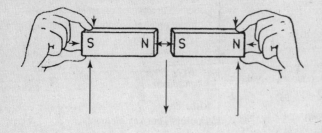

Design Process, question 2, page 178

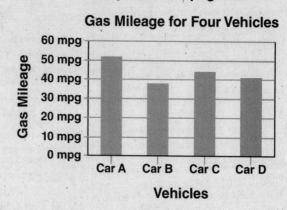